I loved reading this book! With humility, grace, and courage, David has v
of wisdom and practice addressed to his younger self and by extension to all successors and their families,
friends, and advisors. I know David as a teacher, speaker, storyteller, collaborator, and friend, and I greatly
admire and respect his commitment to living his best life and helping others to do the same. There's been a
gap in family enterprise literature—we've been waiting for a book like this!
Michelle Osry
Vice-Chair, Family Enterprise Exchange

David has learned a lot about real life, both through his experience as a family enterprise executive and as a
successor. *Dear Younger Me* includes everything you need to know to set you on the road to success.
Jimmy Pattison
Chairman & CEO, Jim Pattison Group

David provides life-changing wisdom for the emerging generation *and* their mentors. If you want to make a
career impact in your family firm, David provides the well-lit pathway.
Steve McClure, PhD
Chairman, The Family Business Consulting Group

I have known David in a business capacity for over 30 years. He possesses a rare combination of academic
wisdom and practical experience. During his career, he has acquired a breadth of knowledge and experience as
an executive and advisor. In his latest book, *Dear Younger Me*, he offers successors both insight and inspiration.
Tom Chambers
President, Senior Partner Service Ltd.

David's candid self-disclosure provides valuable "lessons learned" from his personal experience as a family
enterprise successor. The challenges he has faced have resulted in him developing a level of humility and
empathy that is rare. By willingly sharing his journey and insights he has helped many families to improve both
their communications and their relationships.
Marjorie Engle
Principal, Engle Advisory Services; FFI Fellow

David has that rare ability to anticipate the needs of his clients, as well as the gifted capacity to guide a family business through unsettling waters while confronting the elephants in the room. He does all this with grace, humility, and a deep sense of caring. He has been, and continues to be, an invaluable and trusted mentor for our family.

J. Lyn Bannister
Founder, Bannister Automotive Group

David has been an awesome facilitator and succession planning advisor, working with our family for over a decade. His new book provides wisdom and insight for all next-gen successors.

Greg Simpson
President & CEO, Simpson Seeds Inc.

David, as always, is very generous with his wisdom—a captivating wisdom garnered through his own extraordinary family business experience together with the years of working with other dynamic business families. The reflections and insights shared in *Dear Younger Me* are truly an inspiration and a road map for the next generation of business family leaders.

Bill Brushett
President & CEO, Family Enterprise Xchange

I have known David for over 40 years; during this time, I have witnessed first-hand his unwavering integrity, empathy, and wisdom. These personal traits, together with his education and experience, are unparalleled in our country. Combining all this with an ability to authentically self-reflect allows him to provide valuable insights for any family business.

Donald Carson
Principal, Carson Automotive Group

David has given his life to the service of family companies. Because of his dedication and a willingness to share his first-hand experience, he has been a great benefit to many. In this unique and very challenging field, I could not recommend anyone more highly.

Bob Gaglardi
Founder & Chairman, Sandman Hotels & Northland Properties

David is a caring individual who has given a great deal of his time to charitable causes and the teaching of family business skills to our community. He is one of British Columbia's most prominent leaders.

David G. McLean, OBC, LLD, FICD
Chairman, The McLean Group, & Chairman Emeritus of Canadian National Railway Company

Dear Younger Me is more than an inspired reflection on life, learning, and success. It is a guidebook for a life path filled with discovery, connection, and growth. I recommend this book to anyone who wants to find a better path.

John A. Davis
Founder & Chairman, Cambridge Family Enterprise Group

David is a master storyteller, and thanks to his invaluable experience as an owner, a thought leader, and a trusted advisor, he now provides us with a priceless resource for family enterprise successors. The wisdom he offers combines his life experience and best practices to stretch our minds and provoke "the change from inside out." His book is a must read for every learning family!

Olivier de Richoufftz
General Secretary, Family Enterprise Foundation

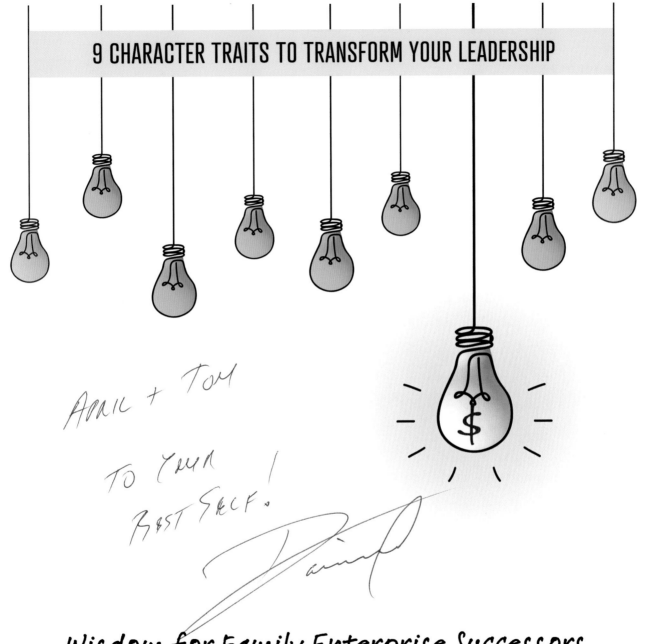

9 CHARACTER TRAITS TO TRANSFORM YOUR LEADERSHIP

Wisdom for Family Enterprise Successors

DAVID C. BENTALL

Published by: Castle Quay Books
Burlington, ON, Canada | Jupiter, FL, USA
Tel: (416) 573-3249
E-mail: info@castlequaybooks.com | www.castlequaybooks.com

Edited by Marina Hofman Willard
Book interior and cover layout by Burst Impressions
Interior illustrations, charts and cover illustrations by www.foundcreative.ca
Images of John Wooden and the Pyramid of Success courtesy of John R. Wooden™ owned and licensed by John Wooden Legacy LLC, c/o Luminary Group LLC
Printed in Canada

Library and Archives Canada Cataloguing in Publication
Title: Dear younger me... : wisdom for family enterprise successors / David C. Bentall.
Names: Bentall, David C., 1955- author.
Identifiers: Canadiana 20200164902 | ISBN 9781988928128 (softcover)
Subjects: LCSH: Family-owned business enterprises. | LCSH: Family-owned business enterprises—
  Succession.
Classification: LCC HD62.25 .B46 2020 | DDC 658/.045—dc23

To my wife, Alison.
Your selfless love for me and our family amazes and inspires me.
I couldn't have asked for more support or a better cheerleader while working on this project.
Thank you for all you have done and continue to do to make my life truly blessed.
I love you with all my heart.

CONTENTS

ACKNOWLEDGEMENTS   **11**

FOREWORD: Ruth Steverlynck, LLB Hons, FEA   **15**

PREFACE   **17**

I THE BENTALL FAMILY STORY   **19**

    1. Aspiring to Lead

    2. Working Together as Family

    3. Struggling with Succession

II WISDOM FOR SUCCESSORS   **45**

    1. Family Enterprise Distinctives

    2. Perspectives on Succession

    3. Preparing for Leadership

III TRANSFORMING YOUR LEADERSHIP   **85**

    1. Humility: *Getting Out of Your Own Way*

    2. Curiosity: *Discovering the Doorway to Innovation*

    3. Listening: *Accessing the Wisdom All Around You*

    4. Empathy: *The Power to Connect with Others*

    5. Forgiveness: *The Secret to Living Free*

    6. Gratitude: *Discovering the Magic in Every Day*

    7. Critical Thinking: *Assessing Options Rather Than Criticizing Others*

    8. Patience: *Waiting Without Frustration*

    9. Contentment: *The Pathway to Poise and Focus*

IV WISDOM FROM SUCCESSORS   **249**

   1. Adrian Fluevog (Fluevog Shoes): *"Humility Is More Than Just A Nice Idea"*

   2. Laura Kusisto (Kenroc Building Supplies): *"Curiosity Creates A Career"*

   3. Andrew Williams (North Prairie Developments): *"Listening Makes A Leader"*

   4. Michelle Jones-Ruppel (West Coast Auto Group): *"Empathy in A Man's World"*

   5. Shaun Plotkin (Plotkin Health): *"Forgiveness Is a Willingness to Let Go"*

   6. Erik Brinkman (Brinkman Reforestation): *"Finding Gratitude in the Amazon"*

   7. Breanne Ramsay (Britt Land & Engagement): *"Hard on Issues/ Soft on People"*

   8. Ellisha Mott (Mott Electric): *"Patience Is A Deliberate Choice"*

   9. MeiLi Coon (Trilogy Excursions): *"Pursuing Your Passion Leads to Contentment"*

V EXEMPLARY LEADERS & ROLE MODELS   **289**

   1. Benjamin Franklin: *Choosing to Cultivate Humility*

   2. Albert Einstein: *Insatiable Curiosity*

   3. Gandhi: *Leading by Listening*

   4. Mother Teresa: *Changing the World With Empathy*

   5. Nelson Mandela: *Forgiveness on A Grand Scale*

   6. Kim Phuc: *Gratitude Rises from the Horrors of War*

   7. Walt Disney: *Critical Thinking and the Magic Kingdom*

   8. John Wooden: *A Dynasty Founded on Patience*

   9. Helen Keller: *Contentment in Spite of Circumstances*

VI HELP ALONG THE WAY   **331**

   1. Taking Action

   2. Assessments & Mentoring

APPENDIX: Corrie ten Boom on Forgiveness   **343**

ENDNOTES   **345**

ACKNOWLEDGEMENTS

This book rests on the shoulders of many colleagues and friends, the many individuals who have truly lifted me up, both in my personal life and in my professional career; the people who have enriched my life by teaching, mentoring, and inspiring me and by being exemplary role models. It is their collective wisdom and insight that have sponsored my pursuit of the nine virtues explored in this book. I am profoundly grateful for their support on this highly personal journey towards greater emotional intelligence.

HELPING ME AS AN EXECUTIVE

To begin with, I want to express appreciation to those who mentored me during the first 20 years of my career. Each of the following executives helped illuminate the qualities and characteristics that *Dear Younger Me* is all about.

Paul Schoeber, my first employer, began by modelling for me *empathy.* My uncle **R. G. Bentall** modelled for me *patience,* especially while waiting for over 30 years to lead our family company. My father, **H. Clark Bentall,** asked great questions and was a superb listener. From him I learned the power and the potency of *listening* deeply. In the life of my grandfather **Charles Bentall,** I was able to observe *humility.* In spite of his iconic success and as a member the Canadian business hall of fame, Granddad never puffed out his chest with pride. While I worked in Calgary with **Bruce Trevitt**, he showed me the value of *curiosity* whenever approaching a new opportunity. While I was in Toronto, **Jim Bullock,** president of the Cadillac Fairview Corporation, introduced me to the value of *critical thinking.* Later, when I returned to Vancouver, **Dick Myers,** CEO of Dominion Construction, showed me the value of living with **contentment** in spite of my circumstances.

As I look back I see that all of these individuals planted priceless seeds of virtue. These may have taken years to germinate, but they were there, deep in the soil of my life.

HELPING ME AS AN ADVISOR AND COACH

When I embarked on my second career, that of an executive coach and family enterprise advisor, I discovered a whole new world, beyond our family business and beyond the real estate and construction industries. During the past two decades, I have benefited enormously from the encouragement, guidance, and mentoring offered by many generous and remarkable human beings. The following individuals have helped me to accept my circumstances, including the challenges and disappointments, and to learn from them. Even more importantly, they have helped me to focus on others and how I could be of service.

First, I want to thank **Philipe** and **Nan-b DeGaspe Beubien**. They were the first to encourage and educate me regarding how to assist other business families. Second, I want to thank **Gord Wusyk,** for believing in me and for being catalytic in helping me to choose a career in this field. Third, I want to express appreciation to **Dr. John Davis, Dr. John Ward,** and **Dr. Ivan Lansberg**. These three professors were my first teachers and mentors in the field. Their support and guidance were critical in launching me as a family enterprise advisor. Fourth, **Dr. Steve McClure** was my mentor both during and after I completed my initial training with the Family Firm Institute. His encouragement and unwavering support enabled me to "jump in with both feet" and to discover that I could make a positive contribution to our field, both as an advisor and as a writer. I am forever in his debt.

On a more personal note, I want to thank my sister **Mary George.** She was the first person to point out to me that God had gifted me to be a teacher. I initially resisted this idea, but thankfully my executive coach, **Laura North,** was able to help me embrace this role. In a similar way I am indebted to **Drew Mendoza**, who assisted me in recognizing that my strengths were perhaps well suited to be a family enterprise advisor. I am also deeply grateful to **Dr. Nancy Langton, Ruth Steverlynck,** and **Wendy Sage-Hayward**. I have had the privilege of team teaching with each of them over many years. Their wisdom and insight, as professionals, educators, and lifelong learners, were life-giving, especially as I have sought to understand what successors need to truly thrive.

HELPING ME AS A PERSON

For over 30 years, my close friends **Carson Pue** and **Bob Kuhn** have faithfully stood by me, encouraging me, praying for me, and believing in me. They have also given me the courage to openly share my mistakes and to do so in a way that might enrich others and assist them along their way. **Dave Phillips** is a friend and colleague who has stimulated in me an ongoing process of self-examination and self-discovery that has been transformative, ultimately showing me how much I lacked each of the traits explored in this book.

My water ski coach, **Chet Raley**, has been my mentor for nearly two decades. Every day he wakes up determined to get better. His example was instrumental in me realizing that I needed a wholesale renovation of my attitudes. Similarly, my performance coach**, Jim Murphy,** has been teaching me how to manage my thoughts and feelings as a competitor. As a result, I have been gradually changing how I speak, not just to myself in the context of my sport but also to others in the context of my work. **Peter Vaughan**, as our counsellor, not only supported Alison and me in rebuilding our marriage but also in seeing how I could learn new patterns of relating more broadly. He gave me hope, as well as tools and guidance in re-establishing a sense of equilibrium in my life. **John Furlong**, former CEO for the Vancouver 2010 Olympics, inspired me to abandon criticism of others. Similarly, **Dr. John Radford** modelled for me how to disagree without being disagreeable and how to communicate a difference of opinion without being critical.

HELPING ME AS AN AUTHOR

Sue Martinuk has been my principle editor and collaborator on this project for over two years. Her dedication, professionalism, and commitment to excellence have been fundamental to bringing structure and order to what I have written. As someone who loves to tell stories, I desperately needed a literary expert like her who was able to sift through my ideas and determine what was worth preserving. Her tireless support was essential in guiding this project to completion. **Jon D. Bentall**, PhD, was my research assistant. Without his scholarly input, I fear this book might have been little more than a collection of stories about all the mistakes I have made. I am so thankful for the fresh ideas he uncovered and for the substantive insights he shared. These have both augmented and reinforced the lessons I wanted to share.

Marina Hofman Willard, PhD, is the senior editor at Castle Quay Books. Her desire for perfection has been relentless. I am so grateful that she insisted that everything be done methodically, so that it would also be done "right." **Amy Johnston** was creative and collaborative, while adding clarity and interest through her memorable illustrations and with the cover design. I also want to thank members of the Next Step Advisors team, especially **Kiran Chatha** and **Zoe Robinson**. They tirelessly tracked down footnotes and photographs, as well as a myriad of other details, in order to get this manuscript across the finish line. Well done!

Larry Willard, the publisher of Castle Quay books, has now provided stalwart support for me for over two decades. His guidance and encouragement have been immeasurably valuable to me in completing this project, as well as my two previous books.

HELPING ME ON THE ROAD OF LIFE

I also want to express profound appreciation to all of **my coaching clients** for the courage and strength they have each demonstrated when facing the challenges that life has offered. I have had the opportunity to learn and grow along with them while walking alongside them on their individual journeys.

Finally, I want to acknowledge each one of **my family enterprise clients.** As I have worked with all of them, I have seen how and where I needed to grow. I am extremely grateful for all of the families who have trusted me to be a part of their lives. As we have planned together, talked together, and even cried together, I have learned so much.

FOREWORD
Ruth Steverlynck, LLB Hons, FEA

Many years ago, I had an unsettling experience with owners of a large family enterprise. They had obtained advice from some of the leading experts in our field and, over several years, had introduced virtually every recommendation they had been given. In fact, they initially appeared to be a textbook example of family enterprise governance and continuity planning.

But, much to my surprise, none of the strategies employed were working!

In the years since this experience, I have seen many similar situations where well-intentioned family leaders and advisors have implemented "best practices" for their family enterprises and yet the results have not lived up to expectations.

The question is "Why?"

Over the past 40 years, much has been learned about "best practices" for family enterprise governance. We have discovered ways to improve communication, clarify values, and create a shared vision; we have developed genograms, codes of conduct, and mission statements; independent members have been recruited for boards, and regular family council meetings have been facilitated. However, in spite of all these governance initiatives, all too often our continuity planning efforts have failed to yield the dividends we had hoped for.

What has been glaringly overlooked is that the success of our systems, structures, and processes hinges on the character traits and personal qualities of the human beings working within them.

Human beings are fragile yet strong; unpredictable yet certain; complicated yet similar. Yes, structures and process are essential and planning is critical, but they have consistently proven to be unworkable without strength of character, emotional intelligence, and relational capacity.

To help us "do better" in our family enterprises, I commend to you the reflections and insights of my dear friend, colleague, and mentor David C. Bentall.

I have had the privilege of knowing David for over 10 years. What has struck me about David, beyond his clear sense of purpose, tireless energy for everything he puts his mind to, and the ability to shine no matter what the situation, is his grace. David epitomizes grace. And it is with grace that he gives the field of family enterprise the gift of this book.

Our field has been waiting for this book. It answers this question: Why are structures, processes, and planning, in and of themselves, not enough to ensure continuity for our family enterprises?

The missing piece in the puzzle of family enterprise, and why some will succeed in the future and others will fade, lies within the wisdom imparted in this book. What distinguishes those that succeed from those that languish are character traits that can be taught, learned, developed, and modelled.

This book, framed as advice David wishes he had received when he was younger, gracefully and practically details the character traits that David now knows would have served him and his family's enterprise well had he developed them decades earlier. Without humility, without curiosity, without the ability to listen, without empathy, forgiveness, gratitude, critical thinking, and patience, there is always limited capacity to both find the pathway forward and realize what truly matters.

I believe that his candid reflections on his past mistakes and the practical instruction he offers represent the next step in the evolution of the field of family enterprise advising. By bringing clarity to what his younger self could have benefited from by learning and developing, David offers an actionable capacity-building guide for successors that can help them to avoid the common pitfalls that so often cause members of the rising generation to stumble.

This book reiterates the importance of family enterprises understanding family systems, creating governance structures, and engaging in meaningful planning—and it invites the people, the human beings, the individuals, within family enterprises to prioritize the importance of character development.

It answers these questions:

What are the character traits that will best serve the structures, processes, and planning put in place for the benefit of the family enterprise?

Why are certain personal qualities essential to the future success of a family enterprise?

How can these personal qualities be learned, developed, and used in service of our family enterprises, as well as in our personal lives outside of the enterprise?

The book closes by showcasing leaders and role models who exemplify the character traits posited. My dear friend David C. Bentall should be included in this inventory of masters.

PREFACE

"Aim High and Strive Hard"

A framed copy of our family coat of arms hangs on a wall in my office, serving as a constant reminder of our strong and proud family heritage. Etched into the plaque, just under the shield itself, is the Latin phrase *Tende Bene et Alta Pete*, which, roughly translated, means "aim high and strive hard." It is a standard that I and many other Bentall family members, both past and present, have sought to faithfully pursue throughout our lives.

"Aim high and strive hard" is a daily reminder of all that my grandfather Charles and my father, Clark, were able to achieve during their lifetimes as they established our family name as one of the primary builders and shapers of the landscape that is downtown Vancouver.

Frankly, I have never had much of a problem with "aiming high" or "striving hard." If anything, my career has suffered from the consequences of pushing too hard and trying to accomplish too much.

When I was a young boy, my father made it clear to me that he expected me to one day become president of our family business. In preparation, I began developing the leadership skills that I thought would be needed and during my time at university studied both business and real estate. Once I joined our family firm, I worked hard to acquire experience and to earn respect as I began working my way up the corporate ladder.

In other words, I was "aiming high" and "striving hard" as I prepared to one day lead our family enterprise.

Unfortunately, my career did not unfold as my father had hoped or as I had planned. Just as I was about to enter the executive suite, I was dismissed from the company. Simultaneously, my dad was forced out of the business, and a tragic rift emerged in what was once a collaborative and cohesive family.

In the process, I came to realize that my education, leadership skills, and years of hard work had done little to prepare me for the realities of a family business and the challenges that were tearing our family business apart. After much subsequent study and reflection, I can see that I was ill-equipped to be a part of the solution because I lacked many of the qualities needed to make a positive contribution to our situation.

Over the past several decades, Western society has witnessed the fall of numerous corporate giants, in many cases because of character flaws in their leaders. As a result, personal character and traits such as listening, humility, and empathy have become common topics of management research, and they are being lauded as essential traits for effective leadership.

The pages that follow include an exploration of nine personal qualities that have been shown to make a radical difference in leadership and relationships.

I wish that I had taken the time to develop each of these personal character traits earlier in my professional career—and, frankly, I wish that I had known how important they are for successful leadership.

Dear Younger Me is, essentially, the book that I wish someone had written for me when I was just starting out in my career. It contains the wisdom that I would offer if I could roll the clock back and have a heart-to-heart conversation with myself 30 or 40 years ago.

Over the past 30 years, since leaving our family company, I have learned much, reflected deeply, and advised hundreds of family enterprise successors. By sharing the insights I have gained during this process, it is my hope to assist family enterprise successors and inspire them to make a positive impact on their businesses, their families, and their relationships.

SECTION I
The Bentall Family Story

Our grandfather Charles Bentall emigrated from England in 1908, and, over the next 75 years, he and our family enjoyed sustained business success. By 1988, The Bentall Group was a fully integrated real estate and construction company, with offices across Western Canada and in California. The company owned and managed real estate assets in excess of 2 million square feet, which were, at that time, valued at approximately $500 million.

Unfortunately, despite his best efforts, things did not turn out as Granddad had hoped for his three boys and his grandchildren. As we struggled with succession from G2 to G3 (generation two to generation three), both our family business and our family relationships were significantly impacted. Over time, everything was sold, largely for lack of a shared vision.

In section I, I summarize what happened to our family and some of the key lessons that can be extracted from our experience.

CHAPTER 1
Aspiring to Lead

I am the youngest of four children. My older siblings were 10, 12, and 15 years old when I came along. I was very fortunate because when I arrived our family business was much more successful than it was when my brother and sisters were born. It is often said that some kids are born with a silver spoon in their mouth. Some might say that about me, and my older siblings would probably agree. As difficult as it is to admit, the expression hits pretty close to home.

My Growing Up Years

I grew up in a beautiful home in an affluent neighbourhood of Vancouver, British Columbia, one of the most livable cities in the world. Our family meals were served in a formal dining room as we sat around a polished mahogany table. A crystal chandelier shone down from above. The surroundings were not opulent, but they probably would have made any king or queen feel quite comfortable. I certainly grew up feeling more like a prince than a pauper.

When I went downtown it would usually be to visit my father at the office complex that bears our family name. The Bentall Centre

The Bentall family home, where I grew up, in Vancouver

> "You can't be president if you don't do your homework."

is a cluster of five office towers at the heart of downtown Vancouver, connected by a series of beautiful plazas and fountains. Looking out from the window of my father's office on the top floor of the tallest building in town, I could see the Royal Vancouver Yacht Club, where our family boat, *Lazee Gal*, was moored. She was a custom-built mahogany vessel, and my summers were often spent on her, cruising the waters off the West Coast with my parents. You could certainly say that I was privileged, but this was just the norm for me in my childhood.

In time, I would come to understand that all of these comforts could be traced back to the success of our family business, known then as Dominion Construction.

My grandfather Charles Bentall had purchased the business shortly after moving to Vancouver. My father, Clark, joined the business immediately after graduating from university and became president in due course. As he approached retirement, my granddad gifted the company shares to Clark and his brothers, Howard and Bob.

My Destiny Is Set

The next generation of our family (G3) consisted of four boys and seven girls; consequently, I was one of 11 cousins who were all potential heirs to our family business. At that time, it was more likely that women would choose to raise a family rather than run a construction company, and the women in our family were, at least initially, inclined to follow that social convention. Therefore, none of them worked for the family business, except for some part-time work or summer employment while attending university. My older brother, Chuck, chose a career in architecture; my cousin Rob felt called to give his life to pastoral ministry; and my cousin Barney became a recording artist. Over time, this would result in me being the only member of the next generation who could potentially lead the family enterprise.

My dad was an advocate of this possibility and would often remind me of my future responsibilities. I recall watching *Casper the Friendly Ghost* on television when I was just 10 years old. My dad saw this as a waste of time and came into the den and instructed me to "Turn off the television and do your homework." I am sure that every child in North America has heard a similar admonishment many times over. However, when I failed to immediately obey, he continued with words that few kids ever hear: "David, you can't be president [of the company] if you don't do your homework."

Clearly, Dad believed that if I worked hard, I could one day be appointed leader of our family firm. Some have said that my father was cruel to put this kind of burden on me at such a young age, but I have never seen it as anything other than a gift. Even now, I cannot recall any sense that my life was somehow constrained because of his expectations. Rather, I remember thinking that my father had an exciting vision for my future, and as I grew older, this gave me a tremendous sense of confidence, knowing that he believed in me. I also saw his encouragement as an invitation to follow in the footsteps of my father and grandfather, and, frankly, I did not plan to disappoint.

I was more than willing to do all that I could to prepare for the day that I would become president. Throughout high school, I enjoyed various leadership roles in athletics and youth programs, and during the summer months, I worked full-time at a camp. Subsequently, while I attended university my summer employment included working as a labourer in our construction company and, later, in accounts payable. In 1979, I graduated from the University of British Columbia with a commerce degree and a major in urban land economics (real estate).

Eager to Impact Our Family Firm

I joined our family company almost immediately after convocation, and my first job was as executive assistant to the general manager of BC Millwork. It was our smallest division and probably not the glamorous start that some might have expected for an aspiring successor. However, I hoped it might be the ideal position for me to demonstrate my capabilities to the top brass. As a recent graduate, I was full of ideas, including the latest theories and best practices for management. Some were put to good use as I developed marketing and human resources plans for the millwork operation and, later on, their first strategic plan.

After just one year, I was invited to the head office by Uncle Bob. At the time, he was president of The Bentall Group, the parent company of Dominion Construction, our flagship business, and the plan was for me to work closely with him as his administrative assistant. In the beginning, we experienced great collaboration, especially as he and I worked together to introduce strategic planning throughout the corporation. I enjoyed this opportunity immensely, and I believed that I was making an important contribution to the future of the company.

But my excitement was dashed as I enthusiastically championed changes that I hoped would make the company better and then realized that all our planning was not leading to action. No matter how hard I tried, all my attempts to implement progressive change were stymied. The message seemed clear—change was just not going to happen.

Although our family business had experienced decades of consistent success and profitability, it was 75 years old, and the entire enterprise seemed to be afflicted by a culture that was dedicated to maintaining the status quo. As the only member of the next generation who was working in the business, I was concerned about our prospects for the future. To make matters worse, even though my dad was chairman of the board and the largest shareholder and my uncle was president and CEO, I seemed powerless to effect the changes that I felt were desperately needed.

My attempts to discuss these concerns were rebuffed, and this only served to exacerbate the growing tension between my uncle and me. After less than a year of working with him, I decided it was time to get out of town, and, somewhat in protest, I went to work in another division of our company. Over the next five years, I set about to learn about our operations in numerous cities and gain exposure to our broad business interests, which included leasing, design, construction, manufacturing, marketing, sales, and real estate development.

Learning and Growing

My first stop was Calgary. It was 1981, and for the previous decade Alberta's real estate market had been over-heated and full of opportunities. I could hardly wait to experience the gold-rush mentality that had gripped the market, and I anticipated that there would be a more progressive environment once I was out of the shadow of head office. Unfortunately, my search for greener pastures was in vain. Dad and Bob needed to approve any deals we proposed, and, since they were not as familiar with the Alberta market, they were even more reluctant to invest in new projects there. In addition, just after I arrived the real estate market virtually collapsed.

After two more years of frustration, I left our firm and joined the shopping-centre division of the Cadillac Fairview Corporation in Toronto. At the time, it was one of the largest publicly traded real estate companies in North America, and it offered me opportunities to work with several great mentors. This included the company's entrepreneurial president, Jim Bullock. I was employed there for two years and found it to be a very refreshing and positive work experience. Working outside the family business proved to be invaluable, as it provided me with the perspective and training that was not available in our family firm, where I constantly worked in the shadow of my last name.

After a short stint working in California, I returned to the company head office in Vancouver. It had been five years since I left, and during that time I was able to enhance my credibility as a successor by gaining relevant experience both outside and inside our company. So, in spite of the tension that still existed with Uncle Bob, I was appointed to the position of corporate vice-president, assuming responsibility for all our real estate development activities in Canada. As Bob approached his 65th birthday, there was a general consensus that he would soon retire.

"I Just Can't Wait to Be King"

Initially, things went pretty well, and it was not long before other senior executives were recommending that I be promoted to the position of senior vice-president. Such an appointment would have put me on par with our three other senior vice-presidents (finance, construction, and property management).

At the time, the men in these positions were the only other potential candidates for the most senior role in the company. My appointment to a similar position would be a clear sign that I also had a legitimate shot at the job.

I was 33 years old and had acquired the education, experience, and credentials to be considered a potential candidate to succeed Bob as president of The Bentall Group. My opportunity to lead was about to arrive … or so I thought.

Unfortunately, like many next-generation successors, I didn't realize how much my sense

Disney Junior/© ABC/Getty Images

Just as Mufasa had expectations that Simba would one day rule the Pride Lands, my dad had similar hopes for me.

of entitlement had profoundly influenced my expectations. In addition, I had enjoyed my dad's unwavering support since childhood. Consequently, my background and my ambition combined to stoke the fires of anticipation.

Quite literally, I could identify with young Simba in the movie *The Lion King*, prancing around with pride while singing his signature tune, "I Just Can't Wait to Be King." Like Simba, I was impatient ("Oh, I just can't wait to be king"), ready to take charge ("working on my roar"), and prepared to lead decisively ("I'm gonna be a mighty king"). Unfortunately, I was also under the mistaken impression that succession meant I would one day be "free to do it all my way"!

> *I became increasingly impatient and critical.*

As time went on, my expectations led me to become increasingly dissatisfied when things didn't pan out as I had hoped. I was eventually overcome with frustration and presumption, leading me to become extremely critical of my uncle in his role as company CEO. These very attitudes revealed how truly unprepared I was for leadership, at least at that time. Sadly, I was blind to my own pride, as well as many other inadequacies in my character, and thus I missed my opportunity to take remedial action. In hindsight, I can see why John Ruskin observed that "Pride is at the bottom of all great mistakes."

Quite understandably, Bob was becoming very uncomfortable with the prospect that I might be appointed as his successor. To make matters worse, there were unrelated tensions between Bob and my dad. As a result, the environment in our offices on the 31st floor of Bentall Three became increasingly dysfunctional. Unbeknownst to me, things were going to get even worse, and I was about to learn some very painful lessons.

CHAPTER 2
Working Together as Family

The name Dominion Construction was virtually synonymous with our family name for over 75 years. During that time, the company's growth and influence far eclipsed the wildest dreams of its founding family. Here are some facts:

- The business was profitable virtually every year (the lone exception was a single year during the 1930s when the company recorded a nominal loss of $120.91).
- By 1988, Dominion had spawned a host of companies that came under the banner of The Bentall Group. The combined businesses had over 1,500 employees and assets of nearly $500 million.
- We had offices in five cities across western Canada that provided an integrated approach to engineering, construction, real estate development, and property management.
- We owned related subsidiaries that offered interior design, electrical and mechanical contracting, and millwork manufacturing services.
- The firm was honoured as one of the 100 best companies to work for in Canada.

By almost any measure, our family enterprise appeared to be doing well. Before I explore how it all fell apart, the next few pages highlight some key events in the history of our business and its leadership.

GROWTH

When my grandfather Charles Bentall left his home in England and moved to Canada in 1908, I am certain that he had no idea of the success he would one day enjoy. Fortunately, our country was undergoing an exciting building boom, and there was plenty of work available for someone who had a degree in structural

The World Newspaper Building, Vancouver, 1911

engineering, was willing to work hard, and was determined to succeed. Upon his arrival in Vancouver, he joined the engineering firm J. Coughlan and Sons, and he very quickly made a name for himself as one of the premier designers in British Columbia. His first assignment was to design the dome of the Vancouver courthouse, now known as the Vancouver Art Gallery. In 1911, he gained further acclaim when he designed the structural frame for the World Newspaper Building, an 18-storey building that was, at the time, the tallest in the British Empire. It is still standing more than 100 years later, now known as the Sun Tower, and its elegance continues to add a touch of old-world charm to the Vancouver skyline.

The next year, Charles joined a well-known building company called Dominion Construction. He soon became the general manager, and it was not long before he began taking steps to acquire the firm. By 1920, he had become the primary shareholder.

A Foundation Built on Integrity and Innovation

In the beginning, Charles was more widely known as an engineer than as a business leader. But his disarming manner and genuine concern for others enabled him to easily make and keep friends. These traits, combined with his determination and Protestant work ethic, soon made him a force to be reckoned with in Vancouver business circles. More importantly, Charles became known as a man of his word, and he developed an unparalleled reputation for honesty and fair dealing. People came to realize that "Charlie" Bentall could be trusted, and his personal integrity became the cornerstone of his success. (His three sons, Howard, Clark, and Bob, maintained those same standards, creating a legacy where our family name was synonymous with integrity.)

By combining his engineering skills with his knowledge of construction, he was able to offer a unique integrated design/build service to customers that allowed Dominion to save both time and money on new building projects. Remarkably, he even won over skeptical potential clients like Scott Paper Canada (formerly Westminster Paper), who had a policy that formerly prohibited the design/build approach for their projects. In the 1930s, Charles convinced the paper company to let Dominion design and build their first plant on the shores of the Fraser River.

> *My grandfather's personal integrity was the cornerstone of his success.*

It was so successful that Dominion Construction was awarded every major expansion contract for Scott Paper facilities for the next 50 years. As a symbol of the close relationship that developed between the two companies, Charles was eventually appointed chairman of its board of directors.

A Sudden Changing of the Guard

As long as Charles was at the helm, the business prospered. He knew that someday he would need to discuss leadership succession, but for almost 35 years, the topic was not addressed. That changed in rather dramatic fashion in June 1955, when a sudden heart attack put him in the intensive care unit at Vancouver General Hospital (VGH). Stunned by the experience, Charles was forced to face his own mortality, perhaps for the first time.

Coincidentally, on that very same day my mother, Phyllis, was also at VGH, in the maternity ward, welcoming me into the world. My dad, Clark, must have experienced the full range of emotions as he shuttled back and forth between the ICU and the maternity ward, keeping his eye on the progress of his father, his wife, and his newborn son. The same could probably be said for Charles, who likely experienced his own emotional turmoil in the aftermath of his near-death experience. As he lay on a hospital bed, reflecting on his life, he realized that his days as Dominion Construction's top executive were over. For the sake of his health and for the continued success of the business, he decided that it was time to step down and transition leadership to the next generation.

Wanting to be fair to his three sons, Charles gifted each one (Howard, Clark, and Bob) with an equal ownership stake in the company. But when it came to leadership, things were more complicated. Tradition would suggest that the heir apparent should be the eldest son, and in this case that would have been Howard. However, with his father's

H. Clark Bentall (left) reviewing the plans under the watchful eye of his father, Charles Bentall (seated)

enthusiastic endorsement, Howard had already decided to pursue a career in ministry and had no ambitions to lead Dominion. Next in line was Clark, who was a structural engineer and had been working alongside Charles for the previous 17 years. The youngest brother, Bob, was also an engineer, and he had worked in the company for 15 years. When Clark visited his father in the hospital, Charles handed him the leadership of the business with the simple words "I guess, son, the business is yours." The next day, Clark went into the office, moved out Granddad's personal belongings, and took up residence in the corner office as leader of the family business.

> "I guess, son, the business is yours."

SUCCESS

Although this transition had been initiated by an unexpected health scare, the leadership transition went smoothly. For the next several decades, everyone seemed content with the arrangements that Charles had made, and the three brothers and their families remained close. Bob and Clark developed into an effective team and enjoyed lunch together almost every day. Similarly, Howard and Clark got along well and spent regular summer holidays together, cruising the waters off the west coast of B.C. in their twin 45-foot custom-built powerboats.

Charles eventually recovered from his heart attack and went on to live happily for almost 10 more years, well into his 90s. He remained actively interested in the business, serving as chairman of the board long after his retirement as president. This provided ample time for him to watch as Clark envisioned and successfully created what would eventually prove to be his, and the company's, crowning achievement.

The Bentall Centre, Vancouver, BC

Dominion Construction Makes Its Mark

In the late 1950s, my father visited the Rockefeller Center, a landmark development in the heart of New York City. As an engineer and a visionary, he was captivated by the multi-building complex with its integrated architecture, soothing fountains, and beautifully landscaped plazas. He immediately began to imagine a similar complex in downtown Vancouver, where office towers, retail space, and parks would be a beacon to attract the most discerning office and retail tenants.

Clark devoted the next 20 years of his life to creating a West Coast version of the Rockefeller

Center, a project that would ultimately be named in honour of his father, Charles. Today, the Bentall Centre encompasses more than two million square feet and is one of the largest integrated office complexes in Western Canada. It includes five office towers and underground retail shops, with stunningly landscaped plazas and fountains.

In parallel with the development of this landmark project, 20 years elapsed with my dad at the helm of Dominion and his brother Bob serving at his side as executive vice-president. For the most part, they worked well together, and the company prospered. Even those who knew them well considered it an exemplary partnership. However, as time went on, Bob became anxious to take on more responsibility and was eager to have "his turn" to lead the company. He had served in my father's shadow since 1955, and his patience was waning. In 1975, it was agreed that Bob would be appointed president and then in 1980 as CEO. Clark assumed the role of chairman of the board.

LOSS

The transition was accomplished without any apparent difficulties. After all, Clark and Bob had worked as a team for decades, and most major decisions had been made collaboratively. Although their roles had changed, they enjoyed equality in virtually all things. They were paid the same salary and had the same sized offices on the 31st floor of Bentall Three. One small but apparently important difference was that Clark's office was in the corner, with Bob's adjacent. Eventually Bob requested that they switch offices, in part to demonstrate that the transition in leadership was complete and Bob was in charge.

Trouble Beneath the Surface

Unfortunately for Bob, his title and the location of his office did not seem to matter, as people continued to treat Clark as the main man. The confusion over authority was exacerbated as Clark, like most successful leaders, found it difficult to "let go" and continued to have a significant influence over decisions. Over the years, Clark had earned the confidence of both employees and customers, and it was difficult for them to go to Bob when Clark was right there. In hindsight, I think that it was actually very difficult for both of them to try to change patterns of authority that had been established over decades of working side by side.

Sadly, as time went on, Clark's very presence in the office and his perceived interference became increasingly frustrating to Bob. As the company's 75th anniversary drew near, internal tensions escalated.

The proverbial "straw that broke the camel's back" occurred one day as Bob was finalizing plans to appoint one of our employees as the vice-president for real estate. A search for the right person to take on this responsibility had been ongoing for several years, and although an official announcement had not yet been made, Bob had offered the job to a faithful and hardworking executive of the company. The official announcement of his appointment was imminent.

However, at the eleventh hour, Clark ran into a business associate and friend who had just left his former employer. He seemed ideal for the position, and Clark offered him the job on the spot. He then advised Bob that he had found the perfect candidate for the new VP role.

Bob recognized that Clark had truly identified an ideal candidate, but the process by which it happened was clearly unhelpful, and this incident caused a tragic breakdown in their relationship. In spite of his best intentions, Clark had undermined Bob's authority, and as far as Bob was concerned, it would be the last time.

As company loyalties became divided and family relationships began to unravel, Clark and Bob decided to hire an independent facilitator to assist them in resolving their challenges. He recommended that each of the three families meet independently to share their desires for the future. Once the goals of each family were known, we hoped to create a shared vision that would satisfy everyone.

A Final Attempt to Create a Shared Vision

Each brother (Clark, Bob, and Howard) convened individual meetings with their children and spouses. (Clark's family met at a downtown hotel.) Instead of having our independent facilitator lead these meetings, it was agreed—at the last minute—that a "trusted" senior executive would be the facilitator because he had intimate knowledge of our business and the value of all our various assets.

Our meeting was attended by Dad and Mom (Clark and Phyllis), the four of us siblings, and our spouses. We were repeatedly asked "What do you want?" and "Would you prefer operating companies, land, buildings, or cash?" After eight hours of deliberations, we unanimously determined that all we wanted was "restoration of relationships in the family."

> All we wanted was "restoration of relationships in the family."

We hoped that this would be an encouraging message to spark productive and reconciliatory discussions amongst the families. But, over the next few days, there was no response from either of the other parties. When Dad and I finally sat down for a face-to-face meeting with Bob, Howard, and their cadre of lawyers, it was apparent that something had been "lost in translation."

We were bluntly told that as 32 percent owners of the business, we had two options: 1) We could buy out both Bob and Howard and acquire sole ownership of the company, or 2) we could endorse Bob's leadership and his four-point plan, which included a requirement that Dad physically relocate to a separate building, moving out of the head office.

Recognizing that Dad only owned a minority stake in the business, we approached our "trusted" senior executive to discuss our options for a buyout. He quickly dismissed the idea as far too risky and utterly unworkable. Shortly thereafter, I was summoned to a meeting where, in the presence of my three older siblings, I was informed that I would be removed from my position at the company. Suddenly, in my father's 50th year with the business, both he and I found ourselves on the outside, looking in.

It was a shocking turn of events, and we wondered how this could be happening to our family.

CHAPTER 3
Struggling with Succession

SYSTEMIC CHALLENGES

In retrospect, it is evident that there were a host of unresolved issues that eventually led to significant family conflict and relational breakdown. These challenges included growing tension between my dad and his brothers; differing opinions regarding the long-term vision for the company; Bob's frustration after waiting 30 years to lead the company; and, perhaps the most vexing, the question of who would be appointed the future CEO.

Most of these issues had been brewing beneath the surface for several years, and had there been better communication, a resolution might have been available to us. But, as is often seen when a family enterprise approaches an intergenerational transition, the most intractable problems were rooted in events that occurred long before things finally unravelled.

In our circumstances, it seems that the final dissolution of our family enterprise may have been emotionally driven. However, in the preceding years, the major challenges that contributed to the eventual fallout could be summarized as problems related to succession, governance, expectations, conflict, communication, and trust.

In my book *Leaving a Legacy*, I explore each of these topics in some detail and consider some of the strategies that we, as a family, might have employed to avoid or resolve them. In contrast, this book is focused primarily on what I might have done as a successor to mitigate these destructive undercurrents.

Before launching into a discussion of what I could have done differently, I would like to briefly consider some of the major themes that every family enterprise must face and how these were at play in our family.

Leadership Succession

As remarkable as it may seem, in our family the process for management succession was never discussed, let alone agreed to, between my dad and his brothers. Hence, no one knew how we were going to select the next CEO.

It was all so simple when Granddad (Charles) handed the leadership over to Dad (Clark). There had been no formal discussions—from the beginning Granddad had assumed that it would be his decision when he would relinquish his title. It should be noted that at that time, 1955, primogeniture (the practice of passing the family wealth or business to the eldest son) was the typical approach for determining the next generation leader for the family business. In those days, the primary qualifications for leadership were birth order and gender. Yet, despite its simplicity, primogeniture is no guarantee that there will be no hard feelings.

In our circumstance, Clark was several years older than Bob and had already been working in the business for 17 years when Charles had his heart attack. Consequently, it was not unreasonable that Charles, faced with his own mortality, decided to appoint the elder brother as president. That said, the process could have been handled more sensitively.

For example, the decision might have felt very different for Bob if his father had spoken to him personally about the plan. Instead, it must have been shocking for Bob to arrive at work a few days later and discover that his father's personal effects had been removed from the corner office and his brother Clark was sitting behind the CEO's desk. Even if Bob agreed with the decision to appoint Clark, he must have felt somewhat slighted by the way in which the changing of the guard had been implemented.

Governance

In addition, there was a lack of appropriate governance for the business, family, and ownership. Although we had received technical advice regarding succession planning, virtually no time was ever given to developing governance structures that would have facilitated open communication and joint decision-making.

My granddad was generally a collaborative and inclusive leader. But as the sole owner and president of the business, he was also free to make the final call on almost every corporate decision. My dad, Clark, observed (and learned) this leadership approach as he worked alongside Charles for 17 years. When Clark was appointed president, he very naturally assumed a similar kind of authority. Neither Charles nor Clark governed autocratically, as both men invited others to contribute their thoughts regarding all important matters. However, both believed that, in the end, the ultimately decision-making authority should belong with the president.

There were no formal board meetings or shareholder discussions when Charles led the company, and this pattern continued into the next generation. This informal approach to governance meant that Bob and Howard were equal owners with Clark, but they lacked equal decision-making authority. In a sense, Clark outranked them because of his senior role in management. That was the reality.

If one considers the *management hierarchy* as presented in the adjacent chart, it is easy to see how Clark (or others) would assume that the president or CEO was the final authority.

Yet, when one looks at the *company hierarchy*, below, a very different picture emerges. Under this structure, Clark was, in effect, an employee in an enterprise where his brothers owned two-thirds of the company. As such, the brothers could easily say that Clark worked for them. As a result, the brothers had radically differing perspectives regarding who should have final authority.

Years later, when my sisters and I partnered in the ownership of Dominion Construction, with the benefit of hindsight it was much easier for me to understand that I held my job only at "their pleasure" and that, in essence, I worked for them. It could be said that we operated with much more awareness of the company hierarchy.

Regardless, the management approach used by Charles and Clark could be described as primarily entrepreneurial, and it worked well for decades. But by 1975, the size and scale of our business meant that the company needed to implement more professional management practices, including strategic planning, individual goal setting, and formalized roles and accountabilities. When Bob became president, he introduced many such changes, focusing on organizational renewal and the development of clear lines of authority and responsibility.

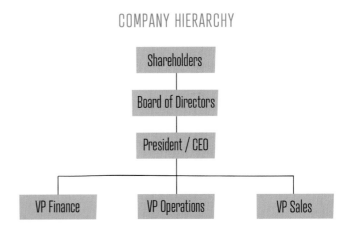

MANAGEMENT HIERARCHY

President / CEO

VP Finance   VP Operations   VP Sales

COMPANY HIERARCHY

Shareholders

Board of Directors

President / CEO

VP Finance   VP Operations   VP Sales

Over the years, Clark had become accustomed to his role as the one ultimately responsible for the day-to-day management of the business, and, even though he agreed to relinquish the formal leadership of the business to Bob, he was still the chairman of the board. Consequently, Clark retained considerable influence with both clients and employees. As a result, the lines of authority became blurred, employees were torn in their loyalties, and clients either did not recognize the change in leadership or simply continued to remain close to Clark because of long-standing relationships.

Different Expectations

Howard, Clark, and Bob each had very different expectations regarding their respective roles and responsibilities as shareholders.

In addition, as time went on, it became abundantly clear that the three brothers had very different visions for the future of the company. Once Bob was in charge, he wanted to make changes that reflected his vision, and Clark found it difficult to support Bob's plans.

In the beginning, Bob's leadership was focused on the professionalization of management. While this was uncomfortable for Clark, it was more a matter of style and not something that was sufficient to cause a major upset in their relationship.

However, as the following bullet points show, their differing visions covered matters at the very core of our family business:[1]

- **Ownership**. Bob wanted to take the company public. In contrast, Clark wanted the company to be passed on to the next generation and to remain privately owned.
- **Strategy**. Bob wanted the business to focus solely on real estate, whereas Clark wanted the company to remain active in both the real estate and construction sectors.
- **Leadership**. Bob wanted no more family involvement in management, while Clark was committed to maintaining our family legacy and wanted me to one day be appointed as president.[2]

> *The transition to professional management practices is always challenging, but ultimately necessary. Most leaders of growing family firms will grapple with this and how they handle it "can determine whether or not the family firm will continue to function harmoniously and to grow and succeed."*
>
> **W. Gibb Dyer Jr.**

It is hard to imagine two leaders with more radically divergent expectations and visions for the future of the same company.

To make matters even more challenging, it would later be revealed that Howard had his own distinctive perspective. Rather than preserve the business and our family's wealth, he wanted to give virtually all of it away to charity. Clearly, this was a noble and generous impulse, but it also represented a third distinct vision for the future.

Conflict

The company had no formal or informal mechanisms for resolving conflict in management or between the shareholders.

Differences of opinion and conflict are inevitable amongst co-owners, so it is important for shareholders to be proactive in planning how to minimize and manage conflict. Charles knew that at some point his three sons might disagree. As a countermeasure, before transitioning ownership of the company to his sons, Charles had the company legal advisors prepare a shareholders' agreement that would "make sure the boys would always remain together." Charles wanted to ensure the company's longevity long after he was gone. Unfortunately, this meant that the three brothers had no "buy/sell" arrangements and no agreed-upon mechanisms for dispute resolution.

Ironically, despite Charles's best intentions, the resulting shareholders agreement eventually created a frustrating situation where Bob and Howard felt "stuck" as co-owners with Clark, even though they disagreed on the future direction of the company. With no pre-agreed method for resolving their disagreements, Howard and Bob struggled to find a collaborative way forward. Eventually, they concluded that decisive action was required.

> *It is critical to have pre-agreed mechanisms for dispute resolution.*

Communication

There was also inadequate communication between the three brothers, especially regarding the future vision of the company.

Differences of opinion often spark an emotional response, but these reactions are typically much stronger in the context of a family business. In retrospect, it is clear that emotions added significantly to the problems our family experienced. The emotional hurt probably dates back to 1955, when Bob felt excluded by the decision to appoint Clark as president. Similarly, Howard's feelings of being left out may have been unspoken for years but eventually were released when major decisions had to be made about the future of the company.

> *Personal frustrations had decades to grow and fester.*

Each one had held back his frustration for years; had these sentiments been dealt with at the time, they may have eventually dissipated. Instead, their frustrations were afforded decades to grow and fester.

On their best days, Howard had a pastor's heart, Bob was a planner, and Clark was a consummate dealmaker. However, on their worst days, Howard could be dogmatic, Bob, defensive, and Clark, stubborn. Unfortunately, once feelings began to dominate, we saw the worst and not the best in each man. Rather than drawing on their strengths, they each relied on their less helpful tendencies. As a result, differences were unresolved, and as events spiralled out of control, fraternal relationships were shattered, and our family business was lost. Sadly, our emotions had gotten the better of all of us.

Misplaced Trust

We placed our trust in a senior executive to help us resolve things, only to discover much later that he had his own personal agenda.

Two years after the breakdown of our family and business, my cousin Rob and I discussed what had happened and the sad reality that there was a permanent fracture between our families. I told him that I still wondered how it was that the family relationships broke down so quickly and so completely after our family had stated that all we wanted was "restoration of relationships in the family."

Rob was taken aback when I told him this. He then informed me that our trusted senior executive had simply stated that "all [we] wanted was cash."

These words were a complete betrayal of our trust. To make matters worse, we later found out that he had been offered a seven-figure bonus to reduce my father to a single line on the balance sheet that read "minority interest," effectively cutting his wealth in half.

Who knows what might have happened if we had the assistance of an honest facilitator? What we do know is that our families continue to experience, 30 years later, the lasting and harmful effects of one man's actions.

It would be very easy to blame everything on an executive whom we should not have trusted. Similarly, it would be possible to point at my dad and his brothers as the source of all our problems. However, there is more to the story, and I feel compelled to consider how I could have made a difference in our situation had I acted or reacted differently.

CHOOSING THE WRONG ROLE MODELS

When I was 12 years of age, our family bought our first colour television, and it was a thrill for me to watch the very first Super Bowl take place *live and in colour*! The Green Bay Packers had a decisive victory over the Kansas City Chiefs, and I have been a dedicated Packers fan ever since they won that epic contest in 1967.

Their iconic coach Vince Lombardi became my first role model for leadership.

During the 1960s, he led the Packers to five NFL championships in a span of seven years. One of his

Vince Lombardi celebrates the NFL championship.

key teaching methods was to focus on getting the basics right, and he became known for welcoming new recruits at training camp by holding up the pigskin and saying, "Gentlemen, this is a football." You cannot get more basic than that.

Playing to Win. More importantly, at least to me, was his legendary determination to win, as exemplified by his famous dictum "Winning isn't the most important thing; it's the only thing." This slogan made perfect sense to me. So, when I graduated from university and entered the business world, I determined that it would be a good philosophy to adopt. After all, his leadership methods were a proven success, and, like Lombardi, I wanted to win.

There was just one problem: claiming Lombardi's philosophy as my own led me to believe that leadership meant winning at all costs. This kind of determination may work well on the football field, but it falls far short of what is required for leading a family business.

In a football game, everyone understands that there will—and must—be winners and losers. After all, that is why they call it a game. But things are very different in a family business, where relationships are of paramount importance; playing to win means there will inevitably be losers, and that can be very destructive to both the family and the business, as I would eventually discover first-hand.

In my working relationships with Dad and my uncle Bob, I was not being collaborative. Rather, I was playing to win almost every day, and that meant I tried to win every argument. It is no wonder that others began to sour on my aggressive and confrontational approach.

Never Give Up. My father, Clark, was an engineer. He had never been to business school or attended any formal courses to study management practice or leadership theories. But he was a voracious reader, and I recall seeing him propped up in bed with a book as I walked past his bedroom door each night. Invariably, he was reading the biography of a world leader or successful executive. Kennedy, Rockefeller, and Churchill were some of his favourite historic figures.

Sir Winston Churchill possessed unrivaled determination.

Not surprisingly, as a young man who wanted to follow in his father's footsteps, I set aside a special shelf in my bookcase for inspiring biographies of great leaders, including Walt Disney, Mahatma Gandhi, and Winston Churchill. Churchill was particularly inspiring to me, in part because of the courage he displayed in standing up to the fury of the German war machine.

He had inspired the British people and many in the Western world to stay strong and to do whatever it took to defeat the threat of fascism. His speeches were passionate and compelling, and some of his most famous quotes stayed with me for years. For example, "Success is not final, failure is not fatal: it is the courage to continue that counts."[3] "Never give in, never give in, never, never, never, never—in nothing, great or small, large or petty—never give in except to convictions of honour and good sense. Never yield to force; never yield to the apparently overwhelming might of the enemy."[4]

As a young man and aspiring leader, I internalized his words, and "never give up" became my personal rallying cry. In the context of business, I applied this strategy to what I considered to be my daily battles—"wars" of words and arguments over ideas. Rather than listening and learning from those who were much older and more experienced than me, I was determined to fight hard and to not give up on any topic.

I built my leadership style largely on the well-known mantras of these two men, Lombardi and Churchill, and their words guided virtually all of my thoughts and actions in the workplace. In hindsight, it is clear that this was not a helpful or healthy approach to leading a family business. I had inadvertently adopted the wrong leaders as role models and the wrong ideas of what comprised successful leadership. That is not to say that the leadership shown by Lombardi and Churchill is somehow unworthy of being emulated. Rather, their leadership styles were very successful and are very effective—especially if you are leading a football team or leading a nation into war. They had the right leadership skills for the tasks they were called to, but these approaches were not well-suited for leading a family enterprise.

I'm not sure why it didn't occur to me at the time, but football games and world wars are obviously very different than a family business. Consequently, the leadership styles required are very different. In a game, there can only be one winner; in a family business, we should be looking for ways to ensure that everyone wins. When fighting a war, many people die. However, no matter how bad things get in a family enterprise, we need not create life-and-death struggles. Instead, we should strive for goals that include love, respect, and family harmony.

> *These heroes dramatically shaped my approach to leadership.*

As a young man and as an aspiring successor, I had chosen powerful, successful leaders as my role models. However, I had chosen the wrong exemplars, or at least to cultivate the wrong character traits of these men, given that my desire was to lead a family business.

Looking Ahead. In the pages ahead, we explore in more depth some of the unhelpful strategies I employed earlier in my career.

Happily, it has been said that in life you do not have to make every mistake yourself (and that you can learn from other people's mistakes). Therefore, I hope you can learn from my mistakes and be guided in taking a different path. In addition, I commend to you other great leaders who might have been better role models for me and who I think could be great exemplars for today's family enterprise successors.

However, before we meet the nine role models I wish I had chosen for my career, we consider some general guidance for aspiring successors, as well as an introduction to the subject of management broadly and the field of family enterprise specifically.

SECTION II
Wisdom for Successors

Over the past four decades, the field of family business studies has blossomed from its infancy to become a mature research-based discipline. During this time, many scholars have endeavoured to determine what are best practices for business-owning families.

Section II provides a broad-based introduction to some of the leading people, ideas, principles, and academic studies that inform the owners and managers of family enterprises today. In addition, it explores some of the most important dynamics at play during the succession process in a family enterprise. Finally, in order to provide a strong foundation for aspiring successors, it includes insights from some of the most influential general management thinkers and practitioners of the past one hundred years.

CHAPTER 1
Family Enterprise Distinctives

Most people (outside of business circles) still consider family business as some sort of "mom and pop shop," with a small storefront and a handful of family members running the place. But the numbers show that this antiquated notion has little to do with reality.

In most countries around the world, family companies are the most prevalent form of business ownership, and they are frequently described as the backbone of our global economy. As an example, in Canada they "generated $574.6 billion [of revenue] in 2017—48.9 per cent of [the private sector] GDP … [and produced] nearly 7 million jobs."[5] Although there can be a perception that they are more transient, the statistics show that they "survive longer" and financially outperform non-family businesses.[6]

> *Family firms last longer and perform better.*

Academic researchers and advisors to business families have devoted the past 40 years to exploring the factors that contribute to the successes and unique challenges of a modern-day family enterprise. In this chapter, we explore these factors and other family business distinctives that successors must understand as they consider how to best contribute to their business family.

FAMILY ENTERPRISE STRENGTHS

More Profitable

Approximately 20 years ago, researchers Danny Miller and Isabelle Le Breton-Miller embarked on an ambitious quest to discover why family-controlled companies tend to perform better financially, and their groundbreaking work culminated in the 2005 publication of *Managing for the Long Run*.[7]

Their study was prompted by their discovery that research from around the world consistently showed that, all things being equal, family-owned businesses enjoyed better financial results than non-family companies.

As one example, the adjacent figure compares the performance of family-controlled companies to all other companies in the S&P 500 Index.[8] During a 10-year period from 1992 to 2002, the 167 family-controlled companies significantly outperformed the 333 non-family companies in terms of revenue growth and total shareholder return (TSR). This comparison revealed that, during that time, family companies also enjoyed a 15.6 percent average annual return, compared to an average of 11.2 percent for all the remaining (non-family-owned) businesses.

Superior Performance by Family Enterprises[9]

Family Controlled Companies
Non Family Companies

Similar results demonstrating the superior performance of family-controlled companies come from a more recent study, completed by the Rotman School of Management. According to their research, over a 15-year period (1997 to 2012) the 23 largest family-controlled firms in Canada outperformed the TSX by an average of 41 percent.[10]

Strategic Advantages

What makes the difference? Miller and Le Breton-Miller performed a rigorous analysis of 16 internationally prominent family companies that 1) had been successful over multiple generations and 2) were the best, or one of the most prominent, companies in their respective industries. Based on those criteria, the study included such well-known family firms as Cargill Grain, Hallmark Cards, IKEA, LL Bean, and Estee Lauder. Following extensive research, they concluded that these family-controlled companies have four unique and strategic pillars that enable them to compete more effectively in the market.[11]

These advantages are summarized as follows:

- **Command:** Family businesses are able to take decisive action and respond more quickly to market challenges and opportunities. (This is because, typically, the CEO of a family-owned business is also a shareholder. This helps create alignment between the shareholders and management, thus avoiding the agency problem that plagues most public companies.)

- **Continuity:** Investment decisions are made with a long-term perspective, rather than the need to focus on quarterly earnings or short term results. (One year in the 1980s, when Cargill Grain had enjoyed record profits, instead of paying any dividends to shareholders, the company allocated 115 percent of that year's earnings for reinvestment and their global expansion plans.)[12]
- **Connection:** Because family enterprise CEOs typically remain in their roles much longer than their non family counterparts, they are able to forge stronger relationships with both customers and suppliers, and they typically reflect a win/win philosophy. (When IKEA was first starting out, one of their component manufacturers was having difficulty keeping up with production, so IKEA loaned them the money to expand.)[13]
- **Community:** They are better able to create a collaborative team of employees and a unified culture. (By employing a personal, more relational style of management, family firms tend to do a better job of "uniting the tribe.")[14]

It is important that successors understand the potency of these strengths, as they are all powerful tools to help a family enterprise compete effectively. For that reason, successors should consider these as key priorities to be preserved, and thus successors should steward them wisely.

FAMILY ENTERPRISE COMPLEXITY

Two Bottom Lines

Complexity is one factor that is often overlooked when considering the various elements that make a family enterprise unique. The family (including interpersonal relationships and family patterns of communication) can have a powerful influence on the success of its business. Conversely, the impact of business issues on family relationships adds an additional element of complexity to the family.

CEOs and leaders of large independently owned corporations are often able to retreat to the sanctuary of their homes after a difficult day at work, but there may be little solace available to the leader of a family business who must head home to further deal with the family issues that are impinging on the business.

In many ways, in a family enterprise, the family and the business are not truly independent or separate; rather, they are interwoven in a dynamic way such that any shift or change in one inevitably has consequences for the other.

Commenting on this, Dr. John L. Ward and Dr. Denise Kenyon-Rouvinez, widely known family business researchers and consultants, have described this duality as two distinct entities that are competing for the attention of the patriarch or the successor. They note that "Both the family and the business have their own needs and goals; each has its own life and each has its own beliefs."[15]

> *A family enterprise has two bottom lines— financial and relational.*

Some leaders make the business their top priority and are willing to put their marriages or family relationships at risk for the sake of the firm. Conversely, some executives put their primary focus on their family, at the expense of paying proper attention to business. (And this can lead to declining financial results or even the loss of the business.) Each situation represents the kind of extreme that family business leaders want to avoid.

The key, as they say, is to pay an appropriate amount of attention to both sides of the coin. At the Business Families Centre at the University of British Columbia, we refer to this as paying attention to the *two bottom lines*—financial and relational.

3 CIRCLE MODEL

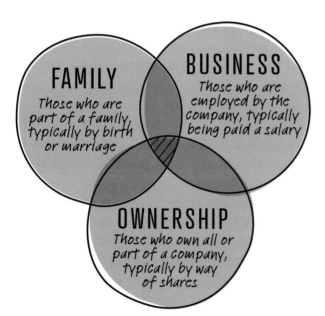

FAMILY
Those who are part of a family, typically by birth or marriage

BUSINESS
Those who are employed by the company, typically being paid a salary

OWNERSHIP
Those who own all or part of a company, typically by way of shares

Three Interrelated Systems

Dr. John Davis is a globally recognized pioneer and authority in family enterprise studies who is also a senior lecturer in the Family Enterprise Executive Programs at the MIT Sloan School of Management. Over 30 years ago, while working on his doctoral thesis, he sought to discern the source of the most common family enterprise challenges. As he interviewed families, he discovered (not surprisingly) that most of the issues had their roots in either the business or the family domain. However, he also made the unanticipated observation that many of the challenges were related to neither. Further analysis showed that *virtually all other problems emanated from the ownership or shareholder realm of the company.*

This discovery gave birth to the Three Circle Model (representing the company, the family, and the ownership) as a means of explaining the interdependence of the three entities at play, as well as the resulting advantages and issues.[16]

In the preceding diagram, the Three Circle Model demonstrates the independent and overlapping systems that are a part of a family enterprise.[17] Each system has its own priorities, preferences, and membership; each one can impinge upon or even compete with the other domains. Membership in each circle is defined by whether the individual is a member of the family, an employee, or a shareholder. The overlapping sections reflect the linkages (and potential tension) between the various groups.

There are many advantages to viewing a business with this model. Most importantly, it clarifies the relationships between shareholders, family members, and company employees by visually demonstrating who rightly has responsibility for decisions in each arena. For example, not every family member is an employee or a shareholder. This may result in some feeling "left out" if they are not included in a business or shareholder discussion. However, just as in every other business, it is inappropriate for those not active in a business to presume they should be able to influence business decisions. The same principle holds true for non-shareholders who may wish to attend a shareholders meeting. It is just not appropriate.

It's critical to clarify which topics should be discussed in which circle.

By using this model to understand and analyze their relationships, all members of a family enterprise can more easily establish which topics of discussion belong in which circle (family, business, and ownership) and who should be involved in making decisions in each of these spheres. Within a family business, there are times when family members may try to insert themselves where they do not belong. The Three Circle Model helps makes the lines of authority (and therefore appropriate behaviour) much clearer for family members, employees, and owners. In short, this can help families determine when individuals may properly have a "voice" but not a "vote."

Obviously, in a new venture or young company, the business founder is usually the main decision-maker in each circle. However, as the company matures and the founder's children come of age, it can be difficult for the founder to share decision-making duties with others. The potential for blurring the lines between circles adds the kinds of complications that make a family business more complex and multi-dimensional than other corporations.[18]

For some, this diagram may appear to make things far more complicated than necessary; after all, each person should know how they relate to the family business, right? Unfortunately, this is often not the case. For these reasons, using the Three Circle Model as a tool to visually define relationships is essential for helping family members to understand where they fit in the grand scheme of things. In addition, the diagram can be extremely useful in helping families develop good governance because it clarifies both decision-making responsibilities and appropriate lines of communication.

For all of these reasons, it is necessary for successors to be aware of the interests of those in each of the different realms so they can better understand their motivations and how these may influence their decisions.

Ownership Complications

In a family enterprise, most of the serious problems arise in the ownership circle. This is because it is the sphere where the real power resides. One of the most common challenges families face is transitioning ownership between the generations. Simply determining how and when to pass authority and responsibility from parents to children can be extremely difficult. (Sometimes parents wait too long, creating frustration and disillusionment on the part of the rising generation.)

In other situations, siblings or cousins may become co-owners in a family enterprise as a result of what some have termed "an accidental partnership." This situation can arise when family members who have no desire to go into business together end up as co-owners or partners as a result of a bequest from the elder generation. In such relationships, it can be a real challenge to develop a collaborative and effective ownership group.

Unfortunately, all too often there is very little mentoring offered for the next generation regarding how to become a capable owner or a good partner. At best, successors are encouraged to learn how to become competent employees. However, owning shares is a fundamentally different responsibility than being a company executive. As a result, when challenging shareholder issues arise, most family enterprise inheritors are ill-equipped to exercise their responsibilities wisely.

FAMILY DYNAMICS

Relational Challenges

Business guru Peter Drucker is often referred to as "the founding father" of modern management and has been one of the world's most influential thinkers on business management. He notes that "any organization is both an economic and social organ"[19] in that every company involves business and interpersonal affairs, and these tend to create an element of tension for business leaders. Since all corporations have limited resources, he argues that the human and commercial aspects of a business always compete for time and money.

> *Family relationships are the most important priority.*

In this respect, all companies reflect the realities of a family enterprise where both personal and business interests are in tension, and this interface needs to be managed. But the relational issues in a family firm are often more complex than the situation described by Drucker because family relationships require attention both within the business and within the family. This may seem very self-evident to some, but I recall thinking as a young business school student that the interpersonal aspects of business were somehow not that important, especially when compared to the business itself and the financial bottom line. So, rather than pay attention to this vital area, I gave it short shrift, both at school and when I started working.

I could not have been more mistaken in choosing my priorities. In contrast, wise family enterprise successors recognize that the relational and interpersonal elements of a family business are perhaps the most important priority, requiring their understanding and careful attention.

Emotions

When I first mention to someone that I work as an advisor to families in business, they are often a bit curious as to what such a role might entail. But when I explain that my primary objectives are to help my clients avoid 1) "the business wrecking the family" and 2) "the family wrecking the business," they inevitably nod knowingly. It is as if they suddenly understand the unique circumstances and complications that can develop.

In our family's story, personal and familial issues eventually came to dominate all the critical decisions surrounding the future of the family business. Sadly, the emotional pain that had festered for years without being addressed eventually overwhelmed the situation and dictated the business decisions that resulted in the business being sold.

It is almost inevitable that emotional issues in the business that are not properly addressed will "spill over" into the family and vice versa. When this happens, either the business or the family is severely impacted, and sometimes both.

In preparing to lead, most successors work hard to gain the knowledge and skills required to understand the business that is associated with their family—including acquiring sufficient knowledge and experience in a particular industry, recognizing the unique factors that allow it to compete successfully in that marketplace, and understanding the priorities of shareholders. However, in a family firm, this simply is not enough. There is also a vital responsibility for successors to also understand what is going on in terms of family dynamics.

Emotional Intelligence

In my early career, I spent several years focused primarily on learning as much as I could about our various business operations. Yet, during this time, I remained largely unaware of the level of jealousy and ill will that existed within our family, not to mention the similar feelings held by other employees and executives. Had I been more self-aware, I would have seen the potential for rough weather ahead, and perhaps I would have realized how much I needed to cultivate productive relationships with other employees, family members, their spouses, and their offspring.

Daniel Goleman, who helped popularize the term *emotional intelligence* (EQ), explains how our EQ is more important to success in life than our intelligence (IQ).[20] According to Goleman, the ongoing and deliberate development of five distinct skills, including self-awareness, self-control, and empathy, contributes to developing a higher EQ. More importantly, it has been shown that a higher level of EQ is generally displayed by the most effective leaders.[21]

> *The most effective leaders have a high EQ.*

Without emotional intelligence, we are susceptible to "flooding," where an emotional response such as anger generates more anger.[22] As executives, when we become angry or flooded, chemical reactions in our brain impair our ability to think and act rationally, and our ability to lead effectively becomes compromised.[23]

In a family business environment, where we may often be interacting with other family members, emotional reactions can be easily triggered, either because of relational baggage or as a result of ongoing family tension. Rather than being able to think clearly, which our business roles require, we can be derailed by our emotions.

With this in mind, it is futile to simply insist that everyone in the business should simply be rational. Instead, those who are part of a family enterprise are wise to work at developing their emotional intelligence and to give careful attention to the relational dynamics that are so critical to effective management. I now realize that this was definitely absent for me earlier in my career, and this lack on my part was instrumental in me eventually forfeiting my opportunity to lead our family enterprise.

LEADERSHIP FOCUS

Management Styles

Leaders of a family firm (especially owner/founders) typically adopt a very different leadership style than other executives. In a family enterprise, the leader's style is often more informal and based on authority derived from ownership. In companies that are not family controlled, the owners generally seek out leaders who possess *professional management* skills. Often it is assumed that family business leaders cannot be professional managers.

Yet, Gibb Dyer Jr. points out that the two need not be in conflict. In his classic article "Integrating Professional Management into a Family-Owned Business," he suggests that family business members can develop professional management skills in the same way as non-family executives would.[24]

He also offers a valuable comparison of the typical characteristics that are associated with each kind of management style (see table).

Obviously, these descriptions are broad generalizations. For example, not all family managers are more relational in their dealings than non-family managers; similarly, not all professional managers can be classified as being exceptionally rational. Nonetheless, it is helpful for successors to be aware of the natural inclinations associated with each style of management, as attributes from both categories can be constructive and contribute to creating a healthy and productive workplace culture.

Comparison of Typical Management Characteristics

FAMILY MANAGERS	vs	PROFESSIONAL MANAGERS
Informal		Formal
Intuitive		Analytical
Personal		Impersonal
Vision-oriented		Bottom-line focused
Emotional		Rational
Relational		Detached
Authority derived from ownership		Authority derived from position

When discussing the advantages and disadvantages of each, my undergraduate and MBA students at the University of British Columbia were virtually unanimous in their preference for the professional management approach. Traits such as analytical, rational, and bottom-line focused seemed particularly compelling. But, as we thoughtfully considered some of the benefits of family management, it became clear that those who reflect these qualities would have stronger, more relational, and intuitive characteristics than the detached, analytical approaches utilized by non-family managers.

After all, who would not prefer working in a company where the culture was informal, relational, and personal? It sounds much better than working with a leader who is formal, impersonal, and detached.

As my students eventually concluded, ideal leaders incorporate some combination of professional management and family management, thus enabling them to employ the best of both.

Vision Versus Bottom Line

Many business executives and management consultants assert the critical importance of maintaining a "bottom-line focus" in business. This emphasis is referenced almost as sacrosanct, and in many ways it is. After all, a company that cannot maintain a healthy bottom line eventually (often sooner rather than later) ceases to exist.

Family businesses are somewhat different in that many are more focused on their mission or vision than their financial results. In essence, they enjoy a strong bottom line *because* they have faithfully pursued a compelling vision rather than financial metrics, and this has led them to achieve great things in the market and for their customers.

One example of this is the development of the Bentall Centre in downtown Vancouver. It was conceived of and developed based on a dream birthed when my father saw the Rockefeller Center in New York City. As a result, he purposed to create a similar complex on the West Coast. The project produced great economic results and was an enduring financial success; but this was due primarily to the tenacious pursuit of a grand vision rather than to a myopic focus on financial metrics.

CONCLUSION

As remarkable as it may seem to some, family businesses are typically more profitable than other companies, and they also enjoy strategic advantages that emanate from them being family controlled. On the other hand, family firms are more complicated. Quite simply, the "family dimension" adds many more variables, including the potential for more interpersonal and emotional challenges, as well as some unique leadership issues.

Consequently, aspiring leaders in a family enterprise cannot think only about rational solutions to the problems they face; they also must consider the emotional and relational impact of their decisions. They need to also consider the company shareholders, who, ultimately, have the greatest power and authority. If they want to make a positive contribution to the family, business, and ownership, wise successors recognize the complexity of a family enterprise and place a high priority on the relational aspects of management and on developing their own emotional intelligence.

CHAPTER 2
Perspectives on Succession

It is almost impossible to complete a 1,000-piece jigsaw puzzle if you have not seen the picture that you are trying to create. Similarly, even if you know what the image is, it is often useful to step back and take another look at the picture on the box. One look helps you to determine how the pieces ought to fit together. In other words, stepping back gives you perspective. This not only enables you to more quickly see how things fit together; it also empowers you to complete the task at hand.

Sometimes succession (or continuity planning) can feel like trying to assemble a giant puzzle. The difference is that if you are struggling to complete a jigsaw puzzle, the challenge may, at worst, hurt your pride. The stakes are much higher with succession, where career ambitions, family relationships, and survival of the business are all potentially at risk. Just like in the puzzle analogy, it is often critical for successors and others involved in the succession process to take a step back and gain some perspective.

In this chapter, we explore several ways of viewing succession in an effort to help both the elder and the rising generations to see how the complicated elements ought to fit together. In addition, we consider some of the best practices that can help families navigate the challenge of continuity planning.

HELPFUL PERSPECTIVES ON SUCCESSION

Succession Is a Process

It has been 20 years since I asked Bill Sauder to tell me his thoughts on succession. At the time, he was the successful CEO of a prominent Western Canadian family business in the forest products industry. When I asked Bill what advice he had for my students and those in family business, he immediately replied, "*Tell them that succession is a process, not a decision.*"

Many people think family business succession should focus on *who* will lead the company, but, as Bill explained, succession is a more complicated process that involves a host of activities, including *discussion, planning, adjusting, revising, and mentoring* (to name a few), and should involve a number of stakeholders, such as shareholders, family members, senior management, and board members.

> "Succession is a process, not a decision."

Bill spent 31 years actively engaged in the process of succession, including all the activities previously noted. His eldest son, Lawrence, was eventually appointed president of their private company, Sauder Industries, and invited to serve on the executive committee of their public company, Interfor. These roles were a natural fit for him, as he had done well and successfully risen within the ranks of both companies. But when Lawrence turned 55, he decided to take early retirement, and that left Bill, at the age of 75, having to rethink things.

Subsequently, when Bill passed away, the board of directors stepped in and assumed a leadership role. One of their first decisions was to invite Lawrence to come out of retirement; he agreed and once again took a leadership role in the family company.

Some might find this story discouraging, but I think it points out the wisdom of Bill's holistic view of succession. Because he saw succession as a process, rather than as a choice, he had worked hard to prepare the board, family, and shareholders for the future. As a result, when changes needed to be made, the company was better equipped to adjust and make wise, timely decisions.

The Sauder family story illustrates the twists and turns that can occur during continuity planning in a family enterprise, as well as how long the process can take. It also shows that succession is more than simply making a choice regarding the company's next leader. Rather, it is a process; and, when thoughtfully approached, it includes at least four main elements:

- preparing the corporation for transition,
- preparing leadership candidates for the future,
- preparing a board who can guide and support the process, and
- preparing the family for change.

Whether the reality of the process turns out to be relatively seamless or somewhat turbulent, one of the most helpful basic postures toward succession is to take seriously that it is a process and to commit oneself and one's family to thoughtful preparation and capacity building.

Many family enterprise experts also emphasize the importance of viewing succession as a *process*, rather than simply as an inevitable moment of transition. For example, John A. Davis and Dr. Sabine Klein explain that succession is a complex process within which there is a common set of patterns and phases, including a *preparatory stage* that anticipates change, a *hot phase* that reflects the actual transition, and a period of *post succession re-orientation.*[25]

Unfortunately, some families naively view succession as a fairly straightforward transition that virtually happens on its own as one generation gracefully shifts into retirement and another rises capably. In contrast, some fear succession and may view it more skeptically, waiting for a sudden moment of inevitable crisis—like a car accident—when those involved can only see the moment coming, brace for the impact, and hope for the best.

How we view succession is vital because it inevitably influences the way in which we approach and participate in the transition. Regardless of whether we view succession with optimism or with fear and trepidation, understanding its dynamics is a critical step in navigating it successfully. Seeing it as a *process* is the first and most important step.

Succession as Collaboration

A casual conversation with successors often includes the innocently spoken yet presumptive question "*When are you going to take over the family business?*" It may be spoken in naivety, but in today's socio-political context, the words *take over* imply an aggressive or even hostile act. For example, the takeover of a public company typically involves a group of shareholders who forcibly seize control; it rarely involves a handshake and congenial handing over of the keys.

> It's unhelpful to talk about "taking over" the business.

Frankly, even some of the more genteel phrases, such as *handing over the reins* or *being given the keys to the kingdom*, still carry the connotation of a successor who is assuming magisterial *control*, with the implication that the elder generation is to be supplanted or discarded.

From the perspective of the elder generation, a conversation with such language is unsettling at the least and frightening at the worst. More dangerously, such analogies can contribute to feelings of impatience, as well as amplify a sense of entitlement.

Thinking of *succession as a takeover* has the potential to create serious intergenerational conflict or to exacerbate any pre-existing elements of tension. The language may be casual, but it suggests an almost cavalier view of succession that works against a spirit of teamwork or partnership, and it ought to be resisted as unhelpful. Rather than planning a "hostile takeover," wise successors look for ways to collaborate with the elder generation and opportunities to learn from those who have gone before them.

Building Succession on Shared Values

An instructive way of viewing succession is advocated by John A. Davis and Dr. Sabine Klein.[26] They compare the succession process to building a house; first comes the foundation, then the structure, the siding, and, ultimately, the roof. The authors propose that the foundation for the succession process be a shared vision and a codification of the family's values. Building on this, the process can include other priorities, such as strategic planning, leadership selection, and suitable governance mechanisms. Unfortunately, many families start their succession planning with who should lead the business, which, according to Davis and Klein, is similar to building the roof of a house before pouring the concrete footings.

Agreeing on a shared vision requires time and careful thought and is usually best initiated with the help of an independent non-family facilitator who can help the family to hear one another and to articulate their hopes and dreams for the future.

Agreeing on a foundation of shared values can be accomplished in a similar fashion. By way of example, the following is a family values statement that was developed by a long-term client as they approached succession between the second and third generations.

Simpson Family Values

1. **Family.** We value family first and foremost and strive to maintain a strong and united family bond for future generations to come.
2. **Faith.** We acknowledge that faith in God is important to many members of our family, and we agree that we will conduct our family affairs in a way that will be consistent with Christian principles.
3. **Integrity.** We look to uphold a standard of honesty and integrity in all our relationships.
4. **Tradition.** We will honour and cherish our family's traditions as a way of maintaining unity and passing on our strengths from generation to generation.
5. **Teamwork.** We will support and encourage each other in pursuing our individual and collective goals, and we will seek synergy and teamwork wherever possible.
6. **Respectfulness.** We will be open minded and be courteous towards one another despite any differences.
7. **Loyalty.** We value one another and will remain loyal to the family and its best interests.
8. **Communication.** We believe that good communication is the key to strong and meaningful relationships within the family.
9. **Excellence.** We strive towards excellence in all we do.

10. Work/Life Balance. We will support and encourage one another to maintain good health and to seek an appropriate work/life balance.

Note that these are statements of family values and not business values. When the family shareholders met with the board to discuss business values, they used the preceding list as a starting place. They then developed a set of values that reflected the owning family's values but were adapted to address the needs of the business.

Working with family clients over the past two decades, I have found that discussing family values is a great way to help build family unity. Clarifying values also provides a foundation for planning and creating a shared vision. Ideally, if shareholders are clear about both their values and their vision, the whole succession process is easier.

> Clarifying family values can help establish a shared vision.

Succession as Passing the Baton

A fourth and complementary view of succession is to think of it like the *"passing of a baton"* while running a relay race. As you think about what is required for succession, consider the similarities with a successful exchange between members of a relay team:

- The party with the baton does not stop running until after the baton is firmly in the hands of the next runner.
- The person receiving the baton must start running before being given the baton.
- Mutual respect and collaboration are needed for a successful handoff.
- No matter how well you run your leg of the race, a poor handoff can spell disaster.
- Careful planning and practice are required to execute this well.
- The baton exchange is not a single moment but rather many moments of collaboration.
- Focusing on your own leg of the race, even with steely determination, is not the way to win the race.

To succeed with intergenerational succession, both generations require an appreciation of the needs of the other and ought to be actively considering how they may assist one another. This is particularly important for successors because likely there will be a longer "collaborative phase" than they might want. Admittedly, too much overlap between generations can be frustrating (for each group), but accepting that succession takes place "over time" rather than "in an instant" is critically important. In preparing for their role in passing the baton, successors and their counterparts are wise to discuss and agree on what their "overlap" is going to look like in terms of the anticipated time and their respective roles.

In an ideal, or optimum, transition, the elder generation mentors the younger generation, and they work together collaboratively. On the other hand, a poor transition takes place when the elder generation is reluctant to transition power and authority to the rising generation, creating frustration and tension for everybody.

The following illustrations compare a situation where there is *too much* overlap—the elder generation overstays its welcome, and frustration is created—with a healthier or *optimum* transition, characterized by mentoring and collaboration.

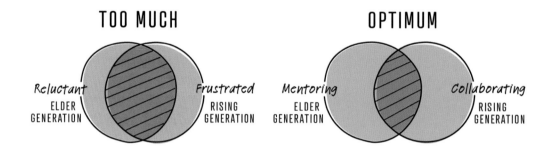

Balancing Tradition and Innovation

Finally, it is important to think of succession in terms of the interplay between the old way of doing things (tradition) and the new way (innovation). By definition, these elements are generally in a state of tension. However, wise successors in a family enterprise recognize that these elements are best understood as two overlapping narratives or stories. Permit me to explain.

The Family Narrative. Being part of a family inevitably means being part of a narrative that includes traditions and a defined heritage. Every family has a unique history, a particular sense of identity, shared values, and a common way of doing things. In the Bentall family, we have all been influenced significantly by several long-held family traditions initiated by our grandfather. These included summer vacations on Keats Island, a habit of working hard, the importance of family, active participation in a local Baptist church, and a duty to give back to the community. Each of these patterns was modelled by Grandpa Charles and his three sons and then passed on to our generation. In turn, we have encouraged our children and grandchildren to follow these important family traditions.

Sometimes there were adjustments made to these values in practice, while still honouring their original intent. For example, my wife, Alison, and I no longer attend a Baptist church today, nor do any of our four children, but we all remain active in a local church community. As I reflect on all of these elements of our lives,

I think Granddad would be delighted to know that we all continue to care about the things that were most important to him.

Theoretically, successors can choose to identify with every aspect of their family's traditions or to reject them completely. But the situation does not have to be an all-or-nothing choice—often the best approach is when members of the rising generation engage with their family heritage in a manner that establishes a healthy balance between tradition and innovation.

For this reason, it is important for successors to consider and reflect upon their family's traditions and to gain an understanding of why things are done the way they are or why a particular tradition is so significant to the family. In the case of our family, my grandfather's personal faith informed everything he did, and his Christian beliefs were the bedrock beneath his integrity in business and the warmth in his interactions with both clients and employees. Without question, the values of his personal life and his business life were inextricably linked.

The Corporate Narrative. Corporations also have their own traditions, although they are more commonly referred to as "the way we do things around here." For example, 30 years ago, when IBM was nicknamed "Big Blue," one of their traditions implied that virtually everyone in the company should wear a blue blazer and grey slacks. However, in more recent years, as business changed, and as culture changed, so too did IBM's dress code. For the clothing company Lululemon, their traditional norms include personal goal setting, an active lifestyle, and regular yoga sessions. While it may be difficult to predict how Lululemon's traditions may change in the future, it is inevitable that there will be changes over the long run.

In fact, in many corporations, if they fail to change from within, they are forced to do so by outside forces, such as changing markets or changing tastes of customers. In a world that is constantly evolving, all businesses must be willing over time to either adapt or die. In other words, some forms of change or innovation are always required for an enterprise to survive long term.

> *Every business must adapt or die.*

Throughout their careers, both my father and my grandfather were required to address the complex dance between tradition and innovation. To begin with, they were both strongly committed to a set of core values, including honesty, integrity, quality, and loyalty. Nonetheless, as leaders, they were also adaptable in terms of introducing new products, starting new ventures, and visualizing new projects. As may be readily apparent, their core values did not need to be compromised in order to innovate in these ways. Such is the nature of enduring values.

In comparison, some of the traditional ways of doing things at the company did have to change. For example, as our company evolved and grew, it was forced to adapt to the growing influence of technology and to adopt new strategies, such as joint venturing to finance new real estate projects.

The following is a partial list of traditions that were eventually replaced with new approaches:

- Granddad confirmed deals with a handshake. Today, business is more formal, and legal contracts are the norm.
- Granddad did all project drawings by hand, and most calculations were done with a pencil and a slide rule. Today, computers take care of both.
- In the beginning, our company only built buildings for our clients—we seldom owned them. Over time, owning and managing the properties we built became two core elements of our business.

(Please note that some of the specifics of these changes are discussed in further detail in section III of this book.)

An Ongoing Dance. Whether we realize it or not, we all participate in various kinds of traditions and changes each day. This tension can be amplified for successors who are constantly negotiating between the stability of tradition and the excitement of innovation while attempting to honour what can be conflicting family and business narratives. The tension is obvious to all, yet the impact of family narratives, tradition, and innovation is rarely acknowledged or discussed in a family enterprise. As a result, there can be resistance from both the family and the business as successors introduce new ideas and seek to innovate. Sometimes it may be unintentional and simply the result of not having a discussion and proper communication about the significance of various traditions within both the business and the family.

> *Family narratives and traditions are too seldom discussed.*

The question is, Is it important to retain anything from our history as we battle for market share in a digital age? After all, it may be argued, at least by some, that the most important contribution that a successor can make to a business is to help improve the bottom line.

The problem is that when we only use financial metrics, the values, traditions, and organizational culture of the company are reduced to matters of little or no consequence. A family company that shows no consideration for these important elements in business inevitably has difficulty retaining employees, maintaining morale, and producing innovative products. In other words, the business likely will not last very long. The implications for family relationships in such a scenario are just as troubling.

So how can successors build on what they have inherited without losing touch with the organizational culture of the business and the core values of the family?

To successfully respond to this challenge and to navigate through such circumstances requires emotional intelligence and an acute awareness of the dynamics at play in both the business and the family. It also involves learning how to balance the competing interests of others that become particularly obvious during times of succession.

In my experience, successors often pay little attention to family history and the heritage or traditions of the elder generation. I have commonly witnessed the scenario where successors have a tendency to want to "throw out the baby with the bathwater." When the process of succession is perceived as being an all-or-nothing scenario, younger leaders may look around, as I did, and, without a mature understanding of the company, see little else but the need for sweeping change. This, then, fuels a temptation to abandon what is in the past without giving proper regard to its significance in establishing the company's success.

In our case, as our business grew closer to its 75th anniversary and the possibility of another intergenerational transition, the tension between innovation and tradition intensified. Yet, rather than a balancing between tradition and innovation, it felt more like a winner-takes-all kind of battle. In contrast, successors who want to avoid such a scenario pay attention to the interplay between tradition and innovation and work with the elder generation to strike a balance between the old and the new.

The elder generation in a family enterprise usually emphasizes tradition, whereas the younger/rising generation tends to emphasize innovation. This is normal, but the tug of war between tradition and innovation can cause great tension in the family and the business, as depicted above.

BEST PRACTICES FOR SUCCESSORS

Think Win-Win

Instead of wrestling for control, a better path is found in collaboration. As Stephen Covey, author of *The Seven Habits of Highly Effective People*, puts it, in describing the fourth habit (of seven) in very simple terms, *think win-win*. Wise successors embrace this approach.

I read about this principle early on in my career and recognized its value immediately. Even so, I failed to adequately employ this kind of thinking and thus failed to enjoy its benefits in my relationships with the elder generation in our family. Decades later, I realized that I am not alone in this. In my consulting work with successors, I often see their good intentions go out the window when the rubber hits the road. They may understand the value of win-win, but in and of itself that is not enough to affect their behaviour in the heat of the moment.

Speaking as a former successor, I recognize that we have a tendency to think we know better than the elder generation and therefore to desire freedom to do things the way we want. Once we have reached the conclusion that we know best, it is easy to forget that our goal should be to find a win-win solution for everyone involved.

In practice, it can also be a genuine challenge for successors to develop trusting, co-operative relationships with their non-family colleagues at work. Successors and other employees can often become suspicious of each other and may sometimes wonder what the other might be thinking. Fortunately, Stephen Covey offers a brilliant, aspirational picture of what successors should work towards and how they can build win-win relationships rooted in a combination of trust and co-operation. In essence, he notes that the more we *develop trust* and *learn to collaborate*, the more win-win relationships we can create.

The accompanying chart presents the two priorities to keep in mind when thinking about our levels of communication. If we seek trusting relationships with others and simultaneously bring a co-operative approach to our interactions, this combination leads to *synergistic* outcomes—in other words, win-win solutions.[27]

LEVELS OF COMMUNICATION

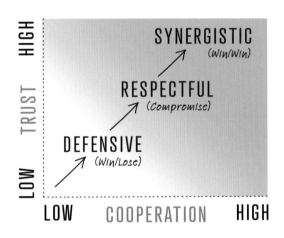

Become "The Best Person for the Job"

For centuries, leaders around the world have desired to see their offspring follow in their footsteps. Whether they were monarchs in years gone by or business executives in the 21st century, they virtually all shared a common hope, that the next generation would successfully assume the mantle of leadership.

In a monarchy, an objective assessment of an heir's competence would be anathema. Unfortunately, some families adopt this same perspective. However, in a family enterprise, the qualifications for promotion to the top job ought to include a suitable education and demonstrable executive competence. Peter Drucker raises a high bar when he writes, "In the successful family company, a [family member] is promoted only if he or she is measurably superior to all nonrelatives on the same level."[28]

He then cites two examples to reinforce this point:

> At DuPont, for instance, all top managers (except the controller and lawyer) were family members in the early years when the firm was run as a family business. All male descendants of the founders were entitled to entry-level jobs at the company. Beyond the entrance level, [however,] a family member got a promotion only if a panel composed primarily of non-family managers judged the person to be superior in ability and performance to all other employees at the same level.
>
> The same rule was observed for a century in the highly successful British family business J. Lyons & Company (now part of a major conglomerate) when it dominated the British food-service and hotel industries.[29]

In my view, the key lesson from these examples is that every family enterprise successor, regardless of birthright, is well served to adopt an approach whereby they "seek to become the best person for the job," regardless of what that job is and regardless of their last name.

Successors should strive to be the best person for the job.

Develop Family Employment Policies

It is often very difficult to bring objectivity to discussions about family members' career advancement in a family enterprise. But the process can be dramatically improved if the family can agree, in advance, to a *family employment policy* to govern family members' participation in the company. Amongst other things, the development of such policies can assist families to consider and agree upon any required educational prerequisites, as well as suitable professional development initiatives.

Family employment policies also help create a balanced approach to hiring and promoting family members and non-family members, without giving undue preference to either. Consider the following helpful excerpts from a thoughtfully crafted family employment policy.

Our children will be happiest with themselves and the world around them when they are strong, independent individuals … Our company cannot be a haven for the weak, or an easy way out of the question, "what will I do for a living?" …

We depend on our employees to run our business. In turn, we owe them an allegiance beyond a paycheque. Their jobs, and ours, will be most secure when we maintain high standards for hiring employees, be they family or non-family …

Just as it is unfair to the family member and the company to hire unqualified family members, it is also unfair to ignore the talents of qualified family members in employment decisions. If a family member and non-family member apply for the same position, both being equal in experience, qualifications, education, and recommendations, we should hire the family member.[30]

Create an Objective Process for CEO Selection

Often the most controversial element of any succession process in a family enterprise is the selection of the future CEO. Not surprisingly, issues such as nepotism, favouritism, and sibling rivalry complicate matters. To avoid these challenges, forward-thinking family owners create an objective and transparent process for selecting the future business leader. In addition, the family employment policy should clarify expectations by including the key qualifications and selection criteria for the CEO.

Create an objective CEO selection process.

While this may take some time and may even seem too formal, clarifying both the process and the criteria helps to ensure that a family member will be appointed as CEO only if they have earned the opportunity, not because they are being "anointed" by the family.

The following table represents an objective selection process that was developed by one of my clients as they contemplated the selection of their next CEO. In order to provide leadership and objectivity to the process, it was recommended that their three independent non-family members of the board serve as a CEO selection task force.

CEO SELECTION PROCESS
(Roles and Responsibilities)

DUTIES AND ACTION REQUIRED	PARTIES RESPONSIBLE
Develop/confirm process	Board of directors
Provide leadership for process	CEO selection task force
Prepare strategic plan	Executive committee
Prepare CEO position profile	Executive committee
Approve strategic plan	Board of directors
Approve position profile	Board of directors
Source and evaluate candidates	CEO selection task force
Recommend future CEO	CEO selection task force
Recommend compensation for CEO	HR committee
Approve recommendations	Board of directors & Family council

All too often the elder generation in a family enterprise is so enamoured of their offspring (like my dad was) that they fail to consider appropriate standards for development before wanting to appoint their children to senior executive positions. Similarly, members of the rising generation are often overly confident in their own abilities (like I was) and unaware of their inadequacies. With some formality and objectivity, both generations can be assisted in making wise choices and getting the succession process right.

CONCLUSION

When properly understood, succession is viewed as a process that takes many years of careful planning and thought to complete. This perspective helps participants visualize the complexity and sensitivities that need to be addressed. Practically, one of the best places to start is for families to determine—and clarify—the values that are most important to them and their business.

In turn, successors should be thoughtful and inquisitive in developing an approach that balances tradition and innovation. They are wise to consider time-honoured approaches to succession that have helped business-owning families around the world to create optimal outcomes. To begin, all aspiring successors can benefit from resolving to become "the best person for the job," rather than being presumptuous about their climb up the corporate ladder.

In addition, successors can encourage their family to develop family employment policies, including an objective CEO selection process. Such proactive planning provides their families with the tools necessary to manage the emotional challenges that are present in a family enterprise. At the same time, paying attention to all of the previously noted strategies gives business families the best prospects for making wise decisions while retaining harmony in their relationships and unity in their family.

CHAPTER 3
Preparing for Leadership

Years ago, I attended a presentation by the president of a family-owned national retail chain. His remarks were direct and to the point. He said that when a family business is planning a transition from one generation to the next, three things are always true:

1. The elder generation wants their offspring to succeed.
2. The younger generation wants to show their parents they are capable leaders.
3. The elder generation decides when the younger generation gets their chance.

For some, this may be disappointing to hear; but the good news is that there is a host of positive and productive opportunities waiting for you … while you wait your turn. This chapter offers a number of suggestions for how you can manage your wait—and make it count.

Get a Great Education

Bill Gates. Mark Zuckerberg. Michael Dell. What do these men have in common?

Undeniably, they belong to the privileged group known as "the wealthiest people in the world." Beyond this, they have (at least) two things in common: they all made billions in the tech industry, and they all dropped out of university.

Today, there are numerous young people who have made millions (and more) from an idea that became a wildly successful app or Web service. Unfortunately, seeing so many of these "computer nerd becomes billionaire" stories play out in the news has led many young adults to question the value of higher education. When asked why, most claim that Bill Gates and Steve Jobs *proved* that a university education is not required for success in life. Of course, they are partially correct in that it was not necessary *for Bill and Steve* to succeed. But we all know that there is no guarantee that every college dropout will follow in their footsteps.

> How will you measure up to those who are better educated?

When I ask young people how they plan to succeed in their careers, the standard answer typically includes some combination of intelligence and hard work. I wholeheartedly agree with this answer, but one question remains: How can you compete successfully with other young adults who are also intelligent and diligent *but also have a great education?*

Because today's global economy is fiercely competitive, I am convinced that those who do not have a solid post-secondary education are potentially at a serious disadvantage. If I was planning my career today, I would not rest all my hopes on my smarts and tenacity alone. I would also want to prepare myself as thoroughly as possible, and that would include engaging in the rigours and disciplines of advanced studies.

There are many business families who think similarly, and some have made the completion of a post-secondary education a prerequisite for any would-be successors wanting to join the family business. For those who aspire to become president or CEO, a degree in business would be expected. Many wise families formalize each of these concepts in their family employment policy.

In contrast, some successors say it is more important to join the business as soon as they can, and they believe that this is how they will learn everything they need to know. However, there is rarely any urgency to join the business, especially when one considers that many members of our elder generation are now able to enjoy healthy and productive lives well into their 80s and 90s. In most cases, there is more than enough time for successors to get a great education. In fact, there is typically more than enough time to get not only an undergraduate degree but also a master's or even a doctorate.

The Value of a University Education

Today, Fisk Johnson is CEO of SC Johnson, the global powerhouse that manufactures a variety of household products, ranging from Johnson's Wax to Ziploc bags, as well as Pledge furniture polish and the bug killer Raid.

While speaking at a family business event hosted by the University of British Columbia, Fisk explained that his father, Sam, was an extremely strong and capable leader, and, as a consequence, it would have been difficult to have much influence in the company as long as his dad was still at the helm. So, rather than joining the family company prematurely, Fisk hit the books. Remarkably, before joining the family firm he successfully completed six university degrees.

All of his degrees were from New York's Cornell University. Remarkably, these included a bachelor of arts in chemistry and physics, a master of engineering, a master of science in physics, an MBA in marketing and finance, and a PhD in physics.

Such a broad education not only prepared Fisk for his future leadership roles in the company, but it also prepared him for the radical changes that the company currently wrestles with in the consumer products industry. Because of his exemplary background he is equipped to provide leadership in such critical and diverse areas as sustainable development, conservation, and international negotiations. Currently he serves as a board member on the World Business Council for Sustainable Development, on the board of Conservation International, and on the President's Advisory Committee for Trade Policy and Negotiations (in the USA).

Preparing well educationally before joining the family business is not something that Fisk pioneered. His father had set the bar high by completing a bachelor's degree in economics and an MBA from Harvard Business School. In fact, the value of a university education is so important to the Johnson family that they have contributed generously to Fisk's alma mater, Cornell, and to the creation of the SC Johnson Graduate School of Management.

When Sam started his career, he was appointed as head of new product development. Ironically, at that time his father was serving as the head of the company and was *extremely reluctant to consider any new products* outside their core wax business. In fact, Sam's first business proposal, for a new bug spray, was flatly turned down because it did not have a wax component. Undeterred, Sam challenged his team to become truly creative, and over the ensuing 12 months, they developed the first bug spray that was able to kill insects without also harming plants.

His prior educational experience was instrumental in enabling him to think outside of the box and to become truly innovative. The resulting product, Raid, has been an enormous success, still enjoying a 60 percent market share globally over 50 years after its introduction.

Work Outside the Family Firm

As discussed earlier, a business enterprise that wants to remain competitive needs to adapt to the changing environment and business landscape in which it operates. Consequently, it must embrace innovation, adaptation, and change. In most cases, as we all know, that is easier said than done. The "old guard" in the company may not be willing to accept new ideas and may hold on to the status quo, whereas the "young bucks" may want to change almost everything.

Thinking strategically, one of the most effective ways to avoid intergenerational stress while simultaneously developing as a leader is for a successor to work outside the family firm for an extended period of time.

(I generally recommend at least five years, and in some cases ten.) Such experience enables successors to develop leadership skills while discovering what genuine accountably feels like, something they can only really get a sense of when outside their protective family bubble.

There are at least three additional benefits to working outside the family company, and they are apparent once a successor returns to the family enterprise:

- Other employees see you as capable and credible.
- The rest of your family realizes that you have gained valuable experience.
- When you look in the mirror in the morning, you confidently know that you are employable and able to make it in the world on your own.

Outside experience is an extremely important aspect of developing leadership capabilities for successors, yet it is often given short shrift by both succeeding and elder generations. I believe so passionately in successors pursuing this path that I devoted an entire chapter to it in my earlier book *Leaving a Legacy*.

Alfred P. Sloan, left, president of General Motors

Optimize Your Career Preparation

Some successors may be tempted to do *just enough* (i.e., the bare minimum) to prepare for their future in the family company. In contrast, I know two entrepreneurial brothers who partnered with their father, a veteran real estate lawyer, to create a new real estate development enterprise. Since its inception, just over 10 years ago, the company has successfully developed over $500 million worth of real estate. However, before they joined forces with their dad, the two boys each completed an undergrad degree and an MBA from a leading North American business school.

One son further added to his credentials by obtaining a CPA designation and then worked in the banking industry for five years. His *preparation* also included several years with a major European bank. His elder brother took a different path and was mentored by a local real estate developer. When they subsequently partnered with their father, these two young men had a willingness to work hard and lots of native intelligence. But they also arrived on the scene with a great education behind them and a strong resumé in their pocket.

I cannot think of any successor in any family business who would not be well served to pursue a similar path. Each of these young men obtained an exemplary formal education and outstanding industry exposure, including five-plus years' experience working independent of their family, each with leading edge companies. This is what can be accomplished when successors are not bent on taking the shortest, fastest route to the corner office.

Learn Responsibility and Accountability

Alfred Sloan was a true captain of American industry who oversaw the growth of General Motors from its infancy to one of the largest corporations in the world. When he was first appointed as vice-president in 1920, GM had a 12 percent share of what was, at the time, a very small car market. By the time he left, 30 years later, the market had grown dramatically, and 52 percent of all cars sold in the United States were GM products.

How did he accomplish this? Essentially, it was through a rare combination of innovation and a knack for administration. As an engineer, he pioneered a number of automotive advances at GM. But, more importantly, he turned out to be a genius at administration, and, as the *New York Times* wrote in his 1966 obituary, he made his mark in the industry "as a planner, organizer, and administrator."

One of his novel ideas was to divide General Motors into five autonomous divisions that would each produce distinct cars within a specific price range, beginning with the basic Chevrolet and then rising in price and prestige to the Pontiac, Oldsmobile, Buick, and Cadillac. Each group operated independently and had its own manufacturing, marketing, and sales groups. At the same time, all administration was centralized.

It was a truly revolutionary step, and one that many considered to be suicidal, given that the five divisions were permitted to compete against each other for customers. However, to the surprise of many, the organizational changes increased GM's efficiency, reduced manufacturing costs, and created higher levels of customer satisfaction. As a result, GM was able to compete more effectively with its main rival, the Ford Motor Company; and, in a relatively short period of time, GM surpassed it as the number-one automaker in America.

Alfred Sloan's genius came, in part, from extrapolating from the astute observation that the most effective way to get anything done is to assign it to one person. That way, there is no confusion as to who is responsible for the task or who is at fault if the job is not completed.

> *Sloan's planning and organizing skills created immense value for GM.*

Essentially, the structural changes he introduced were Sloan's response to one of the paramount challenges of management: how to coordinate the activities of large numbers of people in such a way that each person is productive, effective, and accountable. Sloan determined that GM would be more efficient with smaller operating divisions that could execute their own activities; at the same time, multiple divisions in competition with each other would heighten responsibility and accountability for performance. Through Sloan's reorganization, each division of GM was empowered to identify market opportunities, develop products, and then promote them.

Throughout the rest of the 20th century, large corporations adopted a decentralized divisional structure similar to what Sloan had pioneered decades earlier.

A lot has changed since the days when GM ruled the world. However, many of the lessons that can be learned from Alfred Sloan's leadership are timeless. Perhaps the most important lesson for successors to learn is that management is a science. Sloan's introduction of rigorous planning, organizing, and delegating of authority created immense value for GM. These functions were not just nice ideas but actual skills that can be studied and mastered. In today's popular culture we rightly celebrate creativity, innovation, and entrepreneurship; however, without execution many brilliant ideas simply come to naught.

Running a separate business unit can be an ideal opportunity for aspiring successors to develop their management skills.

How to manage is perhaps the most important skill for aspiring executives to master, and this is why it can be such a great time of learning if successors are given the opportunity to run a division or a separate business unit within the family company. This also strengthens their understanding of Sloan's emphasis on establishing clear roles and accountabilities for both individuals and teams.

Become a Student of Management

What is the job of management? Any aspiring successor should know—and understand—the answer to this question. Perhaps the best source for insight on the topic is Peter Drucker, who many regard as the wisest management guru of the past 100 years.

According to Drucker, all successful executives follow the same eight practices:

1. They ask, What needs to be done?
2. They ask, What is right for the enterprise?
3. They develop action plans.
4. They take responsibility for decisions.

5. They take responsibility for communicating.

6. They are focused on opportunities rather than problems.

7. They run productive meetings.

8. They think and say *we* rather than *I*.

Not only was Drucker amongst the first to study the function and responsibilities of management, but he was also the first to articulate the concept of management by objectives.[31] Typically referred to as *MBO*, it is "a process by which the objectives of an organization are agreed to and decided between the management and the employees, this way the employees understand what is expected of them and help set their own individual goals."[32]

The adjacent illustration depicts the process of MBO.[33]

Drucker wrote about these concepts over 50 years ago, and although many things have changed in the intervening decades, the basic principles of professional management have stood the test of time. Consequently, any family enterprise successor wanting to develop a foundational understanding of corporate leadership would benefit greatly by reviewing Drucker's basic ideas about management theory and practice.

Unfortunately, most of the family enterprise successors I have met are unable to articulate the key roles of management, and still fewer have any degree of proficiency in most of its functions. Yet they are often perplexed by the elder generation's seeming reluctance to transfer greater authority and responsibility to them.

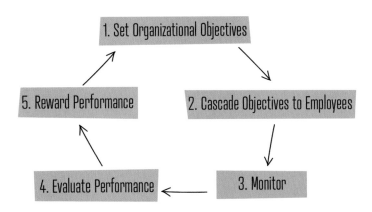

THE FIVE-STEP M.B.O. PROCESS

1. Set Organizational Objectives

5. Reward Performance

2. Cascade Objectives to Employees

4. Evaluate Performance

3. Monitor

In one of his last published articles, Drucker opined that "An effective executive does not need to be a leader in the sense that the term is now most commonly used. Harry Truman did not have one ounce of charisma, for example, yet he was among the most effective chief executives in U.S. history."[34]

This is good news for most family enterprise successors because it counters the notion that effective leadership requires you to be charismatic or potentially to lead in the same manner as the previous generation did.

Welcome Rigorous Performance Reviews

How can successors know if they are doing a good job?

Based on the various roles previously listed, aspiring successors want to acquire a broad range of skills and abilities. So how can they know if they are progressing in their skill development?

Sadly, in most cases, the answer to this question is an emphatic "They will not!" As a result, family business successors tend to have an unrealistic view of their own skills and abilities. (I know that I did.) In many cases, this problem is exacerbated by the protective bubble they live in, where they are not given honest evaluations and the performance feedback that a non-family employee would experience.

The only way they can properly assess their progress is if they have accurate, unbiased feedback on their performance.

In my early 30s, I was literally given a second chance to run one of our family companies when my sisters and I acquired our construction business. I was then invited to step into an executive role that would potentially lead me to become president. As I worked to develop my knowledge of the company, I received regular honest no-holds-barred performance evaluations from our then CEO, Dick Meyers. This was one of the most valuable gifts ever given to me.

> Job evaluations were one of the best gifts I ever received.

As a non-family member, Dick had no motivations or jealousies that would affect his interpretations of me or my actions. In fact, his motives were quite the opposite—he was extremely supportive, and he worked hard to help me achieve my goal of succeeding him as president once he retired.

Dick was known to be rigorous when it came to performance management within the company, and he certainly maintained that rigour in his meetings with me. At least twice annually, he would canvass each of the vice-presidents about my performance and, beyond that, ask for specific examples as to how I could do better. He would then sit me down to carefully review their comments. This input, rather than discouraging me, served to motivate me and challenge me to get better.

These periodic meetings typically began with encouragement and comments regarding some of the things I was doing well. There was always an appreciative comment about my ability to communicate verbally and in writing, and his words were instrumental in growing my confidence in these critical areas. However, he also believed that it was important for me to learn from my mistakes and to be continually improving as an executive. In almost a fatherly way, he went over the comments of others and explained how certain changes in my behaviour would benefit me, as an executive, going forward.

Initially, I feared those meetings because I knew that I would hear about all the mistakes I had made and the things that I had done wrong. It also hurt my pride to realize that I was not doing everything quite as well as I had thought. At first, I was tempted to defend myself or to argue that his assessment of my performance was off base. But this was just a lack of maturity on my part.

In time, I came to realize that Dick was "on my side" and that I needed to brace myself and learn to welcome his constructive feedback. After eating a bit of humble pie, I soon realized that his feedback was essential if I was going to learn and grow as quickly as I hoped to. By adopting an attitude of openness and humility, I was able to take his input and advice to heart. Under Dick's mentorship, I gradually made the changes in my management style and approach that were badly needed. Looking back, I must have made satisfactory progress—within three years he recommended to the board that I be appointed president and CEO of the company. I was grateful that Dick advocated for my subsequent promotion, but more importantly, he helped me know what I needed to do in order to earn it.

Develop Skills for Managing Conflict

Becoming the CEO of a small or large enterprise is not—and should not be seen as—a free ticket to do whatever you wish. There are limits; but the big question is, "*Who is going to hold you accountable when you are the top executive?*"

Many family firms have inadequate governance or, in many scenarios, no functional board at all. Instead, there is just an assumption that the president should have the final decision-making authority on most subjects. However, when the family president is also one of several owners, as with a sibling partnership or a cousin consortium, it is vitally important to clarify the president's decision-making authority—that is, which decisions belong to the president and which ones require the approval of either the board or the shareholders.

As one would expect, not all owners see a business the same way, and they may have different perspectives and priorities. Similarly, all family enterprise successors have times when they have differences of opinion with others. How do we handle these conflicts? If you are the sole owner, you can just make a decision and tell others to fall in line, or else. However, if you are part of a sibling partnership or a cousin consortium, the situation is quite different.

Moreover, if you want to build an environment where decision-making includes respectful input from others, then learning to both collaborate and compromise is essential.

In his *Conflict Style's Assessment Workbook*, Alexander Haim notes that there are only five ways to handle conflict: *collaborate, compromise, compete, accommodate,* and *avoid.* Each has its own merit and may be suitable in certain circumstances. In assessing which style is most appropriate to a particular situation, Haim suggests that we ask ourselves the following two questions: *How important is the outcome?* and *How important is the relationship?*

In a family enterprise setting it is common to have conflict with family members regarding topics such as career opportunities and finances. In cases where both the relationships and the outcomes are important, Haim advises that *there are three styles of handling conflict that are not suitable (avoid, accommodate, and compete). In these situations, compromise and collaboration are the most helpful and most desirable conflict resolution strategies.*

Given that there are only five basic options for handling conflict, it is critically important to determine which style is most appropriate in a given situation. To do this, it is essential to consider the relative importance of relationships and outcomes, as illustrated in the adjacent figure. For example, note that when the importance of the outcome is *high* and the importance of the relationship is *high*, then the best way to handle the conflict is to collaborate. On the other hand, if the importance of the relationship is *high* but the importance of the outcome is *low*, then it is often best to accommodate.

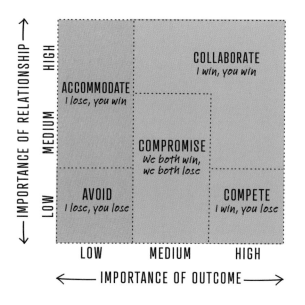

5 WAYS TO HANDLE CONFLICT

Recruit Independent Board Members

Ideally, all business families would have a strategy to minimize and manage conflict without the need for intervention from a third party. But that is not the reality; most families find it necessary to have someone who is independent and capable of facilitating a productive discussion when things get emotional. In some cases, a professional family enterprise advisor can play this role. In more difficult situations, a counsellor or family therapist might be necessary. However, to avoid having issues escalate, the wisest approach is to obtain the support and advice of independent board members.

Beginning in the 1960s, Leon Danco, widely known as the founder of family business consulting, began advocating the benefits of a *working board* with independent non-family members who can offer advice and support to a family in business. Rather than having family members wrestle for control of the enterprise, he encouraged families to create a board that could bring objectivity and rationality to decision-making, build bridges between the generations, and offer sage advice. He emphasized the value of an effective board to provide support and accountability to the company president or CEO.

Danco writes, "No well-run corporation, family owned or not, can operate efficiently without a periodic review of its chief executive officer. Yet, his employees, his managers, and his advisers cannot provide this review. They are the paid help … This is the job for an outside board of directors."[35]

In addition to reviewing and advising the CEO, independent board members can help successors by providing objectivity for decision-making and helping to mentor them as they learn sound business practices. This environment of professionalism and strategic thinking is one within which successors can more easily develop into competent leaders. Knowledgeable directors can be very effective as mentors for the next generation, both indirectly at board meetings and more directly at private meetings.

> "If you only do one thing to help with succession, recruit a board of directors with a majority of independent members."—Dr. John Ward

Given all the potential benefits wise board members can offer, it is no wonder that Dr. John Ward, who today is one of the most widely respected and most published authors in the field of family enterprise, has stated, "If you only do one thing, to help a family enterprise navigate the process of intergenerational succession, recruit a board of directors with a majority of independent members."[36]

Introduce Regular Family Meetings and Strategic Planning

What factors facilitate a smooth succession in a family business?

Joe Astrican at Kennesaw State University (KSU) followed 18,000 business-owning families over a 10-year period in an attempt to uncover the critical factors that help families to prepare for succession. Astrican found three factors that positively correlated with successful transitions:

1. A board of directors with independent members.
2. Regular family meetings.
3. A formalized strategic planning process.

The first is not entirely surprising for those who have studied Leon Danco or John Ward. Transitions go more smoothly when owners endorse good governance by recruiting independent directors.

But the next two factors on the list offered some novel insights. Successful families take time to invest in the family's education and well-being through regular family meetings and by being proactive in developing a strategy for the future. Family enterprise leaders and successors increase the prospects of continuity over the generations if they encourage and support each of these priorities.

Find a Need and Fill It

As discussed in the previous chapter, there is often tension between the elder generation's emphasis on tradition and the rising generation's interest in innovation. One of the most effective ways to manage this tension is through something referred to as *intrapreneurship*. However, this concept has not been well understood or even widely accepted until recently.

When I first heard someone use the term, I thought I misunderstood what was being said. Surely the person was trying to say "entrepreneurship" … and doing it badly. I have since come to understand what an intrapreneur is. It is someone who has the support of an existing enterprise as they pursue the development of a new venture.

In a family business context, successors become intraprenuers by starting a new business with the support and guidance of the family enterprise. This support can be in the form of seed capital or the ability to access the network and administrative functions of the family firm. Becoming an intraprenuer provides successors a large measure of independence without leaving them completely on their own to build a new organization.

> *If you are tired of waiting, start a new venture.*

If you are an aspiring successor and the idea of starting something new seems daunting, it may be helpful to remember the advice of one of American's leading wartime industrialists: the key to business is simply to "find a need and fill it."[37]

Richard Branson, founder of Virgin Group, is a strong advocate of intrapreneurship; he explains it as a process in which "an employee … is given freedom and financial support to create new products, services and systems, [and] does not have to follow the company's usual routines or protocols." He goes on to say that "Virgin could never have grown into the group of more than 200 companies it is now, were it not for a steady stream of intrapreneurs who looked for [new opportunities and then developed them] … often leading efforts that went against the grain."[38]

In the future, I believe that more family businesses will take advantage of intrapreneurship as a way of capturing new business opportunities while providing career challenges for successors. If aspiring successors are either unclear or unsatisfied with their career trajectory, a great option is to start their own intrapreneurial venture in collaboration with their family firm.

Curiously, I have met many successors who say they believe themselves to be extremely capable yet they have never demonstrated their confidence or ability by launching a new business on their own. In some cases, establishing a new division or starting a new venture with the blessing and support of family could reduce tension as a successor waits for an opportunity to lead in the family firm. But this is not just a great idea for learning; it also has the potential to lead to the creation of a meaningful new business. If you are a successor who is "waiting," you may want to propose a new venture with the family firm's backing.

Establish a Family Bank

The concept may be relatively new for some, but Antoine Mayoud's family has a long history of success with intrapreneurship. In 1905, his entrepreneurial grandfather launched a wool manufacturing company in France. Five decades later, in 1961, he provided capital to help one of his sons launch a retailing company, called Auchan. Today, the latter company employs over 350,000 people (eclipsing the original company many times over). The remarkable success of this second company helped to establish a strong tradition in the family whereby subsequent generations have been encouraged to launch their own new ventures, rather than thinking only about what has been done by the elder generation. When they do this, as Antoine notes, the next generation never feels they have to "compete" with their father (psychologically or practically).

In 2007, the family established an investment fund dedicated to helping young family members launch their own companies with family capital. It has been a great success, giving each young family member the potential support of the family, with advice and capital, when considering a new venture. As a result, since 2007, more than 30 family members have launched new ventures with the help of this investment fund.

When young family members are assisted in launching their own businesses, the family investment fund never fully underwrites a new venture. In fact, the amount of financial support is quite modest—typically no more than 30 percent of the capital and no more than $120,000. Because only modest amounts of equity are offered and budding entrepreneurs are required to obtain the majority of their funding from other sources, all new start-ups must obtain a broader base of support, not just help from the family.

Mayoud offers four reasons why their family investment fund is a powerful strategy:

1. It inspires the entrepreneurial spirit in the younger generations; instead of having mistrustful and passive heirs, it cultivates confident, active successors.
2. The younger generations are motivated to become part of the family business because they have their own stake in it.

3. The younger generations are starting their own ventures. As such, they do not feel as though they are competing with the elder generation or aspiring to be the new leader.
4. The family enterprise has the opportunity to build a diverse portfolio by investing in the opportunities identified by the next generation.[39]

CONCLUSION

Most aspiring successors must wait longer than they'd like for their chance to lead. Rather than becoming frustrated or impatient while waiting, there are many things they can do to help build a strong foundation for their careers. Rather than chomping at the bit, wise successors do well to embrace the opportunity to invest in themselves and their personal growth. This can be done by furthering their education and by gaining outside work experience. In addition, there may be potential to create a new business, through intrapreneurship or with the help and support of a family bank. However, regardless of the chosen approach, I am confident that by considering these suggestions and acting on them, successors can greatly enhance their prospects for future success.

Members of the elder generation can play a more supportive role, by embracing new intrapreneurial ventures and by encouraging successors when they seek to gain further education and to obtain experience working elsewhere.

SECTION III
Transforming Your Leadership

Section III explores the nine character traits that I wish I had been wise enough to develop when I was a young executive. I believe that each trait is necessary for successors to develop the skills and relationships required to successfully lead a family enterprise.

They are also the elements required for the growth and transformation of successors into successful family business leaders. I believe that if successors can learn to harness the potential in each of these distinct areas, they will be amazed by the strength and wisdom that results.

Furthermore, those who diligently cultivate these qualities not only find that their leadership improves, but they will also see a dramatic improvement in their relationships, both inside and outside the business.

CHAPTER 1
Humility: Getting Out of Your Own Way

"True humility is not thinking less of yourself; it is thinking of yourself less."[40]

As a 29-year-old executive keen to develop new skills, I was thrilled to be working at the corporate head offices of the Cadillac Fairview Corporation in Toronto. Back then, it was one of the largest real estate development companies in the world and responsible for such iconic projects as the Eaton Centre and the TD Centre in the heart of downtown Toronto. It had no shortage of creative, inspiring executives, and it was intoxicating to rub shoulders with the best and the brightest in our industry.

Exciting, yes. But working with the best also put me into a situation where it seemed that there was no room for error. At that time, the ideal executive projected strength and confidence; it was just assumed that they understood all aspects of the business and had all the answers. I thought that if I wanted to be seen in that same light, I had to project a similar image, and that meant making every effort to conceal my own insecurities about my youth, limited knowledge, and lack of confidence.

These fears often led me to present a facade of understanding ("Hey, I've got this!") even when issues were beyond my comprehension and I should have been asking questions and looking to others for advice.

Although this attitude was fostered by a competitive business environment, it was also fed by my own intellectual arrogance and belief that I was somehow gifted with natural insight and a better understanding of business than most others.

A Humble Admission. Fortunately, all that changed as my executive experience grew. One particular incident that left its mark occurred when more than a dozen Cadillac Fairview executives gathered in the main boardroom to review plans for a $70 million ($170 million in today's dollars) redevelopment of the Polo Park

Shopping Centre in Winnipeg. We were all eager to hear a geotechnical engineer present his findings on how we could add an additional level to the existing shopping centre without having to dig new foundations.

The project was dependant on his analysis, yet his report was complicated, and many aspects of his presentation were simply beyond my ability to comprehend. Even so, when he had completed his remarks and asked for questions, I remained quiet, and so did everyone else.

After a few uncomfortable moments of silence, George Lawtey, our senior vice-president and the most experienced executive in the room, spoke up: "I'm sorry, but I don't understand. Could you please explain it all again?" I was surprised and stunned.

Asking a few follow-up questions is normal after a presentation, but this was the first time I saw a senior executive admit he did not understand. As I thought about it later, I realized that his actions made perfect sense, at least from a business perspective. This was a vitally important project, and, with millions of dollars at stake, it was imperative that those who were responsible for the work fully understood the most critical issues. After all, we had hired a geotechnical engineer to provide his expertise—our job was to listen and to learn from him.

It may seem like a small detail in a much larger context, but this boardroom exchange proved to be significant in my growth as an executive because it set me free from the need to *pretend* that I always understood what was going on. (Thankfully, it also removed the sense of anxiety that typically accompanied my efforts to maintain this pretense.) Even more importantly, this event served as a positive impetus for me to become more vocal and to ask more questions in such situations. As more questions led to more answers, I realized that this new sense of freedom allowed me to expand my knowledge far more rapidly than being a quiet observer ever did.

WHAT IS HUMILITY?

In our society, we often make the erroneous assumption that humility is associated with a low sense of self-esteem or lack of confidence. Even the *Oxford English Dictionary* defines humility as "the quality of having a modest or low view of one's importance" and offers such uninspiring words as "diffidence" and "unassertiveness" for synonyms. Frankly, none of these traits are particularly appealing for life in general, let alone as descriptors of leadership in the competitive world of business.

Yet a host of influential leadership experts emphasize the need for humility at the highest levels of an organization. For example, Jim Collins, author of the best-selling book *Good to Great*, has developed a five-level hierarchy of characteristics necessary for great leadership. At the peak of this hierarchy is humility, accompanied by a strong will. He states it this way: "the most powerfully transformative executives possess a paradoxical mixture of personal humility and professional will."[41]

With this in mind, how can we transition from viewing humility as associated with weakness to seeing it as one of the most valuable characteristics for today's business leaders? Perhaps the best place to begin is to recognize that humility is more about respecting others than it is about denigrating yourself.

Humility Is Respect for Others

Edgar Schein, professor emeritus at the Sloan School of Management at MIT, has devoted much of his career to a rigorous study of humility, and he defines the concept primarily in a relational sense, stating that humility is "granting someone else a higher status than one claims for oneself."[42]

In order to illustrate this and to underline some of the benefits of humility, Schein suggests we consider the profound level of interdependence required for a successful surgical operation. In order to be effective in a hospital setting, teamwork and co-operation between nurses, anesthetists, and surgeons is necessary. However, Schein would argue that there must also be an element of interpersonal humility in order for the surgical team to communicate and collaborate effectively.

As we would all readily recognize, when facing a life-and-death situation (such as open heart surgery) one's posture toward others on the team really matters. On the other hand, if humility is lacking between the participants, there is a genuine risk of potential harm. In order for optimum results in such an environment, it is critically important to recognize that there are times when you need to be deferential toward others. In this way, humility is a personal trait that helps ensure efficient and effective organizational functioning, whether we are in a hospital, on the athletic field, or in a business environment.

> "Humility is granting someone else a higher status than one claims for oneself."

Humility Is a Powerful Asset

In addition to respecting others, humility has a lot to do with how we see ourselves. When properly understood, it is not about thinking poorly about who we are or what we are able to do. Rather, in its truest sense, humility is a powerful asset that embraces the following two essential elements:

- **Self-Awareness**—the ability to have an appropriate understanding of one's strengths and limitations, and
- **Openness (to new ideas)**—including positive and negative feedback that can contribute to an individual's personal and professional growth.

When viewed this way, it is evident that humility is a potent influence for enhancing an individual's personal and professional development.

It is clear that George Lawtey, when he spoke up in the Cadillac Fairview boardroom, was demonstrating true humility by both acknowledging his limitations and being open to learn.

It is interesting that recently published studies reinforce the notion that humility is a powerful and positive trait, while also illustrating some of the confusion often associated with the word. Jennifer Cole Wright et al. report that our understanding of humility undergoes positive change as we age, suggesting that our perspective of this virtue may be related to our level of maturity and development.[43]

For example, as shown in the following figure, their research revealed that more than half of the students in grades 5 and 6 thought of humility in negative terms (such as feeling embarrassed or badly about themselves). By grades 7 and 8, only one-third of students saw humility as a negative trait, and that number fell to just one in ten as they became teenagers (grades 9 to 12). In other words, age, education, maturity, and greater life experience all seem to contribute to individuals having a more positive view of humility.

This evolution of understanding apparently continues as students mature into adulthood.

In a second study, the same researchers asked adults to describe people with and without humility. The vast majority (89 percent) connected humility with people who had a *low self-focus*, defined as being capable of seeing themselves and their abilities in an honest and appropriate way. Similarly, 95 percent of the adults surveyed said that people who lacked humility did not possess these attributes.[44] In other words, if we fail to cultivate humility we risk developing a distorted view of ourselves.

CHANGING PERCEPTIONS OF HUMILITY

Grade	Students who viewed humility in negative terms
5 - 6	56%
7 - 8	33%
9 - 12	10%

Humility Is Self-Awareness

As previously stated, true humility is expressed through two important characteristics that are vital to successful leadership; one of these is *self-awareness*.

In part, humility can be as simple as looking at yourself in a mirror and taking stock. If we take a step back and pause for a moment to look at our reflection, we can get an accurate picture of how we appear to others; but without this self-evaluation, we may have a completely mistaken impression about how we look, leading to the "Why didn't you tell me my hair was messy?" scenario.

In his *New York Times* best-selling book *The Road to Character*, David Brooks writes that humility allows people to see themselves as others do, to recognize their own imperfections, and to acknowledge that their view of things is limited. He states that humility in its simplest terms is "the awareness that there's a lot you don't know and that a lot of what you think you know is distorted or wrong."[45]

> "*Humility enables you to see yourself as others do.*"

Patagonia, a well-known American clothing company, recognizes the benefits of hiring employees who possess humility because they realize that this makes them more self-aware and open to learning, both valuable attributes for an employee. During job interviews, the company actively scrutinizes applicants for these traits by asking them about times when they have failed and what they learned as a result. These are commonly asked questions in a job interview, but in most cases the answers are assessed in terms of how the potential employee recognized what went wrong and ultimately how they fixed the problem. At Patagonia, they probe deeper, using the same question to assess the degree of humility possessed by the interviewee.[46]

Humility Creates Openness to New Ideas

As humility has become a research topic in business, the concept of *intellectual humility* has emerged. It still relates to self-awareness, but the primary focus is understanding the limits of one's own knowledge. Those who recognize their inadequacies are more likely to be open to new ideas and to have a willingness to consider new evidence.[47]

It is not surprising that those with intellectual humility are known to be the best learners and are more likely to learn from others, even those with whom they disagree. We may readily recognize how important this trait could be to debaters (or even politicians); it is of significant value in organizational life as well.

As an example, author Stephen Covey emphasizes the importance of being humble so we are able to consider new ideas and learn from others. He illustrates this by recounting a fascinating story about the beginnings of the Atomic Energy Commission.[48] In the aftermath of World War II, the US government established a group of scientific luminaries to discuss the peaceful development of nuclear power and the best ways to harness it for use in a civilian context.

> If an intelligent person disagrees with me, I must be missing something.

As you can imagine, this group consisted of some of the brightest minds in the world, and they were anxious to get started and to complete the task as quickly as possible. But their appointed leader, a lawyer and public servant named David Lilienthal, had other plans and set aside the first few weeks as a time for members to get to know one another. According to Covey, Lilienthal essentially assisted them in creating an *emotional bank account* by sharing "their interests, their hopes, their goals, their concerns, their backgrounds, their frames of reference, [and] their paradigms."

Lilienthal initially received a great deal of criticism for this perceived inefficiency, but the payoff was huge. As the group began to better understand each other, their individual interactions became more respectful and co-operative; the initial barriers created by personal and intellectual pride came down.

Covey writes, "The attitude was 'If a person of your intelligence and competence and commitment disagrees with me, then there must be something to your disagreement that I don't understand, and I need to understand it. You have a perspective, a frame of reference I need to look at.'"

By first removing potential barriers stemming from intellectual pride, the group developed close-knit bonds and open communication patterns that were creative and synergistic. According to Covey, "The respect among the members of the commission was so high that if there was disagreement, instead of opposition and defense, there was a genuine effort to understand." In other words, the more familiar the members of the group became with each other, the more they were willing to consider each other's ideas and perspectives.

THE BENEFITS OF HUMILITY

Although it may still seem counterintuitive to some, a growing body of scholarly research supports the idea that humility can have an enormously positive impact on the personal and professional development of business leaders.

Professional Growth

Management researchers Bradley Owens and David Hekman have spent years studying the concept of humble leadership in corporations, and they have found that *humility is essential to an individual's professional progress.* They write, "humility appears to embolden individuals to aspire to their highest potential and enables them to make the incremental improvements necessary to progress toward that potential."[49] In other words, humility helps people to advance because it enables them to more clearly see their inadequacies and identify the areas that may require further growth and development.

> Humility helps us see how we need to change.

The idea that humility is a critical factor for success does not appear to be lost on all successors. In a workshop discussion I hosted with several next-generation leaders, they came up with the following positive descriptors of people whom they perceived to be humble.

- Honest about their strengths and weaknesses
- Supportive, but not submissive
- Open to new ideas
- Able to listen to the counsel or input of others
- Willing to seek advice
- Willing to take time to collect all the information required to make good decisions

These characteristics are a good reminder that humility itself may not be a clearly visible attribute; rather, it is more of a hidden strength, and so we can only observe the outward manifestations of that strength. Humility often begins with introspection and an honest appraisal of the self, but when it is expressed outwardly through our interactions with others, it reveals positive personal growth—an obvious advantage in developing better relationships and more successful careers.

PROFESSIONAL BENEFITS

A Competitive Advantage. In a recent workshop for family business successors, we explored the tangible benefits that result when a corporate executive includes more humility in their leadership style. Not only did we discover numerous ways that humility makes for a more pleasant work environment, but we also realized that humility could create a competitive advantage for business.[50]

In discussions, the successors made the following observations about humility in leadership:

- When a leader demonstrates humility, employees feel respected and more like equals.
- Employees then become more collaborative and more willing to share their opinions openly (including the good and the bad).

- This leads to change, new ideas, and innovative thinking.
- Ultimately, this can result in the company developing new products and services that give them a competitive advantage in the marketplace.

Remarkably, this sequence shows how one small change at the top (a leader choosing to demonstrate greater humility in their relationships with fellow employees) can lead to a better and more competitive business.

The potency of the potential linkage between humility and competitive advantage is illustrated in the adjoining diagram.

Edouard Michelin: The Original Michelin Man. There is perhaps no better example to demonstrate the impact that a humble leader can have on innovation and competitive advantage than Edouard Michelin; if it had not been for his humble leadership, Michelin Tire might never have become a household name.

Edouard (1859 to 1940) was the family patriarch and CEO back in the 1930s. As a general rule for hiring employees, he told the head of personnel, "Don't judge by appearances … Remember that one must chip away at the stone in order to find the diamond hidden within." That principle came into play when a very ordinary fellow by the name of Marius Mignol sought work at Michelin. Although he had no formal education, he had some experience as a typographer and was therefore hired and assigned to the company's print shop.[51]

One day, Edouard passed by Mignol's desk and noted a rather strange ruler-type device lying there. Being curious, Edouard had to ask Mignol what the contraption was. Mignol responded by explaining that it was a self-made slide rule that he used to quickly convert exchange rates. Edouard knew then that Mr. Mignol was a very gifted man; Edouard declared him to be "a genius" and immediately transferred him to the tire research division.

This occurred at a time when conventional tires were reaching their safety limits because of a tendency to overheat at high speeds. The first radial tire had already been designed in the United States, and although it offered superior performance, little was known about it, and European motorists did not have access to it.

Over the next few years, Mignol designed a new tire, with its sides replaced by radial metallic cables separated by spaces. In 1946, the design was patented, commercialized, and sold as the Michelin X—the first radial tire for European automobiles. Because of its revolutionary design, it provided tremendous advantages in durability and fuel economy, and it soon became the most popular tire in Europe and Asia.

All of this happened because Edouard Michelin had the humility to show respect to a lowly typesetter, to inquire about an interesting object on his desk, and to look beyond Mignol's lack of education to see "the diamond within."

Edouard truly believed that humility was a basic condition for business success, and he was widely known for his sense of *fraternal humility*, the habit of serving others and offering the utmost respect to all employees.

This respect for all was continued under the leadership of his successors. For example, his grandson Francois believed that it was his job to serve each "unique and irreplaceable person" and stated that the one thing that "counts above all" is to "help a person become himself."[52]

Edouard Michelin, CEO of Michelin Tires

Michelin Tire became one of the leading tire manufacturers in the world because the Michelin family-owned business adopted a leadership style rooted in humility.

Employee Loyalty. Further discussion with family enterprise successors yielded the additional insight that there is a strong connection between humility and employee loyalty. According to workshop participants, employees have a greater sense of trust in, and admiration for, an executive who demonstrates humility. This influence on the work dynamic can create a host of positive benefits, such as,

1. There is increased dialogue and trust in the workplace.
2. The workplace has a greater sense of safety for employees; and safety is fertile ground to nourish a sense of empowerment and creativity.
3. Employees have a growing enthusiasm for work and are inspired to work harder.

4. Employees realize that they are important to the success of the company, and their loyalty grows because the business is no longer just about the leader.

The adjacent figure shows that humility is like a fountain that produces numerous positive benefits, including increased dialogue, a sense of security and increased enthusiasm. Taken together, such interpersonal factors can help to create an environment that stimulates employee commitment and loyalty.

In summary, successors in our workshops concluded that leaders who demonstrate humility cause a significant shift in the work culture of their companies, potentially creating employees who are more innovative, empowered, dedicated, and loyal. With these potential payoffs it seems that humility is not just a nice idea; it is a potent generator of business success and, consequently, a trait that all successors are wise to cultivate.

Better Teamwork

Phil Jackson is widely considered to be the most successful basketball coach in NBA history. He led the Chicago Bulls to six NBA championships from 1989 to 1998 and then, after a brief retirement, came back to lead the Los Angeles Lakers to five championships between 2000 and 2010. In his most recent book, appropriately entitled *Eleven Rings: The Soul of Success*, Jackson reflects on his illustrious career and provides insights into his intimate working relationships with two of the NBA's greatest players, Michael Jordan and Kobe Bryant.[53]

It is tempting to think that Jackson's success was the result of having two of basketball's biggest stars playing on his teams. While their talents were critically important to the 11 championship rings, Jackson writes that their giftedness created difficult situations in which he had to deal with star players who failed to recognize their need for the rest of the team.

Jackson knew that team success would only happen when these athletes learned to put aside their egos and bought into the concept of playing as part of a team. His challenge was to figure out how to communicate that, at different times and in unique ways, to his superstars.

In Chicago, Michael Jordan had a remarkable talent and an exemplary work ethic, but after five years playing in the league, an NBA championship remained elusive. So Jackson bluntly told Jordan that there would be no championship rings until he learned to share the stage with his teammates. When their initial discussions proved insufficient, Jackson sought a new way of encouraging change. He knew that Jordan loved a challenge, and so he "challenged him to imagine a new way of relating to his teammates."[54] That is, Jackson encouraged Jordan to, rather than trying to carry the team on his shoulders, "try to envision ways he could serve as a catalyst to get all the players to work together."

Gradually, during the ensuing season, Jordan began to demonstrate a less selfish style of play. The turning point apparently came during a 1991 playoff game against Detroit where Jordan began to truly play team ball, and as his teammate Scottie Pippen observed, "for the first time I can say he's not going out there looking to score."[55]

A similar situation was present when Jackson first took charge of the Lakers. Soon after arriving in Los Angeles, he noticed that Kobe Bryant was somewhat of a loner; he kept mostly to himself, did not socialize with his teammates, and generally failed to acknowledge them or his need for them. His then-teammate Shaquille O'Neal even went so far as to publicly say, "I think Kobe is playing too selfishly for us to win."[56]

As with Jordan, Jackson realized that Bryant's pride and self-absorption were standing squarely in the path to his dreams. For the team's sake, he needed Bryant to put aside his pretensions, humble himself, and commit to being part of a team. Only then would the rest of the team be willing to work harder and play the supportive role that was needed for success.

In a bid to rectify the situation, Jackson arranged for Jordan to meet with Bryant, hoping that "Michael might help shift Kobe's attitude toward selfless teamwork."[57] He encouraged Jordan to share the importance of being more inclusive, both on the court and in the locker room.

Sometime later, Jackson addressed the entire team with these words: "You can't be a selfish player and make this offence work for the team's good."[58] He did not single out Bryant with this comment, choosing instead to remind *all his players* that they could not win unless they were each willing to develop more unselfish habits.

At that point, Bryant finally came to realize that he could not achieve his personal goals if he continued on his current path. Gradually he started paying more attention to his teammates, both on and off the court. This shift eventually translated into an attitude of "we" in the locker room, and this inspired the team to come together on the floor. As we all know, the payoff was substantial—five world championship rings.

Phil Jackson brought many skills to the table in helping both Jordan and Bryant to achieve their goals. Perhaps the most important gift that he gave these immensely talented athletes was self-awareness—and the ability to recognize their need for some genuine humility if they were going to reach their goals.

HUMILITY IN FAMILY BUSINESS

Humility is an important quality required by those who aspire to climb the corporate ladder, and it is a particularly critical trait for ensuring family enterprise success. Once we properly understand it (and how it relates to characteristics such as pride, confidence, and arrogance), we are more likely to develop an appreciation for this virtue and the need to cultivate it in both our personal and professional lives.

The importance of humility to a family business is similar to the oil in the engine of a car. Everything runs smoother when it is plentiful; but when the oil is low, things can very easily get overheated.

Humility Leads to Better Relationships

As leading management experts have noted, humility is a powerful characteristic that warrants both emphasis and cultivation. It is of particular importance in a family business, where humility has a decisively positive impact on family relationships, especially between the elder and younger generations.

Over the past 20 years, I have observed hundreds of successors and their interactions with siblings, family members, and employees. As a result, I have witnessed the benefits that stem from adding even a small dose of humility in such relationships. Unfortunately, on far too many occasions I have also noted the need for humility in these same relationships, primarily through its absence.

The chart on the following page lists seven major benefits available to successors in their professional lives if they are willing to cultivate more humility. Also noted is a brief explanation of why humility is so valuable in a family business and what happens when it is absent.

These observations emphasize the need for healthy conversations where questions are asked and ideas are laid open for honest discussion. Unfortunately, some families (and corporations) frown upon asking questions and tend to place greater value on knowing the answers or speaking assertively. However, successors who cultivate humility are willing to ask questions in a respectful manner because they value the advice of others and want to learn and to develop their skills. By valuing others in this way, they promote strong and open relationships.

Humility Helps with Career Growth and Development

For the past 10 years, I have worked with clients who run a family business that exports lentils to 80 countries around the world. It is currently owned by three brothers (who are second-generation owners), and six of their offspring work in the company. These cousins are all intelligent, dedicated, and experienced young executives.

WHAT ARE THE BENEFITS To Cultivating Humility?	WHAT IS THE DOWNSIDE When Humility Is Absent?	WHAT WILL BE DIFFERENT When Humility Is Present?	WHAT WILL HAPPEN If Successors Are More Humble?
1. Increased Trust	Others won't trust you or be willing to delegate responsibility to you.	Others will trust you because you won't be so self-absorbed.	Elder generation will be willing to delegate more authority and responsibility.
2. Personal Growth	Your growth and learning will be severly hampered.	You will realize that you don't have all the answers.	You will grow and develop more quickly as an executive.
3. Better Listening	You will be talking too much, not listening.	Your mind will be open to others' perspectives.	You will be able to listen— with the intent of learning.
4. Rational Discussions	You will be opinionated and prone to argue.	You won't need to defend your own positions.	You will advance your ideas with a spirit of "give and take," leading to innovation.
5. Conflict Resolution	You will tend to believe you are always right.	You will discard the notion that you are always right.	You will become respectful when interacting with others.
6. Mutual Respect	You will see others as less intelligent.	You will value others' insights and experience.	You will become more open to other people's ideas.
7. Increased Openness	You will not realize your own blind spots.	You will be able to hear constructive feedback.	You will be able to receive mentoring and coaching.

As part of our work together, I asked each of them to create a career development plan that would prepare them for their potential leadership roles in the next five to ten years. Initially they did not see a need for this since they had each developed a remarkable amount of business savvy through their prior work experiences. However, once they began to concretely consider their possible future roles with their current skill sets, each of them was required to think beyond their present abilities.

In a sense, this was an exercise in humility: in order to plan, they were forced to undertake deep introspection and then realistically consider—and share—what they believed to be their vulnerabilities and weaknesses. This was essential for them to realize their need for, and the value of, further training and mentoring.

WHY DO WE RESIST HUMILITY?

The personal, relational, and professional benefits of humility may be obvious when viewed on the pages of a book, but in the day-to-day realities of business many of us are still reluctant to be known as humble. As described earlier, I often masked my fears and insecurities by putting on a pretense of bravado and confidence. Years later, as a family business advisor, I have witnessed many other executives and family business successors do the same.

The obvious question is, Why? I would like to suggest at least five reasons:

We Think We Already Know the Answer

We assume that we know what others are going to say and have predetermined that we do not want to hear it. After all, if we know what should be done, why waste time listening to the input and suggestions of others? This is particularly true when we sense that their comments may threaten or undermine our own ideas, perspectives, and priorities.

> *With humility, you can learn from even those you disagree with.*

Nonetheless, current research shows that intellectually humble adults (who are open to other perspectives) are likely to learn something from a discussion, even when it occurs with people with whom they disagree. Additionally, according to Dr. Tenelle Porter, a postdoctoral researcher in developmental psychology at the University of California, Davis, "disagreements tend to be more constructive" with intellectually humble adults. The catch is, of course, that the individual first must have a sufficient degree of humility in order *to want to hear* what the other person has to say.[59]

We Think Our Situation Is Different

We *assume* that our particular circumstances are special or unique. But such an attitude is simply rooted in pride. As a result, we are not open to hearing what someone else has dealt with—perhaps successfully—in a similar situation. However, by choosing to believe that our experiences are somehow special or different, we become defensive about others' comments and cut ourselves off from the very people who could be of assistance. This not only prevents us from hearing valuable advice but also keeps us from taking action and moving forward. In short, choosing pride over humility is often a choice to remain stuck in our circumstances.

The key to overcoming these assumptions and their resulting inertia is humility—to humbly accept that others have something to teach us. Humility opens our minds to what others have to say, and in many cases their insights can provide the inspiration and insight necessary to resolve our most challenging situations.

We Do Not Want Others to Tell Us What to Do

It is a natural response to not want others to tell us what to do. We first begin to resist authority when we are toddlers (e.g., "the terrible twos"), and we gradually gain independence and autonomy as we age. By the time we are adults, we tend to believe we have the knowledge and maturity to make all our choices independently and, essentially, do as we please. But if we fail to consider the viewpoints of others, we are sentencing ourselves to a life that is limited to our own narrow perspective.

I have seen first-hand how this desire to be free from the advice of others can result in disaster, even for the most intelligent and capable entrepreneurs. In fact, I know of more than one instance where those who had experienced remarkable success in their first business venture followed this up with an equally spectacular failure. Because of a previous success, some leaders become convinced that any future ventures will be similarly lucrative. After all, they have a proven track record, and as a result others may be eager to invest in their next big idea.

Unfortunately, all too often, rather than embracing wise counsel, some entrepreneurs in this situation assume that they always know what to do and start to shun the advice of others. Such overconfidence can become a fatal flaw.

The problem is clear: too much self-confidence or pride can lead to a downfall. It does not matter if you are a recent graduate or a seasoned business leader; the consequences of hubris do not discriminate. As the ancient proverb warns, "Pride goes before destruction, and a haughty spirit before a fall."[60]

In contrast, leaders I have known who possess humility are willing to listen to others and seldom assume that they are always right.[61] They are also confident enough in their own ideas that they are willing to expose them to the objective scrutiny of others.

We Value Self-Esteem

In traditional cultures and throughout history, there long existed a broad consensus that pride was at the root of much that was wrong with the world. But that notion has been largely cast aside in Western culture, where sociologists, psychologists, and popular writers often assert that a lack of self-esteem is the root cause of many of our problems, both as individuals and as a society.

Consequently, our education system and many of our institutions have become convinced that one of the main things we need to do as a society is raise everyone's self-esteem. In many ways, this is almost the opposite of cultivating humility. For this reason, in many circles humility is no longer valued as it once was, and it is seldom promoted as a virtue to be desired, especially for leaders.

Well-known author and speaker Tim Keller highlights this issue:

> As a result of this seismic shift in thinking we want to build ourselves up to be more confident. We now focus more on encouraging our youth to believe in themselves and to take pride in their work. If they are struggling, we support them in efforts to cultivate their self confidence and their self esteem.[62]

This line of reasoning is difficult to oppose, because it seems self-evident that developing a positive self-image, or improving one's self-esteem, would be an asset for everyone, including students, athletes, scholars, and business executives.

However, although developing poise and confidence can often be helpful in pursuing our goals, improving self-esteem is not the panacea many had hoped for. In fact, recent research studies demonstrate that self-esteem doesn't have a really strong impact either way. As Professor Baumeister notes,

> Either high or low self-esteem doesn't have nearly the consequences … [that I] certainly … hoped [it would] when I started studying this 20, 25 years ago. I thought it was going to be a really important key to understanding lots of behavioral phenomenon, but it just doesn't pan out.[63]

We Are Highly Intelligent

While teaching in the MBA program at the University of British Columbia, I often enjoyed spirited discussions with my students and teased them that, in truth, MBA stands for *money, brains, and arrogance*. Without exception, these individuals were highly intelligent, confident, and well-educated; yet, in spite of these attributes, I was concerned for their future. This is because I have witnessed countless MBA graduates enter the corporate world and place their entire identity and confidence in what they believe are their greatest assets—their intellect and their education.

Unfortunately, when intellectual confidence is taken to the extreme, it can cross the line to become arrogance—which can then become a major liability. This attitude does not sit well with co-workers, and it can lead peers and superiors to reject a person's best ideas simply because of an overconfident and prideful approach.

In Greek mythology, arrogance and pride were often responsible for the downfall of even the most powerful, and they continue to be a threat to those who walk in the halls of power and the corporate boardrooms of today. To be blunt—no one liked a know-it-all in ancient times, and that has not changed over the centuries. With this in mind, I have urged my graduate students to cultivate humility as a part of their professional development. But even as I shared admonitions, the response from my students made it clear that most of them were not entirely convinced.

DEAR YOUNGER ME …

As I reflect on the early years of my career, I am struck by how badly I overestimated my own abilities and importance. At that time, humility may have been viewed as a desirable personal trait in some circles, but it certainly was not emphasized while I was attending business school. Similarly, humility was not celebrated or promoted in any of the popular books of that day. However, more contemporary research and current respected management experts emphasize the importance and relevance of humility in leadership, and we see clearly how this virtue can have a broad and positive impact for our roles in business.

For business families, humility plays a particularly important role in establishing and maintaining healthy relationships between siblings and between generations. Consider, if you will, what would happen if each family member associated with your family enterprise made a commitment to humility. I am convinced that it would have a remarkable impact.

Looking back over my years working in our family enterprise, I am convinced that just a modicum of humility on my part could have made a significant difference in my career. Even more importantly, my own humility could have had a far-reaching and potentially positive impact on the succession challenges that my dad and his brothers faced. Rather than being a source of tension, helping to drive them apart, I could have possibly been a bridge builder.

> ## THE BOTTOM LINE
>
> Humility builds better relationships, stimulates employee loyalty, and cultivates innovation.
>
> *David*

CHAPTER 2
Curiosity: Discovering the Doorway to Innovation

"The wise man doesn't give the right answers, he poses the right questions."[64]

Back in the 1980s, I approached the CEO of our family enterprise with the idea of establishing a division to develop seniors' housing projects. My rationale for the project was based on three essential facts.

First, North America was heading towards a demographic "grey tsunami," whereby a tidal wave of aging baby boomers would place unprecedented stress on our societal institutions, such as housing and health care. People were starting to search for solutions.

Second, The Bentall Group already had some experience in building and managing retirement homes. My brother-in-law had pioneered this work, establishing a charitable foundation that had built successful projects in both Calgary and Vancouver, operating under the name Trinity Lodge.

Third, both my grandfather and father had established a sterling reputation in the marketplace as men of integrity who could be trusted. Under their leadership, our company had been active in Western Canada for nearly 75 years, and as a result, any project bearing our company name would give potential clients an added measure of confidence as they considered future accommodations for themselves or their elderly parents.

My idea was met with uncertainty by our executive committee, but since I had presented a clear rationale for the concept, the company decided to at least conduct some market research. We hired William (Bill) Turner to explore the seniors' marketplace in Western Canada and to provide us with his insights. I expected that Bill, through his research, would confirm a solid opportunity for my proposed new seniors housing division. (As most people in the business world know, market research is often little more than an elaborate exercise that involves paying someone to tell you what you want to hear. However, Bill brought both integrity and a genuine curiosity to this assignment.)

As he travelled across the western provinces, speaking with Canadians about their expectations for housing in their retirement years, he began to hear a familiar refrain: Seniors wanted to stay in their own homes for as long as possible. More specifically, they wanted to 1) stay in a familiar neighbourhood near family and friends, 2) be able to cover medical expenses and fund in-home assistance as necessary, and 3) have more income to allow them to travel. A clear majority also made it abundantly clear that they did not want to move into a nursing home, a congregate care facility, or an assisted-living complex. In short, what they really wanted was more cash and more freedom.

As Bill considered what could be done to meet these expectations, he came up with the idea of borrowing against the equity in people's homes so they could continue living in their own houses and have more disposable income during their golden years. From these insights, Bill developed the concept of a reverse mortgage and founded the Canadian Home Income Plan (CHIP), which ultimately led to a national company that pioneered this revolutionary option for seniors. In essence, Bill's curiosity birthed a whole new industry in Canada!

As a result of Bill's leadership, reverse mortgages have become commonplace in Canada, and many elderly people have been able to stay in their own homes for many additional years. (For those who may be wondering, the concept allows for any remaining equity in a person's home to be transferred to the next generation through their estate, if desired.)

> *Curiosity created a whole new industry.*

The point to this story is that Bill did not begin his investigations with the idea of radically changing the way that Canadians live out their retirement. But when his questions led to answers that failed to support our plan to build more nursing homes, he did not stop asking questions. He continued his probing and his quest to deeply understand what people truly desired.

He was genuinely curious, and his curiosity led to some out-of-the-box thinking that eventually resulted in a whole new concept in retirement living.

WHAT IS CURIOSITY?

In essence, curiosity is a hunger to know more and have a greater understanding; it is a drive to discover and to expand our horizons. It is also a God-given gift and a very natural part of life. Think about young children and how they are innately wired from birth to explore the world around them. This rapidly evolving process of exploration starts with grabbing, touching, and feeling. Objects go into their mouths, fuzzy toys are caressed, shiny necklaces are given a tug, and favourite books get chewed. (Naturally, many of the items that they investigate are the very things we do not want them to touch!)

Then comes the era of never-ending questions that start with "Why?"; and parents everywhere are left wondering how on earth their children keep coming up with questions that they cannot answer. Interestingly, a 2017 study of British parents found that a four-year-old child asks their parents between 73 and 93 questions each day.[65] Since the definition of curiosity is to ask questions to uncover the "why" behind something or someone, these typically innocent questions represent the spirit of curiosity in its simplest form.

Although curiosity is a natural state for most children, it did not come easily to me, and I never felt that I was particularly skilled at asking questions. Ironically, as I began my training to be an executive coach, I learned that the most important skill required to be a coach is the ability to ask good questions. Our instructors noted that most individuals already have the answers to their own questions deep inside them; they just need someone to blow away the clouds of confusion so that they can clearly see which direction to go.

In the beginning, I considered this emphasis on questioning as both artificial and manipulative. It did not seem to me like a very efficient way of accomplishing anything. However, in hindsight, I recognize that the real problem lay with me—I would rather tell people what I thought they should do rather than help lead them to their own conclusions.

One of my mentors, Laura North, is an outstanding professional coach who, 20 years ago, helped guide me through my initial training as I became a certified life coach. Early on, she noted my propensity to instruct those I was coaching rather than question them. Using a metaphor, she said I was like a man who had "a strong right bicep and a weak left one." She observed that my natural teaching skill was a strength that enabled me to help my clients to learn and grow (my strong right bicep). However, my lack of curiosity was keeping me from using questions as a means of truly helping my clients. (Hence, this left me, symbolically, with a weak left bicep.) In short, Laura was trying to help me realize that my coaching skills were out of balance.

She encouraged me to correct this by learning to ask more questions. She put it something like this: "David, you might be a great teacher and a great storyteller, and you have lots of knowledge and insight to share. But if you are ever going to be a great coach, you need to develop your sense of curiosity!"

Genuine Interest. There is an oft-told story about a dinner attended by Mahatma Gandhi, the distinguished activist who led the fight for India's independence from British rule, and Prime Minister Winston Churchill, the extraordinary man who led Britain to success during World War II. At the formal function, one of the female guests was invited to sit between the two of them over dinner.

At the end of the evening, a friend asked her what it was like to sit between two of the most remarkable men in history, and her response was very telling. She said that the prime minister told her about the Boer war, his experiences in Parliament, and what it was like to lead the war cabinet during the Second World War. She found the whole experience spellbinding and concluded by saying, "I've never met anyone who was more interesting!" When asked what it was like to sit beside Gandhi, she became more reflective and spoke softly, almost reverently, saying, "I never met anyone who was more interested in me."

What a contrast! Churchill was *interesting*, whereas Gandhi was *interested*. I have never been able to confirm whether or not this is a true story, but I am inspired by it nonetheless. It vividly illustrates the personal impact that may result when we engage our curiosity to show a genuine interest in another person.

HOW CURIOSITY BENEFITS BUSINESS

Knowledge and experience have long been at the top of the list of characteristics that are desirable in employees and leaders. While these qualities are obviously necessary, they are not enough to keep leaders at the top of their game when the only constant is change. Innovation, new technology, and information overload make it almost impossible for one person to know all the answers. Perhaps the best way for executives to keep up is to unleash the power of curiosity in their professional life.

> *Today, executives need the power of curiosity just to keep up.*

Curiosity is so important in today's technological age that when Michael Dell, founder and CEO of Dell Technologies, was asked to name one attribute that would best help current CEOs to succeed, he said, "I would place my bet on curiosity."[66]

Curiosity Stimulates Learning

In *H3 Leadership*, Brad Lomenick writes about how important it is for aspiring leaders to *be humble, stay hungry, and always hustle*. He has worked with numerous leading executives and notes that many of them possessed "unbridled curiosity" in the early stages of their careers. But as time went on and they achieved greater success, they became less curious. By allowing this important quality to fall to the wayside, they began the process of limiting their potential to learn.[67]

A desire to learn stems naturally from curiosity, and Lomenick writes that we must maintain a sense of curiosity to keep learning and growing as professionals. He offers some relatively easy ways that each of us can cultivate and sustain our curiosity:

- Take time to write down—and then ask—strategic, open-ended questions,
- Listen to others,

- Spend time with different groups of people ("people who are so different they make you uncomfortable"),
- Surround yourself with people who are smarter than you, and
- Ask yourself, at the end of each day, if you have learned something new.[68]

Coasting through the later stages of a career is the easy route, but, according to Lomenick, "if you're not learning, you're not leading to your full potential." He then reminds his readers what former UCLA basketball coach the great John Wooden said when he bluntly put this concern into perspective: "A leader who is through learning is through. And so is the team such a leader leads. It's what you learn after you know it all that counts."[69]

> "It's what you learn after you know it all that counts."

Popular *New York Times* columnist David Brooks agrees that curiosity is integral to continued learning, in part because it eliminates our need to keep up the pretense of having all the answers. Brooks advocates that instead of putting up a false front and pretending they know it all, aspiring leaders who are wise develop the skill of asking the right questions, of the right people, so that they can grow in their understanding and expertise.[70]

As noted in the previous chapter, I formerly felt the need to put on pretenses to mask my lack of understanding. Fortunately, I later experienced the freedom that comes from dropping such a facade in favour of asking more questions. This has accelerated my learning and growth in every area of life.

Curiosity Cultivates Humility

As also mentioned in the previous chapter, Edgar Schein is a noted professor at MIT's Sloan School of Management, and he has studied the significance of humility in business, documenting many of its benefits. He has also learned that curiosity is an effective tool for cultivating humility. Speaking very practically, Schein notes that powerful leadership emerges when individuals commit to "asking instead of telling." He refers to this process as the skill of *humble inquiry*—which he defines as "the fine art of drawing someone out, of asking questions to which you do not already know the answer, of building a relationship based on curiosity and interest in the other person."[71]

This suggests that curiosity can be a humble, nonthreatening tool for building relationships. It implies that the point of curiosity is not merely to ask questions for the sake of asking questions (like a toddler who continually asks "Why?"). Rather, the mature skill of curiosity is actually very deliberate and based on a legitimate desire to learn about something.

Curiosity Spawns Entrepreneurship

In recent years, we have witnessed disruption in many industries, including transportation and broadcasting, and previously unknown names, including Netflix, Hulu, Uber, and Lyft, have burst onto the scene. What is fuelling these innovators? In a word, it is curiosity.

> Curiosity is the fuel of industry disruptors.

In her 2017 book *The Beauty of Discomfort*, Amanda Lang suggests that embracing the discomforts of change brings about resilience, adaptability, and success.[72] She begins her book by recounting the story of Uber's founding.

Apparently, two friends, Garrett Camp and Travis Kalanick, became frustrated as they tried (unsuccessfully) to hail a cab one snowy afternoon in Paris. Lang writes, "rather than just grouch about it to each other as most of us would, [they] … asked themselves whether there was a better way to match available cars to riders."[73] As we all know, the "better way" that they came up with is called Uber, and the company has been so successful that it was valued at more than $70 billion in February 2020.

Their frustration when coupled with *curiosity* inspired them to create an innovative business that has revolutionized the taxi industry. By disregarding traditional business models, they invented Uber as an alternative to corporate-owned taxi cabs, provided many car owners with part-time employment, and offered consumers a convenient, lower-cost service.

The crucial point that Lang makes is that while the invention and implementation of this new business model is unprecedented, the idea could have occurred to any cab driver or taxi company. The problem, she suggests, is that those who operated within the business-as-usual taxi industry had become complacent.[74] In contrast, Camp and Kalanick responded to their inconvenient situation with *curiosity*, and that provided the catalyst for this remarkable innovation.

Curiosity Uncovers Opportunities and Solutions

Curiosity can be an asset in any industry. When I became the president of Dominion Construction, Dad had just retired, and we needed to identify other rainmakers who could bring in new clients to replace the steady flow of sales that my dad had created in the past. Recognizing that we would need more than one person to achieve this objective, we hired sales training expert David Kennedy to assist us in developing a company-wide sales training program. He focused on teaching our executives to ask questions that would help us uncover how we could best serve our clients.

Prior to working with him, most of us thought that "selling was telling," and so we expected him to teach us how to more effectively explain Dominion Construction's capabilities to potential customers. It was a radical shift for us when we discovered what my dad had known all along—"selling was asking."

Once we understood this, it was abundantly clear that we needed to develop our curiosity and learn how to ask better questions. During our training, I discovered a question that has since become one of my favourite questions of all time, partly because it has such broad application, both in business and elsewhere. The question is *"What would the ideal solution be for you?"*

The Marine Drive Golf and Country Club

Marine Drive G&CC is an exclusive private course in Vancouver, with a history that is almost 100 years old. In 1994, the membership created plans to enlarge their clubhouse, add more space to the lock-

Marine Drive Golf and Country Club, Vancouver, BC

er rooms, update the dining room, and, in general, modernize their facilities. They had conceived the project over several years by conducting extensive surveys, doing space planning, and establishing preliminary budgets. These consultations ultimately led to a final plan that would double the size of their clubhouse. At that point, they invited Dominion Construction (and four other companies) to review the architectural drawings and submit competitive quotes for completing the work.

When the chairman of their building committee came by my office to drop off the plans, I asked if he had a few minutes to talk. We discussed the process they had been through and what their hopes were for the expansion. As the meeting was wrapping up, I asked, "What would the ideal solution be for you?"

This profoundly simple question opened up an entirely new stream of conversation, and I discovered that their ideal solution was to tear down the existing clubhouse and build something completely new. However, anticipated costs had forced them to make a number of short- and long-term compromises, such as forgoing a new building. They remained frustrated because an expansion would not provide them with all that they wanted. He summed up his thoughts by saying, "Ideally, we would like to build a brand-new facility, as long as it does not cost much more than the planned expansion."

> *One of the most powerful questions is What would be the ideal solution for you?*

His words were music to my ears. Since we would already be looking at their expansion plans, I asked if we could evaluate the costs of tearing down the existing building and starting from scratch. I ventured that perhaps we could find a cost-effective way to deliver on their ideal solution. He agreed that we could give it a shot, but I could see that he was skeptical.

UNCOVER CUSTOMER'S NEEDS

DEEPEN RELATIONSHIPS

ENCOURAGE ENTREPRENEURSHIP

STIMULATE LEARNING

DEVELOP LEADERSHIP

CURIOSITY

Several weeks later, we presented two estimates (one for the expansion and one for a full rebuild). As it turned out, we were able to offer the "ideal" solution for only a fraction more than the cost of the proposed addition. The chairman of the building committee and the membership were ecstatic. Today, a beautiful new clubhouse exists because we were sufficiently curious to ask about what they really wanted.

Today, "What would the ideal solution be?" is my favourite question for business and, frankly, for almost any situation. It can be used to discuss your next family vacation, a new car, or even plans for a night out on the town with your spouse. As an added benefit, not only does this question tend to reveal improbable solutions; it also tends to motivate and energize people's creativity.

Curiosity Is a Key That Unlocks Many Doors

Curiosity can help uncover customers' needs and stimulate learning; it helps to deepen relationships and assists individuals to develop as leaders; it also encourages entrepreneurship. As shown in the illustration above, curiosity is a key that opens many doors!

CURIOSITY IN A FAMILY ENTERPRISE

Curiosity Uncovers the Desires of the Elder Generation

During a workshop session with members of a successful family business, one of my professional colleagues witnessed an emotional outburst from a client who was the patriarch. Apparently, his adult children did not agree with his views, and so he let them know how he felt about that in rather emphatic terms. This was not the first time his feelings had gotten the better of him, and, as my friend had witnessed previously, the result was that the other family members immediately shut down, becoming passive and largely silent.

Rather than tell him what to do, my friend employed her curiosity as a means of generating change. She followed up with her client and asked if he was happy with the meeting. Frankly, he was not. When asked what disappointed him about the interactions with his children, he replied, "Their silence." He explained that it implied that they were not interested in the topics he wanted to discuss.

Probing further, she asked, "Why do you think they were so quiet?"

He initially did not know, but when asked how he thought his emotional outbursts affected his interactions with his children, he sheepishly admitted that he might have contributed to their communication shutting down. He also admitted that he could see how his desire to make all the decisions had paralyzed the process and was counterproductive to him achieving his goals.

My colleague then asked one of the most helpful questions anyone can ever ask the elder generation of a family enterprise: "What would you like to see for your family in 20 years?"

This profound and brilliantly curious question motivated her client to share his desire that his children would become deeply engaged in the family business, that they would one day see it as

> *Ask the elder generation, "What would like to see for your family in 20 years?"*

their own, and that they would become a team that could build on the legacy he had worked so hard to create for them.

Concluding the dialogue, her following query clinched the point: "If that is what you desire for them, and for your business, what can you do to help create an environment that helps make your dream a reality?"

This combination of curiosity and thoughtful questions assisted an aging legend to realize that he needed to change his communication patterns, and gradually, with supportive coaching, he was able to control his emotions more effectively. He also learned the importance of asking questions and being curious. This led him to ask questions of his children and then to use more questions to probe and understand their answers. Over time, this paved the way for the adult children to contribute more wholeheartedly to the family meetings and to the shareholder decision-making.

What was the key to resolving this issue? In large measure, it was the artful use of curiosity, which helped uncover the client's vision for the future and assisted him to understand the changes he needed to make in order to achieve his goals. Subsequently, he became more curious when interacting with his children and involved them in the process of creating a future that they all could be excited about.

Curiosity Builds Strong Relationships

Some people work very hard at building a professional network, keeping a list of the people they meet at events and promising to stay in touch. A few decades ago, this involved collecting as many business cards as possible. Now, thanks to technology, we use tools like LinkedIn to establish connections with a host of people, including those whom we have never met.

In contrast, my dad built his network, as they say, "the old-fashioned way"—by meeting people face to face, and typically for lunch. He then used the power of curiosity and his own mastery of asking questions to build genuine relationships. For example, when he was president, our company had an executive dining room on the top floor of the Bentall Three office tower in the heart of Vancouver. From the 32nd floor there was a commanding view of the downtown harbour and Stanley Park, and this provided a perfect setting for entertaining business associates, along with members of our senior executive team. Dad would typically host lunches two to three days a week, and he was widely known for his gracious hospitality and for taking an interest in every aspect of others' lives.

Every one of his guests felt important because *they* were the focus of his attention. That is, *when they were with him, he was with them*. Although he asked questions, they never felt that they were being put on the spot; instead, they felt honoured as they were asked to share their lives and business interests with him. He was a master of curiosity in that he knew how to ask the kind of questions that led to deeper conversations and, ultimately, to loyal clients and lifelong friendships.

Conversations over lunch would follow a familiar pattern as the meal progressed. Dad would start by asking his visitors about their families and personal interests. From there, the conversation would move into current events and business news. As these relationships developed, conversations very naturally turned to business. By the time lunch concluded, everyone at the table would have gained insights into our guests' personal lives, what was important to them in terms of business, and, if appropriate, what mutual business opportunities might exist.

> Curiosity displays an interest in others.

Curiosity was a very natural and essential element of his approach to business. Dad always sought to establish a rapport and personal connection with clients, and that involved coming to an understanding of what their needs were and how we could meet them. To help confirm his understanding of a prospective client's needs, he kept an 8 by 11-inch notepad and a sharpened HB pencil at the ready. He summarized what he learned as he asked questions about budgets, prospects, plans, and locations. His questions not only helped him to understand their needs but in some cases also led clients to discover their own needs.

Numerous well-known executives in Vancouver acknowledged that Dad was the best salesman that they had ever met, and he developed this reputation because he focused on understanding the clients' needs and not on selling our services. He accomplished this through the power of curiosity.

Curiosity Maintains Relationships

Within a family enterprise, disagreements *between generations are sometimes rooted in assumptions that have the power to curtail curiosity*. For example, if members of a family business assume that they already know how other family members feel about a given situation, they are not likely to ask them for their ideas or input on decisions. This shuts out family members, bypasses what could have been extremely helpful dialogue, and has the potential to create a great deal of turmoil and regret.

To illustrate, one of my colleagues acted as a mediator between two co-owners of a family business who had not spoken for 25 years. They were struggling to reach an agreement in what had become a protracted dispute. When the mediator probed to find common ground through the use of curious questioning, the two brothers eventually experienced a breakthrough. By utilizing curiosity, the facilitator of these discussions also helped these men uncover the real source of their conflict. Tragically, 25 years before, the co-owners had each made incorrect assumptions about the other, and this had led to a complete break in their relationship for over two decades. If either one of them had only been curious enough to ask a few questions, they could have potentially been spared all those years of heartache.

> Curiosity helps us to discover others' thoughts and feelings.

Curiosity helps us to understand what others are *thinking and feeling*. It is an important element in all of our relationships, and is particularly important in a family business, where it can be tempting to "assume" you know what your partner/sibling/family member is thinking, or feeling, simply because you may "think" you know them so well.

Curiosity Leads to Innovation

Many family enterprises and companies have been born out of curiosity—that is, founded by individuals who were experimenting with new ideas, inventions, or products. For example, the first vehicle that Henry Ford built was the Quadricycle. Introduced in 1896, it was powered by a 4-horsepower motor and had only two forward gears and no reverse. Nonetheless, it would take Ford another 12 years of experimenting and tinkering with various ideas in order to develop the breakthrough Model T. "Previous models were the guinea pigs, one might say, for … development of a car which would realize Henry Ford's dream of a car which anyone could afford to buy."[75] To build a prototype of the Model T, he created a special room where he and his team could unleash their curiosity, trying out different design ideas.

As his team searched for ways to manufacture more quickly and more cheaply, Ford was ever curious about new materials and new methods of production. For example, when he was first exposed to vanadium steel, Ford enthused, "we can get a better, lighter, and cheaper car as a result of it."[76]

The Challenges & Payoffs for Successors

LACK OF CURIOSITY Without curiosity, successors will tend to…	WITH CURIOSITY When they become more curious successors will tend to…	PRACTICAL IMPACT Successors will also discover that curiosity helps to…	POTENTIAL PAYOFFS Curiosity also helps successors to…
Assume they "know it all"	Ask more questions	Build rapport with others	Facilitate postitive relationships with non-family executives
Be aloof and disinterested	Be more eager to learn	Accelerate their understanding of the business	Grow in knowledge & skill
Have an arrogant approach to problem solving	Humbly ask for input from others	Establish respectful interactions with others	Be respected by members of the elder generation
Be unwilling to consider other people's ideas	Search for "out of the box" ideas	Spawn entrepreneurship	Create new business opportunities
Jump to conclusions quickly	Explore issues thoroughly	Uncover new opportunities	Open new markets, and add value to the company
Be unable to think creatively	Create new solutions	Introduce innovative products & services	Demonstrate to others that they are a team player

Similarly, while exploring ways to reduce the time to build a new vehicle, Ford kept puzzling over how to move materials from storage to the assembly area more efficiently, and this led to one of the decisive breakthroughs in manufacturing history. Instead of taking parts from inventory to the vehicles being manufactured, Ford and his team decided to move the partly assembled vehicles to where the parts were kept. Simply by dragging the partially built cars from storage room to storage room, the assembly line was invented. This innovation, fuelled by curiosity, reduced the production time for a new car from 12 hours to 2½ hours.

Part of the magic that led to such remarkable success was Ford's determination to create an automobile that would be affordable for the masses. However, it was Ford's insatiable curiosity that served as the primary stimulus for most of the innovations that made his dream a reality.

A Lack of Curiosity Inhibits Progress

Unfortunately, when a well-established company grows complacent or accustomed to things being done a certain way, it can stifle a natural sense of curiosity about how to change things or do them better. Once curiosity is gone, it is only a matter of time before a business loses its openness to change and, subsequently, its quota of new ideas. Such companies are at risk of being eclipsed by those that maintain their curiosity and, as a consequence, spawn more innovative solutions. Such scenarios are particularly challenging for family enterprises to navigate because new ideas and a desire for change are often championed by the younger generation who are wanting to innovate, whereas the elder generation may be more content with maintaining the status quo.

In addition to spawning business innovation, curiosity leads to remarkable interpersonal payoffs.

WHAT INHIBITS OUR CURIOSITY?

Once we understand the enormous benefits that curiosity brings to business, it seems ridiculous to think that business leaders would not make it a high priority to develop and utilize this skill in their daily activities, interactions, and management decision-making. But, even though curiosity is an innate human trait, there are many factors that tend to negate or stifle it.

Giving Advice

I have been involved with numerous business groups throughout my career. Some of them function like a board of directors, offering confidential feedback and support to members facing business challenges. One such group that I joined included eight professional peers who were all highly intelligent and extremely accomplished executives. When meeting, we were all encouraged to share our respective challenges, and although I enjoyed learning from their experiences, it was several years before I had sufficient confidence to share with them a particular challenge that I faced as the president of Dominion Construction.

There were strict guidelines governing the process, including the primary rule that we were not allowed to give advice. Instead, we were to follow three strategies as we made our comments:

1. Those who had similar experiences could share what they had done and why.
2. We could ask questions.
3. We could share our thoughts about what we would do if we were in the same circumstance, but our comments were to begin with the phrase "If I was in your shoes, I would."

Essentially, this approach was designed to permit feedback, ignite new ideas, and provide a sense of support, without telling an individual what to do or putting greater pressure on them by saying "you should."

Eventually, I shared my situation, beginning with some background: The average bottom-line profit for a well-performing construction company (at that time) was about 1 percent of its sales. That is, our company could expect one million dollars in profit for every $100 million in revenue. Although our company was private, we knew that 1 percent profit was the standard for even the best publicly traded corporations in our industry.

However, Dominion Construction had a unique advantage over other firms in that we had an in-house design group of 80 engineers and designers. When coupled with our engineering and construction services, our design team enabled us to provide our clients with value engineering services as well as cost guarantees much earlier on in the construction process than our competitors (who had to work alongside design teams from other companies).

A classic example of this was the construction of a 20,000-seat indoor sports arena in downtown Vancouver. Currently known as Rogers Arena (formerly General Motors Place), it is home to the Vancouver Canucks NHL franchise and the former home of the Vancouver Grizzlies, an NBA team that eventually relocated to Memphis, Tennessee.

When the project was put out for tender in the early 1990s, all five competing construction companies came in with bids that exceeded $100 million, substantially more than the $75 million budget. This resulted in a scramble to find ways of dramatically reducing costs. Our in-house design experts pored over the plans, looking for any kind of cost reduction through changes in design. During a three-week evaluation, we managed to find $18 million in savings, while maintaining the size and integrity of what would be a world-class facility. Those changes allowed us to win the contract, and we proudly completed the project in 1992.

Because of the clear advantages that we offered through our design and build capabilities, we believed that we could and should be generating higher profits, and we had set a target of 2 percent, twice the industry average. Yet, even though we had recently been successful in doubling

Rogers Arena, Vancouver, BC

our volume and our profits, our earnings remained at 1 percent.

After explaining all this background information to my business colleagues, my question to them was simply "How can we increase our profit margins?"

But my expectations for helpful feedback evaporated as my presentation progressed. This was obviously a crash course in construction economics for them, and they seemed preoccupied by just one fact—the standard 1 percent profit margin. They all represented business sectors where profit margins were much higher, and they were so incredulous at the norms of the construction industry that they were unable to offer any help.

Instead of receiving questions, I got advice. Instead of curiosity, I got negative feedback. Rather than constructive brainstorming, I was admonished to get out of the construction business and given directives to "sell" and "sell soon." In the end, there were no attempts at finding a solution. Their responses were disheartening, to say the least.

I remained in the group for some time afterwards, but this disappointing exchange drastically changed my feelings about its benefits, and, over time, I quietly withdrew. The most helpful part of the experience is that it provided a vivid and memorable illustration of how a lack of curiosity can derail an opportunity for improvement and innovation.

This encounter made me resolve to become the kind of person who asks questions rather than give in to the temptation to always dispense advice. I admit that it is difficult: it requires a great deal of self-discipline *to not offer* quick words of advice, but I now know how much better it is to be curious and to ask questions rather than to share advice and to tell others what they should do.

A Lack of Patience

Although some parents may take great delight in the constant questioning that is typical of young children, some find the experience time-consuming, frustrating, and, at times, embarrassing. So they tend to shut down curiosity in their kids because it requires more time and patience than they feel they have. Being constantly shut down may be one of the reasons why our curiosity typically begins to erode when we are just four or five years old.

Structured Academics

Most academic institutions put a greater emphasis on book learning than on individual discovery. Consequently, from a very young age, we are taught to search for the answers in a textbook (or online) rather than to think things through and explore the possibilities that might exist by asking questions such as "Why?" As Albert Einstein has said, "Logic will get you from A to B, but imagination will take you everywhere else."

Intellectual Pride

It is tempting for highly intelligent people to believe that they have all the answers. But if intellectual pride is not kept in check, it can diminish or destroy our openness to new ideas and our natural curiosity. In other words, a great mind is a gift to be celebrated, but it may rob a person of the desire or even the need to be curious.

Sadly, I have seen this occur all too often with family enterprise successors. As they say, "the apple does not fall far from the tree," and successors, like the generation before them, are often highly gifted, entrepreneurial, driven, and motivated. Unfortunately, this makes it very easy for them to become judgmental or critical towards others, including members of the elder generation.

Like I did, young leaders tend to assume that they can do much better than their predecessors. As a family business consultant, I have had clients in their 20s tell me that they need to "take over" the family business before their parents "ruin it." In very rare cases, this might be true. In most cases it is not and is simply a reflection of arrogance, pride, and impatience on the part of the successor.

Rather than assume that they know better, successors are wise to take the time to ask members of the elder generation why they do things in a certain way and then pay attention to what they say. Personally, because I lacked curiosity as a young successor, I failed to build a strong rapport with other senior executives in our firm. In addition, with my peers I forfeited the opportunity to show that I could be a team player. Most damaging was the fact that I didn't gain the respect of the elder generation in our family, especially my uncles. As a result, they ultimately chose to have me removed from the company.

Personal Pride

While some highly intelligent people curb their sense of curiosity because they are convinced that they know the answers, others are afraid to ask questions because they don't want to look stupid. As described in a previous chapter, some elect to stay quiet rather than risk looking bad in front of others. Perhaps their pride pushes these people to follow the school of thought inspired by Mark Twain's famous quote "It is better to keep your mouth closed and let people think you are a fool than to open it and remove all doubt."

DEAR YOUNGER ME …

I know that my experience in our family enterprise could have been radically different if I had had the humility to recognize that my father and my uncle had plenty to teach me and if I had employed more curiosity. Not only would I have learned a lot, I am confident that their view of me would have been much different if I had asked them more questions and if I had displayed the maturity and wisdom to listen to their answers.

When I was a young executive, because I thought I knew everything and was not very curious, I was typically unwilling to consider other people's ideas. I also failed to be curious about why things were done the way they were, so I missed the opportunity to be mentored and trained by the people I worked with. This led to a rather superficial understanding of the business, rather than a deep knowledge of what had made us successful in the past and what our true strengths were. Instead of arriving at the office thirsty to learn, I arrived assuming I knew it all.

I have also come to realize the benefits of curiosity in my personal relationships, but it does require focus—a determination to utilize questions as a means of getting to know others. Not long ago, my wife, Alison, and I were on a bicycle trip in Slovenia and Croatia. There were 15 cyclists in our group, and 13 of them were total strangers to us as our trip began. It was a great opportunity to meet people from around the world, but after the first few evenings, I realized that my interactions with others made me appear to be interesting (like Churchill) rather than being interested in others (like Gandhi).

On the third day of our itinerary, I made a commitment to myself that, for the rest of the trip, when talking with a new person I would not share anything about my life until I had first asked at least three questions about the other person. This simple strategy stretched (i.e., forced) me to be much more curious and, over the next five days, strengthened my interactions with virtually everyone. Questions encouraged them to open up and share about their lives, and that immediately started our conversations down a more personal and meaningful path.

As this experience illustrates, curiosity has the power to transform our relationships, help us to uncover new ideas, and assist us to solve problems more effectively. It may not be a natural instinct for some, but the payoffs are enormous if we can make a conscious commitment to become more curious.

THE BOTTOM LINE

Curiosity helps us be more engaging relationally and more innovative professionally.

David

CHAPTER 3
Listening: Accessing the Wisdom All Around You

"Wisdom is the reward you get for a lifetime of listening when you would rather have talked."

Attributed to Mark Twain

The name Jimmy Pattison is legendary in Canadian business circles and beyond. He opened his first car dealership in 1961 and, from there, established a multi-billion-dollar international empire consisting of car dealerships, grocery stores, real estate, broadcasting, and media. His broad range of holdings even extends to *The Guinness Book of World Records* and Ripley's Believe It or Not.

He is consistently listed near the top of Canada's wealthiest individuals, and he is widely respected for using his vast resources to champion a variety of charitable causes through the Pattison Foundation. As an example of his community-mindedness, for seven years Jimmy volunteered his time to lead the effort to bring Expo '86, the international world's fair, to Vancouver in 1986.

In 1987, I had the privilege of joining him at a meeting to select a chair for the fundraising committee for Vancouver's new downtown library and public plaza. All three levels of government (federal, provincial, and municipal) had pledged their financial support, but the committee was charged with raising the final $30 million.

Unfortunately, just after the fundraising campaign was launched, the high-profile executive who had agreed to serve as chair abruptly left town, leaving the project in jeopardy and raising concerns about the reason for his rapid departure. Given these circumstances, it was not an easy task to find a replacement, and one afternoon I joined a group of about 20 senior executives for a discussion on who we could invite to take on this strategic role. We were all painfully aware that we could not afford a second misstep in selecting the new leader, and so we began by carefully considering our criteria for selection.

One member suggested that we get someone who could appeal to wealthy potential donors; another thought we needed someone who could appeal to the broader community, so we could enjoy a large base of community support. Another proposed that the new person needed to have a name that was synonymous with downtown Vancouver, and we all agreed that the perfect candidate needed to have a sterling reputation, fundraising experience, and sufficient time to focus on the job.

As we continued to talk, the list of requirements and the list of potential names kept growing. There was no sign of stopping, and it seemed increasingly unlikely that we would be able to come to any kind of consensus. As you can imagine, people were growing impatient.

I offered a few ideas but mostly stayed quiet and paid close attention to what others were saying. In particular, I wondered what Jimmy Pattison was thinking. Our meeting was at the four-hour mark, and he had yet to say a single word.

He didn't say a word for four hours!

Thirty minutes later, Mr. Pattison finally spoke. The group immediately leaned forward to hear what he had to say. (It reminded me of the popular 1970s TV ad that depicted a group of professionals all speaking loudly at a dinner party until one fellow mentioned that his broker was E. F. Hutton. Suddenly the chatter stopped, and everyone leaned in to listen. The tagline? "When E. F. Hutton talks … people listen.")

Jimmy began by summarizing, point by point, what he had heard during our discussion, including the qualities and characteristics that we were looking for in a new chair and virtually all of the key ideas that we had shared. As he spoke, people nodded their heads in agreement.

He then said, "If we all agree that this is what we are looking for, then I think Kip Woodward would be the perfect man to lead this effort."

The room went quiet. Jimmy had clearly stated what we needed and named someone who met all of our criteria. He had hit the nail on the head, and we all happily agreed with his recommendation. Our meeting adjourned within minutes.

A few days later, Kip accepted the job. He successfully led the fundraising, and over time the landmark project was completed.

This is a powerful lesson in listening. At the beginning of our meeting, I had expected a man of Jimmy's experience, prominence, and brilliance to take charge of the discussion and perhaps even be impatient when listening to the thoughts of others. Instead, he gave a master class on the art of listening. As the rest of the group brainstormed and evaluated a vast array of ideas, Jimmy listened. He was engaged; he did not interrupt or criticize. He respected each of us enough to hear our comments before offering his own thoughts.

That is genuine listening, and this experience shows us why "when Jimmy Pattison talks, people listen."

HOW TO BE A GOOD LISTENER

What exactly does it mean to listen or, more importantly, to listen well? This might not seem like the most profound question, and yet you may be surprised at the value of this virtue once we explore its utility.

What Makes a Great Listener?

People typically say that they are good listeners. But the problem with such estimations is that most of them have come to that conclusion through self-assessment, and, as reported in *The Harvard Business Review*, "People's appraisal of their listening skills is much like their assessment of their driving skills … the great bulk of adults think they're above average."[77]

So what does it take to be an above-average listener?

In an article entitled "What Great Listeners Actually Do," Jack Zenger and Joseph Folkman describe their efforts to define the characteristics that distinguish truly great listeners from the rest of us. As experts and researchers in the field of leadership development, they analyzed the behaviours of 3,492 leaders as they participated in a program designed to help managers excel.

> *The best listeners ask good questions.*

They summarized their analysis of great listeners into four main findings.[78]

1. **Good listening involves interaction.** The best listeners are those who ask questions that promote greater discussion and insight. Apparently, the "silent nod of understanding" that many of us use does not provide the speaker with an assurance that they are being heard. In contrast, responding with one good question tells the speaker that their words have been heard and understood to the extent that they can engage in an active two-way dialogue.

2. **Good listening enhances self-esteem.** According to Zenger and Folkman, "The best listeners made the conversation a positive experience for the other party." That is, they conveyed a sense of confidence in them and support for them that, ultimately, established a safe environment for open discussion.

3. **Good listening involves co-operation.** Good conversations were characterized by a healthy exchange with "feedback flowing … in both directions and neither party becoming defensive." Good listeners engage and listen with the intent of providing positivity and help; poor listeners listen to find fault. Poor conversations were characterized as "competitive," and the participants seemed more like debaters in that they consistently challenged what others were saying. In addition, poor

listeners were focused more on preparing their response than on listening to what was being said. Author Stephen Covey summarized the problem well: "Most people do not listen with the intent to understand; they listen with the intent to reply."[79]

4. **Good listeners make suggestions.** Not surprisingly, it is easier for us to accept suggestions from someone who has first taken the time to listen to us. Rather than just give a nod of encouragement or focus intently on what the person is saying, truly great listeners provide feedback in a way that others are able to accept and opens up alternative streams of thinking.

This last point describes Jimmy Pattison's actions in the meeting recalled at the beginning of this chapter. He spoke in a way that offered no offence to any person or to any of the ideas that had already been presented. He did not condescend or find fault with our input; instead, he affirmed our contributions by going through our suggestions, point by point, before presenting his solution.

It has often been said that a good listener is similar to a sponge in that they readily absorb what is being said. But according to Zenger and Folkman, absorbing the words of others is not enough to make you a good listener.

> Great listeners are like a trampoline, letting others bounce ideas off them.

Instead, they believe it is much more accurate to compare good listeners to a trampoline that provides feedback as you bounce your ideas off of it. Good listeners can also "amplify, energize, and clarify your thinking. They make you feel better not by merely passively absorbing but by actively supporting. This lets you gain energy and height, just like someone jumping on a trampoline."[80]

The trampoline analogy not only portrays listening as a far more active behaviour than the sponge analogy; it also calls to mind the joy we can bring to others by truly listening (which may be quite similar to the great delight our grandkids experience when bouncing on the trampoline at our summer cottage).

Being Present

Most of us have experienced a situation where we are in a conversation with others and things are going great … until a cellphone rings. Suddenly the other person disappears to take the call, and we are left hanging, feeling second best.

I have been guilty of this on many occasions, with both clients and family. That changed on the day that I found myself in a car with someone who was on the phone when I desperately wanted to speak with him.

This person lives a considerable distance from me, and opportunities for us to speak face-to-face are rare. As a result, when I knew three months in advance that I would be in the same city, I made plans for us to have dinner together. His wife would also join us, but prior to that we had a 30-minute drive together, and I had hoped to use this time to get his advice on a few matters.

But when the appointed time arrived and I was just settling into the passenger's seat of his vehicle, his phone rang. He apologized for the interruption, and since it was one of his clients, I understood the need for him to respond. But the conversation went on … and on. Instead of enjoying a special time of conversation (as I had long anticipated), I was watching the scenery fly by as he spoke with someone else. I began to resent the intrusion and grew more frustrated with each passing mile.

As I lay in bed that night, I slowly came to the realization that this is exactly how my friends and family must feel every time that I allow a phone call to interrupt our conversations or family occasions. This time, I was the one who was left feeling not valued or respected. It was a painful lesson.

Since then, I have become more sensitive to the impact it may have on others when I answer my phone. As a result, I am more likely to let calls go to voicemail or to send the standard text "Sorry, I can't talk now."

THE BENEFITS OF LISTENING

Listening Earns the Right to Be Heard

One habit that Stephen Covey encourages us to develop is to "seek first to understand … then to be understood." In other words, if you want people to understand you, or even to listen to you, you need to listen to them first.[81]

This suggestion is based on far more than courtesy and reciprocity; it is founded on the idea that we must earn the right to be heard. This stems from the ancient Greek belief that there are three levels of intimacy in conversation: *ethos* (character and credibility), *pathos* (emotion), and *logos* (logic).[82]

Ethos. The Greeks believed that it was best to begin with our character when seeking to be understood by another. Hence, if we are able to begin by establishing a positive *ethos*, others will consider all that we say within that context and what they know about our character and our credibility. Clearly, if we have a stellar reputation (e.g., we are known to be reliable and honest), then others are more likely to listen carefully to what we say.

Considering this, how can we demonstrate the kind of character that inspires others to listen to us? Simply by showing a willingness to listen to them first. This sends the positive character message that we are not self-absorbed. In turn, this increases the likelihood that they will listen to us when we have something to say.

Pathos. Once character has been established, a relational or empathetic element that the Greeks termed *pathos* can be added to the communication. That is, as we demonstrate empathy and concern, others are more likely to listen to our words. As a result, *pathos* can enhance, deepen, and strengthen both conversations and relationships.

Logos. After a listening relationship has been built on *ethos* and *pathos*, we can begin to discuss our ideas, opinions, and facts. This is known as logic (*logos* to the Greeks), and at this point we can reason with one another because we are truly listening to one another.

As a young executive, understanding the concepts of *ethos, pathos,* and *logos* would have made such a difference in how I communicated my ideas. I had plenty of them; many were logical, and I think some also had merit. Yet most of my ideas went unheard because of the way in which they were presented. At that time, I placed all my emphasis on the *logos* or logic of my ideas, without first building credibility (*ethos*) and demonstrating empathy (*pathos*).

Listening Develops Credibility

In 1993, our son, Jon, began attending St. George's School, and a few years later I was asked to join the board of directors of this highly respected institution. Once a month, nearly two dozen of us would meet to consider and plan for the future of this great school. At first, I felt somewhat out of my depth and was reluctant to speak up, in part because I had never been educated at a private school and I was also not particularly knowledgeable about academic affairs.

As I contemplated how to navigate in this unfamiliar territory, I recalled Jimmy Pattison and how effectively he directed us in our meeting to find a fundraising chair. I decided to try his strategy at the school board meetings, and so I made a commitment to myself that I would listen long and hard before contributing. In other words, I would keep my mouth shut, listen, take notes, and observe.

When new topics were raised, I would write my questions and comments down on a notepad and then wait for the others to speak. At times, I found that my questions and/or comments were addressed by others, leaving me to cross the topics off my list while quietly listening.

On other occasions, if my ideas were not covered in the discussion, I would ask the chair if I could share my observations. The experience was almost surreal ... just as I had witnessed with Jimmy Pattison, people leaned in to listen as I began to speak. At first, it was so noticeable that it was almost distracting, but I soon came to expect it. By respectfully listening to others before speaking, I created an environment where others were much more interested in what I had to say.

As this became my routine at school board meetings, I began to consider how many times I had spoken too freely and/or too often during meetings at the office, particularly on occasions when I was in familiar territory and confident in my knowledge. I began to realize that I had a tendency to interject before allowing others ample opportunity to contribute. These realizations motivated me to utilize the "listen first; speak last" approach in more of my meetings.

Listening Builds Better Relationships

According to clinical psychologist Dr. Rachel Naomi Remen, "the most important thing we ever give each other is our attention."[83] In fact, she believes that *the gift of listening to each other is often more important than the words that we share.*

An excellent example of this comes from one of my good friends, a gifted, successful executive who helps entrepreneurs to finance new real estate ventures. He also travels a lot, working on opportunities throughout North America and beyond. Taking calls from his clients is a priority 24-7, and that means his cellphone is almost permanently attached to his ear.

The one exception to this rule is his family. He always puts down his phone for them. Why? Because he wants to be available to them and to let them know that they are more important to him than his next deal. As he consistently follows through with this discipline, he sends the messages "you are important to me," "I love you," and "I want to be *present* and *prepared to listen* when I am with you."

In addition, his active efforts to listen to his children have created a rapport and mutual respect that serve as a solid foundation for their relationships, and those benefits will last a lifetime.

Listening Communicates Respect

There is perhaps no more important place for this than in a marriage. As I have discovered on many occasions, to be genuinely heard is to feel both respected and understood. A memorable example from early in my marriage illustrates this. At the time, Alison and I were experiencing some difficult relational challenges, and so we sought the help of a professional counsellor. Prior to this, I had thought I was a good listener, but I soon came to the painful realization that listening was not one of my strengths. Much to my chagrin, I came to understand that I had particularly not been doing a good job of listening to my wife.

To help us hear each other better, our therapist encouraged us to develop and utilize a technique known as *reflective listening.* It involved listening to each other without interrupting and then repeating back to one another the words that each of us had heard. This approach allowed us to discover what the other person thought we were saying and gave us the opportunity to either confirm or correct their understanding.

One thing that I like about this technique is that it does not require me to agree with Alison; it just makes me responsible *"to confirm that I have accurately heard what she has said."* For Alison, I think the main benefit to using reflective listening is that *she can know with certainty that she has been heard.* As we have discovered, sometimes knowing that you have been heard is far more important than winning an argument.

One Thursday evening Alison asked if I would be willing to look after our kids the next night so she could go out with some of her high school friends. I was immediately irritated by the request—not because I wanted to deny her time with friends but because I had been trying for months to arrange a date night for just the two of us. It was frustrating to see that Alison had time for her friends but not for me. I was less than thrilled with this situation!

Later that night, Alison and I talked about why I was so unhappy. I explained that I was hurt because it seemed that going out with the girls was a higher priority than spending time with me. Putting our new-found skills into practice, Alison replied, "If I understand correctly, you are feeling hurt because you feel like I'm placing more importance on my school friends than on you as my husband."

"Precisely," I said, feeling very relieved to finally be understood. She had not only *listened* to me; she had also *heard* me.

When Alison asked me what I wanted her to do, I surprised her by saying that I would be fine if she went out with the girls.

Why the sudden change of heart? *Because I had been heard and now felt understood.*

People do not always agree, even in relationships when they truly listen to one another. But knowing that our point of view is being heard often means far more than winning an argument or getting what we want. I had really wanted a date night with Alison, but even more important than that, I had wanted to be heard and understood.

Being a Good Listener Is a Powerful Asset

The ability to listen, to *really hear* what others are saying, is one of the most powerful tools we have for building strong relationships. While our words may communicate a message that is properly understood, the experiences of listening and being listened to send even more messages, including ones of love, respect, and belonging. In addition, a dialogue that involves genuine listening stimulates both learning and growth as people respectfully "talk things through."

The following illustration highlights some of the key benefits that stem from the simple act of listening. They include creating awareness (by demonstrating to another that you genuinely care about their ideas and opinions), building respect (by letting others know they are important), establishing curiosity (showing that you are open to input from others), and enabling learning (by holding "space" for another individual to explore concepts and increase their understanding through discussion).

In summary, when someone listens to me, it has the power to help me to *grow*, to feel that *I am respected*, to sense that *I belong*, and to know that *I am loved*.

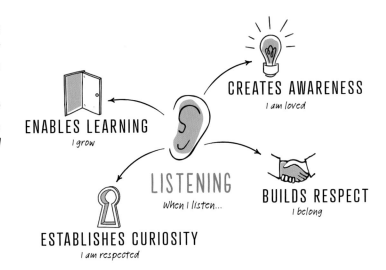

HOW LISTENING BENEFITS BUSINESS

Listening Is the Best Qualification for Leadership

Francois Michelin served as CEO of Michelin Tires from 1955 to 1999, and under his leadership the company became the number-one manufacturer of tires globally. While reflecting on his illustrious career during an interview, he was asked to comment on the most important characteristic of a business executive.

He responded by explaining that before you can lead others, you have to know how to listen to them. "You have to listen from the right and the left to really grasp any situation and to learn for yourself. It is a joy to listen to everyone, whatever their level in the hierarchy or social status."[84]

"Look at my ears," he would say, genuinely believing that they were his best qualification for leadership. It may be a rather odd way for this world-renowned entrepreneur to summarize his leadership, but, in his own way, Michelin was saying that he believed the most important role of a leader is to be a good listener.

> *Listening is the most important skill of a negotiator.*[85]

Listening Makes Us Better Negotiators

Negotiations can be a large part of an executive's professional life, and the ability to negotiate effectively is essential when seeking to reach agreement with customers, suppliers, government agencies, and employees.

What is the most important requirement for a top negotiator? Listening.

World-renowned negotiation expert William Ury says, "If you study the behavior of successful negotiators, you find that they listen far more than they talk."[86] An emphasis on listening offers three benefits to negotiators:[87]

1. It helps you to understand the other side.
2. It helps you to connect and build trust with another human being.
3. It makes it more likely that the other person will listen to what you have to say.

So how do we listen well? According to Ury, our ability to listen to others is dependent on our ability to listen to ourselves. It is an intriguing concept; in effect, he is saying that we can become more effective listeners (and therefore better negotiators) if we are aware of the motivations, feelings, and desires that are going on in our own mind. For example, if I am desperately trying to earn my year-end bonus and need one more sale to hit my target, I can become so preoccupied by this thought that it impairs my ability to make the sale. Rather than listening to the customer's needs, I may be at risk of simply trying to convince them to buy what I am selling.

In contrast, good listeners clear their minds so that they can focus, and this includes taking time to identify and manage their own thoughts and emotions before an important conversation.

Listening Leads to Learning

As discussed previously, an openness to new information and a willingness to learn from others are invaluable assets. Similarly, developing our listening skills creates new opportunities to learn and can lead to a lifelong habit of learning.

I will never forget the first time I met Ron Shon, the young scion of a successful family enterprise in Vancouver. His father had died rather suddenly, leaving Ron in charge of their real estate portfolio at a relatively young age. Ron was not unprepared—he entered the business world armed with a keen intellect and a degree in business. Perhaps even more importantly, he had an inquisitive nature and intentional listening skills.

One memorable day, he was a guest in our executive dining room at the top of Bentall Tower 3. As was his custom, my dad asked Ron lots of questions, trying to learn more about him and his business. But rather than offer answers, Ron asked questions. It was actually quite comical to watch, as Ron was just as determined as Dad to be the inquisitor.

Instead of being presumptive or arrogant, Ron was thirsty to learn from his interactions with others. As a result, when he was suddenly thrust into a leadership position, he was able to wisely steward the family's assets and avoid the common pitfalls that many successors experience when they believe that they "have all the answers."

Listening Helps to Avoid Conflict

We all know of families who have been torn apart by financial or business squabbles. In their excellent book *Deconstructing Conflict: Understanding Family Business, Shared Wealth and Power*, authors Doug Baumoel and Blair Trippe observe that families tend to "fight over legacies, cling to narratives of loss and humiliation, and show an unwillingness to compromise over values they hold deeply."[88] When faced with changing values or legacies, they feel threatened, stop listening to each other, and hold on even tighter to what they are afraid they may lose. Yet, research by neuroscientists and social psychologists has shown that it is easier for people to consider other perspectives when they do not feel threatened.[89]

Furthermore, "Conflict and reconciliation within family-owned companies is no different than conflict and reconciliation around the world. It begins by acknowledging our shared humanity, our common need to be heard, understood, and included in fundamental decisions that shape our future."[90]

In 1988, my siblings and I acquired Dominion Construction from The Bentall Group, its parent company. It is one of the most powerful examples of how listening well helped avoid conflict in our family. I say this because all four of us had radically different goals, and yet, by listening to one another's needs and preferences, we were able to come up with a business solution that accommodated each of our individual needs while simultaneously preserving our relationships.

At that time, my brother, Chuck, desired more independence, so we made arrangements to buy him out of the business. We were able to provide him with complete liquidity within five years. My sister Mary wanted to invest in the business but had no interest in being on the board or in management. My other sister, Helen, was looking for something in the middle, wanting some measure of liquidity as well as a role in the business. Finally, I was looking for a full-time management role and an opportunity to invest.

As a result of our arrangement, Chuck became a former owner, Mary became an investing owner, Helen, a governing owner, and I took on the title of managing owner.

On the following page is a summary of how we accommodated each sibling in our generation.

Our experience clearly demonstrates that family members who listen to each other can still collaborate and accomplish something amazing, even when all members want different things.

Listening Creates Unity and Consensus

For more than three decades (1968 to 1999), four family members (three Nordstrom brothers and their brother-in-law, Jack MacMillan) shared the leadership at Nordstrom, the luxury department store chain. Under their leadership, the company expanded and flourished. During the entire time, they were co-CEOs, and although

	SHAREHOLDER	BOARD	MANAGEMENT
CHUCK BENTALL *Former owner*	✗	✗	✗
MARY GEORGE *Investing owner*	✓	✗	✗
HELEN BURNHAM *Governing owner*	✓	✓	✗
DAVID BENTALL *Managing owner*	✓	✓	✓

this may sound like a nightmare to some, this leadership concept worked extremely well for their family enterprise. When I spoke with Jack about why this had worked so well for the four of them, he offered two reasons:

1. They had a simple tradition of eating lunch together daily. Because they spent so much time together and knew each other so well, "reaching decisions by consensus didn't seem that difficult. It almost happened by osmosis."
2. Collaboration was a deeply rooted and long-held value in the company's culture. According to Jack, "Unless the four of us were unanimous about a given strategy or decision, we didn't proceed."

The Nordstrom family's experience shows that spending time together and truly *listening* to one another can build understanding, improve decision-making, and create unity. Ultimately, this can be a powerful strategy for sustained growth and success.

HOW TO IMPROVE OUR LISTENING

The truth about one family's ability to listen to each other emerged relatively quickly during a consultation about the family business. Our discussion on communication methods had barely begun when one person blurted out, "In our family we don't take turns speaking and listening; we take turns speaking and waiting for our turn to speak."

This remark would have been truly comical had it not been such a tragic indictment of their listening skills.

As I reflected on their experience, I realized that most of us are guilty of this. Rather than actively listening to others as they speak,

THREE KEY STEPS TO BECOMING A BETTER LISTENER

	Action	Strategy	Outcome
STEP 1	Quiet your mind	Set aside distractions	Remove roadblocks to listening
STEP 2	Pay attention	Actively invest in the process of listening	Absorb what is being said (without analyzing)
STEP 3	Seek to understand	Engage your intellect	Make a genuine effort to uncover what the other person wants you to hear

we are often preoccupied with trying to think of a clever response or attempting to marshal our arguments.

In my experience, listening requires three main elements or steps, as pictured above.

It seems simple enough, but we all know that becoming a good listener is no easy assignment. So how can we improve our listening skills? The following are additional strategies that I have found to be helpful.

Pay Attention to Tone of Voice and Body Language

What we say is only a small part of what we communicate. As the following pie chart illustrates, the vast majority of the messages we send while talking come from our tone of voice and our body language. No wonder we often miscommunicate.[91]

ELEMENTS OF INTERPERSONAL COMMUNICATION[92]

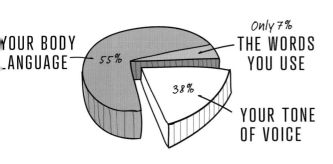

YOUR BODY LANGUAGE — 55%

Only 7% THE WORDS YOU USE

38% YOUR TONE OF VOICE

The implications are clear. Good *listening is more than hearing words*; it involves interpreting the speaker's tone of voice and watching for visual cues, such as body language.

Listen to Hear What Is Not Being Said

Years ago, my wife and I were at Smoke Tree Ranch, our family's home in Palm Springs. A new manager had recently been appointed, and as we met with one of the long-time residents for tea, we were eager to hear what she thought of him. Our friend responded to our query by making a short comment about some minor change the

> *Listening is more than simply hearing others' words.*

manager had implemented on the property and then quickly directed the conversation to a new topic.

That night, Alison and I discussed how our friend's support for the manager had been less than effusive and wondered if her reluctance to express an opinion might have been an indication that she was not particularly keen on the new boss. It seemed likely that she was practising the social rule "If you can't say anything positive, don't say anything at all."

Sometimes, what is "*not said*" speaks volumes. By being tactful and respectful, this wise woman said a great deal without saying a word.

Set Aside the Distractions of Technology

One of the greatest benefits of technology is that we can be in touch 24-7; unfortunately, many of us are finding out that being in touch 24-7 may not be the gift (or solution) that we want in our lives.

I used to think it was important to be available on my phone at all times. This was especially true 30 years ago, when we were trying to create an exemplary sales and marketing culture at Dominion Construction. More recently, I continued this practice while launching Next Step Advisors as a consulting business. Since I am the founding principal of the company, I thought that constant access to me was necessary, and I wanted to be known as someone who was available all the time. The problem with this approach is that I was often interrupted by someone on the phone when I should have been listening to the people I was actually with.

Text messages are an even bigger challenge, since we only need one or two seconds to glance at them. Yet this can disrupt our attention on those we are speaking with. If our phone is always on, it can be hard to resist the urge to look and respond quickly, even while we are in conversation with others.

Dr. Brynn Wingard is an award-winning professor and expert in business-brain science. At the 2018 Family Enterprise Symposium held at Niagara-on-the-Lake, she referred to our brains as "three pounds of supercomputer brilliance" and shared some of the secrets of its inner workings. For example, our mobile devices can be distracting to us even when they are not in our hands and just sitting nearby. As she explained, we are still attuned to their call; they are "like a new baby," and we are like the mother who is always on alert "waiting for them to signal."

To avoid this problem, she advises clients to "put the phone in another room for a while, so you don't need to worry about it." I have tried this, and it is amazing how much it increases my ability to focus on others or on my work. I invite you to try this the next time you are having a meeting with a colleague or even a conversation with a family member. You will be amazed at the calming effect and improved listening that results.

Check Your Devices at the Door. My physiotherapist, Paolo Bordignon, always takes the time to ask me how I am doing and then, even as he is treating me, listens carefully to my response. I always leave his office feeling better physically (from his excellent treatment) and emotionally (because

> *Put your phone in the other room so that you can be fully present.*

he has listened to me). We talk about work and my relationships with my family members. I know that he hears me, and the gift of being heard is profound.

Paolo carries this same attitude into his home. There is a basket in the front hallway, and whoever comes through the front door is expected to drop their smart phone into it for the duration of their visit. In other words, he expects his visitors to be fully present during their conversations with him. It is a simple idea, but it has great value and is probably something that more of us should consider implementing in our own homes.

Listen with a Pen in Hand

Even though we strive to retain the words of others, research suggests that humans have a listening efficiency of just 25 percent. That means we really have to work to hear the other 75 percent, and this takes practice and intent.[93]

I am convinced that one of the best ways to develop a listening ear and retain information is with the help of paper and pen or, if you prefer, an iPad or laptop.

When I was a young boy, my dad helped me to develop the habit of note-taking by giving me a small golf pencil and piece of paper to keep me occupied during church. He expected me to take notes during the sermon, and this type of active listening gradually became a lifelong habit. Even today, I continue to take notes when I speak on the phone or meet with a client or business associate. My iPad has now replaced the golf pencil, but the habit remains and helps me to focus on what others are saying.

As a successor and/or an aspiring leader, note-taking is a powerful habit to develop, and not just as a reminder of a conversation. Note-taking visually demonstrates that you have an interest in the conversation and shows respect to the one speaking (especially if you ask permission first).

DEAR YOUNGER ME …

As I look back, I realize that I often failed members of my immediate family by not listening as well as I could have. One of my biggest regrets is an encounter that I had with our then-teenage son, Jon.

He was a typical teenager in that he could be quite disagreeable when dealing with rules and expectations. For example, he often wanted to borrow the car but didn't think that he should have to put gas in the tank. We had expectations that he would help around the house, but he would usually rather be with his friends. While he was living under our roof, we expected him to be home at a reasonable time each night, but our definitions of "reasonable" were rarely the same.

I recall standing in the doorway to Jon's bedroom one evening, having the same old argument. I was frustrated with him for constantly challenging my rules, and on this occasion I was even more irritated because he kept interrupting me as I was speaking. I remember standing in his bedroom as our discussion deteriorated, pointing my index finger at him and wagging it menacingly as I yelled loudly, "Now you listen to me!"

It was definitely not one of my finest moments as a parent. However, as I reflect on this experience now, what troubles me the most is not how fair our rules were or who was right or wrong. *What I regret most is how little I listened to him.* I was so determined to communicate to our son that I spent very little time listening to anything he had to say.

I consider this experience one of life's difficult lessons, and it still saddens me whenever I think of that encounter. The remembrance serves to motivate me to listen more to others, regardless of the circumstances.

About 150 years ago, American philosopher Henry D. Thoreau famously wrote, "The greatest compliment that was ever paid to me was when one asked me what I thought and attended to my answer."

It is telling that these words still accurately convey a truth that is common to all of us. No matter who we are, we appreciate it and are honoured when others are genuinely interested in us, ask us to share our thoughts, and listen to us.

Today, more than ever, we should recall Thoreau's words and consider how we can pay this "greatest compliment" to others.

THE BOTTOM LINE

Listening strengthens our relationships and makes us better leaders.

David

CHAPTER 4
Empathy: The Power to Connect with Others

"I think we all have empathy. [The problem is] we may not have enough courage to display it."[94]

I first met Carson Pue more than 40 years ago, when we attended the same school in Calgary. I recall during the first week of term finding him sitting cross-legged in the furnace room holding a big slice of ham-and-pineapple pizza. There were strict rules prohibiting food in the dorm, so when I began to self-righteously reprimand him for having pizza there, Carson grinned. Without batting an eye, he said, "This isn't the dorm; this is the furnace room!" I had to admit, in that moment, that this guy was special; it was the start of a lifelong friendship.

Fortunately, the two women whom we chose to marry connected with each other the first moment they met. In time, the four of us became close friends and supported each other through marriage, raising children, building our careers, and, inevitably, as we faced some tough times.

"When we honestly ask ourselves [who] … in our lives [means] … the most to us, we often find that it is those who, instead of giving advice, solutions, or cures, have chosen rather to share our pain and touch our wounds with a gentle and tender hand."[95]

I was always inspired by the tenderness that Carson and his wife, Brenda, showed to each other and their ever-deepening level of love and commitment. I know very few people who have what I would consider to be a good marriage; I think Carson and Brenda's was a great one.

Tragically, about a year before her 60th birthday, Brenda was told that she had cancer and advised that she did not have much longer to live. Soon after her diagnosis, Carson left his job so he could care for her, remarking that he had vowed to love her "in sickness and in health," and now that her health was failing, he was going to do whatever it took to be there for her. Their children, families, and grandchildren became their main priorities during the last months of Brenda's life. Alison and I saw her as much as we could, but we knew that she needed her strength to spend as much time as possible with her family.

Feisty and courageous to the very end, Brenda lived another 588 days, and Carson loved her faithfully and tenderly on each one of them. When she died, Carson lost his best friend, the love of his life, and the woman he had worked beside for decades. He was left with a gaping hole in his heart.[96]

In many ways, Carson had exemplary support during his time of grief. After Brenda died, his eldest son, Jason, along with his wife, Kristin, and their two boys moved into the family home so they could be with him. Carson loved having his family close, and on Friday nights all three of his sons and their wives and children would regularly gather together to play games, reminisce, and remember Brenda. As a well-known leadership consultant, Carson had friends around the globe, and his inbox was constantly flooded with notes of encouragement. Wisely, he also attended a grief support group and obtained professional support from a counsellor.[97]

As his friend, I realized that I could not fix things for Carson; I could not take away the hurt, and I could not bring Brenda back. But I knew that I could make sure that I was there for him, take time to enter into his world, and seek to understand how he was feeling. In other words, to empathize.

Being empathetic means that I let Carson set the tone for our time together. As a result, I consciously avoid pushing my own agenda and let him lead us into having the conversation that he needs. At first, I found it difficult to know what to say, and there have been times when conversation has felt awkward. I do not want to constantly remind him of his loss or overwhelm him by incessantly asking how he is doing.

As time goes on, I am getting used to talking about whatever he wants to talk about or doing whatever he needs to do. Sometimes he wants to talk about the future; at other times, the past. There are days when Carson has been in the mood to laugh; sometimes, to cry. I have been silent, listened, helped him with projects, and extended a hearty man hug when that is what he needed.

> *Empathy communicates "that incredibly healing message of 'You're not alone.'"*[98]

I am certainly aware that I could have done more, but I was greatly encouraged last year on Thanksgiving Day when Carson sent me a note that read, in part, "You have prayed and comforted me in my sadness, and your companionship in times of loneliness by phone, text messages, or visits has been sustaining."[99]

I still have lots to learn about how to support my grieving friend, but I am grateful to know that my efforts to offer him love and empathy have given him strength during this difficult time.

WHAT IS EMPATHY?

While there are multiple definitions of empathy, they are essentially variations on the theme of *feeling with* people—that is, understanding their situation and feelings *through their eyes, not your own.*

For instance, Dr. Brené Brown, a world-renowned expert in empathy, describes it as an act that establishes a unique connection between people.[100] It offers a sense of comfort to one and shows the empathizer that their perspective is not the only one.

Another leading voice in helping people to understand the nature and significance of empathy is Daniel Goleman, an author well-known for his pioneering work in the broader area of emotional intelligence. According to Goleman, empathy is "the ability to sense others' feelings and how they see things. You take an active interest in their concerns. You pick up cues to what's being felt and thought. With empathy, you sense unspoken emotions. You listen attentively to understand the other person's point of view."[101]

> *Empathy is "the ability to sense others' feelings."[102]*

Empathy is not complicated, and, based on the insights of both Brown and Goleman, it begins by getting beyond a preoccupation with our own thoughts and feelings. Instead, we learn to "*think*" and "*feel*" as others do. This is an obvious asset in relationships and business and at the point they intersect—family business. *That means it should be a top priority for successors to cultivate the virtue of empathy.*

Empathy Is a Choice

Empathy is not a passive attempt to be in touch with another person's emotions. Rather, it is an active consideration of another person's situation as well as their emotions in a way that affects your interactions with them. In other words, empathy involves a deliberate choice to put your feelings aside to focus on the emotions of another.

The idea of empathy as a choice is supported by a recent study at the University of Cambridge where researchers compared DNA samples from 46,000 people. These subjects completed a questionnaire that measured their levels of empathy (i.e., their empathy quotient), and scientists then compared each individual's genetic makeup to their empathy quotient.[103]

The result? Apparently only 10 percent of our capacity to empathize comes from our DNA. This means that 90 percent of how we respond to the needs and feelings of others stems from what we have learned in our homes, from our friends, and in our work environments.

> ## TRUE EMPATHY:
>
> *"The friend who can be silent with us in a moment of despair or confusion, who can stay with us in an hour of grief and bereavement, who can tolerate not knowing, not curing, not healing and face with us the reality of our powerlessness, that is a friend who cares."*
>
> Henri Nouwen

In other words, this research shows that empathetic people are primarily made, not born. Those who argue that they cannot show empathy because "it's just not who I am" no longer have a legitimate excuse.

This research supports the ideas of Dr. Brené Brown and Daniel Goleman, who are both adamant that empathy is a skill that can be learned, practiced, and cultivated.[104] This is good news for all of us; it means we each have the potential to display empathy and to change the degree of empathy that we show to others.

Empathy Is "Being There"

Over the past 40 years of married life, I have gradually come to realize just how important empathy can be in a marriage relationship. As men, we typically have a natural inclination to try to "fix things," and it is often our first response when others tell us of their challenges. This may work sometimes, but often I find that my wife, Alison, wants a listening ear and an understanding heart rather than a plan of action.

Not long ago, there was a day when I noticed Alison was feeling rather overwhelmed as she designed new shelving space, took care of the grandchildren, and did who knows how many other things to help others that day.

Rather than tell her where I thought the shelves should go (*which was my first thought*), I sat down on the bed with her (*to be closer to her*), held her hand (*to let her know that I was "with her"*), and said I was sorry that she was feeling so frustrated and overwhelmed (*so she would know that she was not alone*). I then asked her what she needed from me (*so she felt supported*), and, as we sat together for a few minutes, I felt that I was able to feel her feelings and think her thoughts with her.

It was a lovely moment for both of us, and a week later, while we were having dinner, she remarked how much she appreciated me coming alongside her that evening and being there for her. I am humbled to report that this is not my typical response in such situations, but perhaps this old dog is beginning to learn some new tricks.

Being there for someone else does not always mean sitting close and holding hands. For example, as my friend Carson has had to adjust to life without his wife, Brenda, I have tried to be available to do a host of little things with him in the hopes that it would fill some of the day-to-day void created by her absence.

The following are examples of occasions when I have been able to support Carson through very ordinary yet practical actions. They have given me the opportunity to *just be with him*, and on some days, that is all he needs—a buddy to hang out with. I share them to give you an idea of some of the practical ways in which you may be able to also show empathy to others.

- Providing Carson with rides to and from the airport, especially for international flights, when the memories of travelling with Brenda can be most poignant.
- Organizing papers. I love to get things shipshape, and on several occasions, I have used my "need for order" to help Carson sift through papers and sort personal effects. I have even helped to tidy his library so that he can have a quiet space to read and pray in the mornings.
- Joining Carson in tackling the fall garden cleanup. This was particularly appreciated by Carson because he was accustomed to doing this annual duty with Brenda.
- Working with Carson to organize his garage when it was overflowing with hockey equipment, storage boxes, and items that Jason and Kristin, his son and daughter-in-law, had to store as they temporarily moved in with him. He and I spent several afternoons together organizing, discarding, reorganizing, and giving away items we found in the garage.
- Enjoying dinners out together; sometimes it is just the two of us, but there are times when my wife, Alison, has joined us.
- Cruising together in the summer, as was our custom with Carson and Brenda, on our boat the *Lazee Gal*. We were reluctant to continue this tradition, knowing that it would inevitably bring back memories of Brenda that could exacerbate his grief. But Carson loves being away on the water, and we are thankful that he has been able to continue to share these occasions with us, even as he grieves and adjusts to the new realities of his life. For the last two summers, we arranged an itinerary that specifically accommodated his schedule so he could join us.
- Joining Carson and his family for Family Camp at Barnabas (located on a beautiful island, just off the coast of Vancouver, British Columbia). Again, we were initially reluctant to impinge on their family get-together, but Carson encouraged us to join in, and it has helped all of us to create new memories and establish a new normal for Carson.

I am not an expert at helping a friend grieve or demonstrating empathy. However, I know that my role as Carson's friend is to walk beside him on what must be the most difficult road a married man can travel. It has been a privilege to be his friend and soulmate during this time.

Empathy Is Not Sympathy

Although *empathy* is often used interchangeably with *sympathy*, there are important differences, and the two are not synonyms. One way of distinguishing the two is to consider their Greek origins, as summarized in the following table.

THE DIFFERENCE BETWEEN EMPATHY AND SYMPATHY
(according to the Greeks)

EMPATHY	SYMPATHY
… from two Greek words: *em* meaning *in* and *pathos* meaning *pain*. Therefore, empathy is when you are *empathos* or in pain with another. Practically speaking, empathy relates to feeling another's pain.	… from the Greek *sym* meaning *together*. When combined with *pathos* (pain), it means you are together with someone who is in pain.

Another way of looking at the differences is to notice the level of emotional connection that is involved in each action. Sympathy can be described as an intellectual understanding of the situation that others are in;[105] that is, you may notice that they are having a hard time, and you may even try to cheer them up, but it does not establish a connection with them or help you to understand how they feel in that situation. It is a more superficial or safer choice than empathy.

In contrast, empathy allows you to identify with the feelings of others and even share or feel those same feelings.[106] It is a far more vulnerable choice because you can feel what they feel. As Dr. Brown describes it, empathy is "communicating that incredibly healing message of 'You're not alone.'"[107]

Empathy Is Not Fixing the Problem

We cannot fix other people's problems, and yet, until we realize that this is not the answer, we typically try to do so. It is embarrassing to write about this, but I recall a time years ago when my wife, Alison, and I were living in Toronto, and she had just given birth to our third child, Jennifer.

In the weeks that followed, Alison, a beautiful, athletic woman, struggled to regain her pre-pregnancy weight and figure. One day she was feeling very discouraged and said to me, "Honey, I'm feeling fat and ugly."

Without thinking, I responded with a "fix," foolishly saying, "You will continue to feel fat and ugly unless you get out and run."

This truly is one of those moments in life where one desperately wishes they could have a do-over. I could have recognized it as a golden opportunity to show empathy towards my wife, and I could have considered her feelings before I answered. I wish I had said, "You are not fat or ugly, Alison. You are strong and beautiful." Then I could have sat beside her and listened as she shared her feelings.

I have since apologized to Alison for this lack of sensitivity, and she has forgiven me. But memories of that day serve as a reminder of how important it is for me to take a moment to consider what the other person is feeling before responding (in any situation).

THE BENEFITS OF EMPATHY IN BUSINESS

While Brené Brown's insights have been influential in driving a cultural awareness of the importance of empathy in relationships, Daniel Goleman and others have urged us to consider the value and utility of empathy in the context of leadership and organizational health. They argue that empathy is critical in the business world, as the world of commerce is fundamentally about relationships (with customers, clients, potential buyers, shareholders, and employees). Perhaps even more importantly, the success or failure of a family business is often determined by the health of the relationships among family members.

Empathy Is "Tipping Your Umbrella"

Slack Technologies is a highly successful technology company that designs software to facilitate communication and collaboration between employees in large corporations. Remarkably, just four years after its inception the company had already reached a market valuation of over $14 billion by June 2020.

Without a doubt, the company must be doing some things right, and a host of business writers and researchers have begun to take note of the successful company culture that Slack has created. At the core of that culture is a list of six rather unusual corporate values—empathy, courtesy, craftsmanship, playfulness, solidarity, and thriving. It is noteworthy that the top corporate value for this dynamic and influential company is empathy.

Why empathy? According to Slack's co-founder and CEO, Stewart Butterfield, empathy gets the top spot because it is about paying attention to the needs of others. He has observed that empathy starts with one person and then follows a chain reaction that makes its way throughout the company's culture. Butterfield says, "people love it, and the reason they love it, is because we pay attention to their needs, and the way you get that is empathy."[108]

No wonder Slack's company culture is referred to as a community that has empathy at its heart.

The group's main headquarters is in San Francisco, but it has also established a satellite office in the trendy Yaletown district of downtown Vancouver. Both cities are known for their cloudy winter days and excessive rainfall. So it is appropriate that Butterfield has a rainy-day story that he shares with all of his new employees to illustrate the simplicity and importance of empathy in everyday interactions.

One afternoon, he and his creative director had stepped out for a short walk on Yaletown's streets when a sudden downpour began. Most Vancouverites are prepared for this scenario, and so, as they opened their umbrellas, the streets were instantly cluttered with colourful canopies.

> *Empathy causes us to ask what we can do to make things better for someone else.*

The problem is that Yaletown's streets and sidewalks are particularly narrow, and it was not long before a simple walk in the rain became a hazardous sport. People were forced to zigzag, duck, and dodge as they passed by dozens of sharp metal points protruding at eye level from the rims of umbrellas.

Butterfield and his colleague were rather amused by the scene and began to take note of how many people bothered to tip their umbrellas and hide the metal tips from those who passed by. It was such a small courtesy and involved so little effort that Butterfield began to wonder why it was not a standard response.

They came up with two explanations for the phenomenon: people were unaware of the problem and its effects on others *or* they had no idea of what they could do to fix it, even though all it would take is a small tip of the umbrella. Butterfield believes that the key to being someone who will "tip your umbrella" is *empathy*—considering the situation from someone else's perspective, then doing something to make the situation better.

Slack Technologies has adopted the term "tipping your umbrella" as a metaphor for empathy.

The words are used to encourage employees to take time to reflect and assess whether there may be a negative impact related to what they are doing or, conversely, if there is even one small thing that they can do to make their workplace more pleasant, simpler, or more productive for others.

By putting empathy first in the list of the company's core values and encouraging employees to act on it, Butterfield has built a cohesive corporate culture and a winning team.

This does not mean that companies must have empathy as a corporate value in order to witness its benefits. Remember, empathy starts with one person showing empathy to a fellow employee or customer. Like a chain reaction, empathy invades more and more interactions. This inevitably leads to improvements in both their working environment and their customers' experience.

EMPATHY IS ...
AS SIMPLE AS TIPPING YOUR UMBRELLA
(so you don't poke someone in the eye)

Empathy in the workplace has many positives, including recognizing the needs of others, improving culture, and motivating employees. Employees love an environment where empathy is present, and the combination of all these factors contributes to improved corporate performance.

Empathy Makes Better Leaders

As noted in earlier chapters, one of the best ways to build loyalty and rapport with employees is to understand the business from their perspective and to let them know that you genuinely value and consider their input.

Within Companies. Effective leaders use empathy to thoughtfully consider and understand the desires, values, and needs of their employees. This attracts the loyalty of employees and, subsequently, has a positive effect on the overall health of relationships within the business. Ultimately, this leads to more concrete benefits, such as increased teamwork, creative collaboration, and improved productivity.

In his best-selling book *David and Goliath*, Malcolm Gladwell suggests that employers who have failed to treat their staff with empathy are contributing to a diminished respect that their employees may have for those in authority. Whether they realize it or not, leaders who are aloof or who find it wearisome or beneath them to connect with their employees are actively creating a work environment that lacks loyalty, motivation, and respect for leadership.[109]

In the simplest terms, successors have a choice to be leaders who demonstrate empathy to their employees and establish environments of loyalty, respect, and motivation or leaders who refuse to connect with employees and produce workplaces of unmotivated and disloyal employees.

> *Empathetic leaders stimulate loyalty and motivation.*

Outside of the Company Walls. Management expert Edgar Schein believes that this failure to connect to those within a company can extend

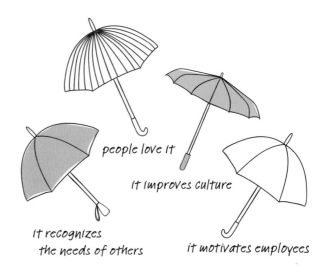

EMPATHY MATTERS BECAUSE …

people love it

it improves culture

it recognizes the needs of others

it motivates employees

RESULT = CORPORATE PERFORMANCE IS ENHANCED

to working relationships that reach past the company walls. With the growth of international trade, corporate leaders must become comfortable doing business in different countries or, at a minimum, with employees from different social or ethnic backgrounds. Yet, according to Schein, we "cannot hope to understand and work with people from different occupational, professional, and national cultures if we do not know how to ask questions and build relationships that are based on mutual respect."[110]

In other words, empathy is a particularly valuable asset in our globalized and culturally diverse world, and the best leaders are able to empathize with those inside and outside their company.

Empathy Shows Our Humanity

In business, senior executives are often paid handsomely to solve problems and find solutions for their corporations. In doing so, they sometimes minimize the human element that may be affected by cancelling a contract or making changes to produce a better bottom line. In such cases, leaders may claim ignorance of the human impact or remain stoic in the aftermath of decisions that hurt their employees.

Such leaders miss out on the opportunity to reveal a human connection with their people. On the other hand, when leaders take the time to listen and connect with employees during tough times, this can demonstrate their humanity and help communicate a genuine concern for their staff. This can potentially be as motivating as it is comforting, especially during difficult times.

Sometimes all an employee needs is an empathetic ear.

When acknowledging an employee or offering empathy, there is often an overwhelming temptation to tell them about a similar experience you have had, give encouragement, offer advice, or even break the tension with (what you believe to be) a witty remark. Unfortunately, this is not empathy. Just sitting with another, in silence, can be uncomfortable, but, as each of us has likely experienced at some time in our lives, silent solidarity can let others know, simply by our presence, that we are truly feeling their pain. We are all human, and in times of challenge we all need others to offer us empathy.

THE BENEFITS OF EMPATHY TO FAMILY BUSINESS

Enhances Intergenerational Relationships

In his classic article "The Succession Conspiracy," Ivan Landsberg writes about the difficulties that families often have when it comes to having an open discussion about succession.

One fundamental challenge is the idea of asking an aging entrepreneur to let go of the business that they have created. They have invested a lifetime of effort, time, emotional toil, and stress in their business, and it can be emotionally difficult—and perhaps even downright terrifying—to suddenly be cut off from a daily routine that may be decades old.

On a subconscious level, stepping down can be accompanied by fears of no longer being needed and/or suddenly losing their status in the business and family. Inevitably, thoughts about being at the end of their productive years lead to thoughts about their own mortality.

No wonder members of the elder generation are resistant when younger successors push to have conversations about their retirement.

> Empathy is the most important gift we can give to someone facing retirement.

It is both unfeeling and unrealistic to expect our elders to simply walk away once members of the younger generation determine that they are ready to lead. Instead, the elder generation should be treated with empathy and respect by family successors, family members, and others involved in the business. In the midst of the challenges of succession, the most important thing we can do for the elder generation is to offer them our empathy.

Honouring 50 Years of Service. In 1988, my dad completed his 50th year with Dominion Construction, our family business. For five decades he had put in long hours and made sacrifices to build our family firm. Yet, as I discussed in chapter 3, this long history of loyalty and dedication meant nothing in the end as he was forced out of the business in a rather unceremonious fashion. This experience was devastating, and he never recovered from the relationship breakdown between him and his brothers.

Thankfully, my sisters and I were able to buy our family's flagship company and keep it in our branch of the family for the next decade. Given Dad's deep hurts, we recognized the need to empathize with him and take whatever actions we could to restore his damaged spirit. We made three corporate decisions motivated, at least in part, by empathy for his situation.

First, we appointed him as our chairman of the board and invited him to play an active role in governance for the business. Second, we built and furnished him with a large corner office that provided a place where he could go each day and feel honoured and recognized. Third, we created an executive dining room in our new premises so that Dad could continue his long tradition of hosting lunches for clients and business associates.

On a more personal level, I made a personal commitment (just between me and God) to have lunch with Dad two to three days a week for as long as he was physically able to do so. Over the next decade, we shared many lunches together or with other executives and clients. Dad was always engaging and warm and had great stories to tell and lots of experiences to share. Everyone loved having him there, and it was one of the ways that his family and the company could honour him for all that he had accomplished.

When Dad's health declined, we appointed Dick Meyers to be the chairman of the board, and he moved into Dad's corner office. But we still did not send Dad out the door; rather, we honoured him by naming him chairman emeritus and creating another suitably appointed office for him, just down the hall. When he could no longer drive, we hired a driver to pick him up at home, bring him to the office, and look after him during the day. We made sure that Dad knew he was always welcome and would always have an office and welcoming staff.

By being empathetic, we were able to share something of Dad's deep hurts, and for the rest of his life we did what we could to honor him, to show him respect, and to treat him with the dignity he deserved.

Honouring Dad as he aged has been one of the most gratifying experiences in my life. We provided a safe place for him to spend his days during the final decade of his life, and in turn he continued to be a powerful resource for friends, family, and staff. It was my privilege to have him around to guide me, both personally and professionally.

Our empathy for Dad did not go unnoticed; others eventually joined us in finding ways to appreciate him. These efforts culminated in two special events: a 75th birthday party attended by 150 of our employees and a Golden Heart of the Year Awards dinner, held in his honour and attended by 1,000 colleagues, friends, and family. Dad was deeply loved, and I am so glad that others joined us in paying tribute to him.

Improves Understanding and Diminishes Conflict

Successors in a family enterprise have multiple stakeholders to consider, including family members, management executives, and shareholders. Building rapport with such a diverse group requires adaptability that is greatly enhanced through empathetic listening. This is especially true within the context of decision-making and conflict.

As Baumoel and Trippe observe, business families should not be seeking to resolve all conflict so much as to manage conflict well. After all, conflict is inevitable, so rather than working to avoid it, we might as well develop the skills that are necessary to understand and manage it.[111]

> Empathy helps us to understand and to resolve conflicts.

If we probe beneath the surface, most of us would acknowledge that disagreements in family businesses are seldom about money or power (even though this is what they may seem to be about). Rather, these are the surface issues that represent the deeper—or real—issues at play, such as "identity, being respected, and being acknowledged."[112]

For example, it may appear that two siblings are wrestling for control of the family company, and in fact their dispute may have devolved to this scenario. But if we re-wound the tapes, we would likely see that the root problem stems from someone not feeling heard, appreciated, or loved.

Empathy is a quality that is extremely helpful in dealing with such emotions. Unfortunately, cultivating empathy can be particularly challenging in family relationships where we know our parents or siblings so well that we may find it difficult to see or feel their pain. Yet, without empathy, damage to relationships can be enduring, and this can ultimately create problems for the business. The eventual consequences of unresolved conflict is life-altering—and not in a good way. Instead, wise successors seek to empathetically manage conflicts in a way that supports both business success and family harmony.[113]

All of this suggests the importance of learning to understand each other and the perspectives of other people involved in the family enterprise before explicit conflicts arise. Developing empathy, understanding, and a willingness to listen is an ongoing process, and these efforts can help families to anticipate, manage, and resolve issues in healthy ways.

Improves Interpersonal Connections

One challenge common to almost every family enterprise is the risk of one or more family member becoming increasingly isolated or disconnected from what is really happening day to day in the company. This separation can create the perception that there is a hierarchy of employees in the workplace, with family members at the top and non-family members on the bottom. Whether or not it is true does not matter if the feeling is a reality to non-family employees. Consequently, empathy is crucial in understanding how employees in this situation may feel.

> It is critical to empathize with employees who are not family.

My dad and grandfather were masterfully empathetic. They were the kind of leaders who would make genuinely caring inquiries about an employee's personal life or family in addition to how things were going at work. They took time to consider each employee's circumstance and to provide support. If an employee felt overwhelmed, they would explore how to lighten the load or provide assistance. On the other hand, if a staff member did not feel sufficiently challenged, Dad and Granddad would try to find or create a new opportunity that would allow the employee to feel more fulfilled at work. Dad felt such a strong responsibility to care for his employees that he once told me, "The sacred mantle of management is to provide continuity of employment for our people."

Giving all staff members a Christmas turkey may be regarded, at least by some, as an archaic practice. But years ago it was a symbolic gesture of care and interest in employees and their families. In difficult years,

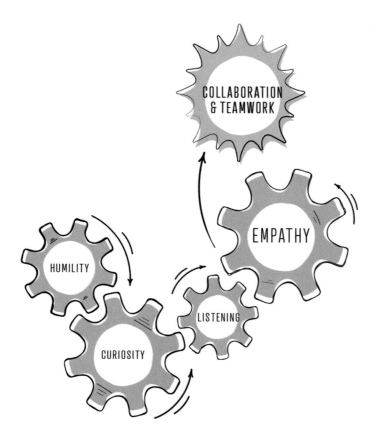

it became a gesture that, for Dad at least, was almost sacrosanct. It was his way of saying to our employees, "We notice you; we appreciate you, and we want your family to know that we value your contributions to our business."

Reinforces and Amplifies Other Traits

In previous chapters, we explored the profound benefits of humility, curiosity, and listening. When taken together, these traits have tremendous synergy. In addition, empathy enhances all of these qualities, adding a final extra gear that can help successors to develop collaboration and teamwork in their organizations.

The power and interrelationship of these forces is pictured in the adjacent illustration.

WHY ARE WE NOT MORE EMPATHETIC?

As a young successor, I struggled with showing empathy because I was often too preoccupied with myself, thought I knew all the answers, and was raised in a relatively affluent bubble. I did not understand or easily relate to the lives of others. However, I have spent the past 25 years seeking to become more self-aware and more empathetic. As I consider my own progress and the many discussions that I have had with business families since then, I realize that many successors face similar challenges.

We Are Too Self-Focused

I recall struggling to relate to the physiological and psychological realities—at times painful—Alison experienced while having a child growing inside her for nine months (and through four pregnancies). Alison was aware of the changes occurring in her body every day; she shared an emotional and physical bond with our child that I did not. Nor did I experience any of the discomfort or back pain. Because it was not happening to me, I had a difficult time understanding the physical and emotional changes going on in her body.

I was fast asleep when Alison woke me to say that her water had broken and asked me to time her contractions. It was just prior to the birth of our first child, Christy, and I knew that Alison was struggling with fears about the pain of labour and pending birth. I tried my best to encourage her, but no matter how hard I tried, I kept falling back to sleep.

It was a moment in which she needed empathy; even the smallest attempt to understand how she felt would have helped. This happened over 35 years ago, yet I still regret that I failed to support Alison when she genuinely needed me. Although it is a painful memory, it serves as a poignant illustration of how important it is for all of us to demonstrate empathy on a daily basis.

Unfortunately, when I later joined our family company, I brought a similar self-focused perspective to the workplace. I was so intense about progressing in my career that I gave little attention to what was going on with other employees. How could I develop empathy for their circumstances if I was hardly even aware of them? I am embarrassed to admit how myopic I was, but I hope that sharing my experience might help other successors to recognize the same tendencies or patterns in their own lives.

We Think We Are Always Right

As a young man, I often found myself frustrated when people failed to see things from my perspective. This became very apparent when I joined the family company shortly after completing my university degree in business. I was immediately thrust into dealings with our senior executives, who were, of course, all well-educated and intelligent. One would think this was a great opportunity for great minds to creatively solve problems and collaborate to generate new ideas, but that did not happen. Instead there was a disconnect in our perspectives.

At the core, the disconnect stemmed, at least in part, from our training; they were mostly engineers (including my father and uncle), while I had a degree in commerce. We had each been taught to evaluate problems in remarkably different ways. Yet it is surprising that we never took this into consideration when trying to resolve our differences or make decisions.

When others did not see things my way, my initial responses tended toward anger and frustration. I was so convinced of the "rightness" of my own logic that I was blind to the thoughts and feelings of others. But empathy involves getting past our own feelings, and that includes the feeling that we are right.

Imagine the potential impact on our relationship if I had taken the time to empathize with Bob about how he felt as I began working with him. He had waited for 30 years to be appointed president of Dominion

Construction. During that time, he had always been required to defer to my dad, his older brother and head of the company. Now that he was finally leading the company, his brother's son arrives on the scene and starts challenging his every move. No wonder he bristled at my youthful insistence that we do things "my way" instead of his.

Unfortunately, some of our earliest encounters badly damaged my relationship with Bob and initiated a downward spiral in our communications. Our relationship never recovered.

We Are Infected by Affluenza

While the benefits of wealth and privilege are significant, psychologists and social scientists have observed that they can have a detrimental impact on the emotional development of next generation inheritors.

The problem has been appropriately termed *affluenza*, and it gained plenty of attention in the court case of a 16-year-old Texas teen by the name of Ethan Couch. On a warm June night in 2013, he got together with friends, stole some beer, threw a party at his parents' home, drank too much, and then made the fateful decision to go for a drive with seven of his (also drunk) friends as passengers.

While driving almost twice as fast as the speed limit, he swerved into a group of people who were helping a stranded motorist. He killed four of them and left one of his friends paralyzed and suffering from a severe brain injury. Hours after the crash, Couch still had a blood alcohol level of 0.24—three times the legal limit.

The resulting trial gained international headlines when a psychologist blamed Couch's irresponsible actions on his family's wealth and called it "affluenza." His lawyers claimed that this condition of being raised in a wealthy and privileged family who did not set limits for him made him unable to understand the consequences of his actions.

While this is an extreme example and there is no empirical evidence to support a diagnosis of affluenza, there is plenty of anecdotal evidence to suggest that it is a real phenomenon. In short, it describes successors and inheritors from wealthy families who have a sense of entitlement, are irresponsible, and make excuses for poor behaviour.[114] As a result, there can be a noticeable delay in the development of their social skills, and they tend to be narcissistic and typically less attuned to the suffering of others, indicating that they lack social skills such as compassion and empathy.[115]

What are the common patterns that successors and inheritors ought to be alert to if they want to avoid the unhelpful influences of affluenza? First, well-meaning parents often shelter their offspring from difficult or challenging experiences. Second, successors and individuals from wealthy families tend to limit their relationships to those with a similar social standing. In short, many inheritors are exposed to fewer difficulties and have a restricted social circle where everyone has the same social status and a similar lack of experience in real life.

This "sheltered life" can delay their emotional and social development and produce unhealthy or suboptimum behaviours. As both our intuition and respected research would suggest, "abundant wealth has a way of separating heirs from the grist of life."[116] Psychologist and family enterprise consultant Dr. Dennis Jaffe says that consequently it

> "It can take people (with money) an extra 10 years to grow up."

can take "people (with money) an extra 10 years to grow up and develop some of the same social and personal maturities as others because they lack certain experiences and challenges."[117]

These factors offer an important warning, suggesting that successors may be raised in such a way that they develop less empathy towards others. However, if you are from a successful business-owning family, you can work to counteract these factors by deliberately seeking to cultivate empathy in your own life.

DEAR YOUNGER ME …

I was raised in a manner that might be similar to those young people who develop affluenza. As a result, I think I developed some of the symptoms of the disease. Although my parents were not lavish spenders, I definitely encountered some challenges when trying to empathize with those who had less than we did.

In addition, as a young executive I had limited awareness of the benefits or relevance of empathy in business. If I had thought about empathy, I likely would have considered it a "nice" trait that would help some people have deeper relationships. However, as I have come to realize, empathy is a potent tool in establishing connection with others as well as a gentler way of relating. As a result, it is a potent and powerful force for effective leadership and a characteristic that can help cultivate more engaged and productive employees.

With empathy comes wisdom.

Perhaps that is why those who are truly wise seek to cultivate this important and transformative quality.

THE BOTTOM LINE
Empathy can transform the culture of your business and your family relationships.

David

CHAPTER 5
Forgiveness: The Secret to Living Free

"Forgiveness says you are given another chance to make a new beginning."

Attributed to Desmond Tutu

I've shared many stories related to the breakdown of our family business, but I will never be able to fully describe the pain, the personal hurts, and the disappointment that settled over many of our family relationships. Over the years, distance grew, and when various attempts at reconciliation were unsuccessful, relationships turned cold. In this sad and disappointing scenario, the relevance and importance of forgiveness within a family, as well as a family business, has become increasingly evident.

Background. As explained in section I of this book, my grandfather Charles transferred the leadership of Dominion Construction to my father, Clark, in 1955. At the same time, he gave an equal share of the ownership to each of his three sons, Howard, Clark, and Bob. Howard was the eldest son, who, many years prior to this, had chosen to enter the ministry. His father and brothers all honoured that decision, and Charles would often comment that Howard had chosen "a higher, better path."

As a result, Howard was a significant owner of Dominion but not actively involved in the day-to-day management of the company. Clark was the appointed leader, with Bob serving as his right-hand man. For most of 30 years, they worked effectively together, and the company prospered. Unfortunately, over time Bob became unhappy with having to defer to his older brother and began to suggest that he would like "his turn" to lead. In response, my father ultimately stepped aside as CEO but remained active in the business as chairman of the board.

This arrangement seemed reasonable on paper, but it did not always work that well in practice. For the next decade, to many clients and employees, Clark was the de facto leader, and this eventually created mounting tension in the office. Bob felt that he was functioning in Clark's shadow, and when this situation became unbearable, he turned to Howard. In simplest terms, he asked if Howard believed that, after 30 years of waiting, he (Bob) should have his turn to lead the family business. In retrospect, it is easy to see why Howard was inclined to support the idea.

Ultimately, this decision resulted in Bob and Howard signing an agreement to create a permanent voting bloc, essentially eliminating Clark's input into the company's decision-making process. Soon afterwards, Howard endorsed my departure from the company.

Those two decisions radically and permanently altered the trajectory of our family business, my career, and my father's retirement. This placed a huge strain on relationships within and between our families. I had admired and respected Uncle Howard for many years, but I now wrestled deeply with the personal and family upheaval that had arisen. I carried resentment that I knew was harmful.

Anger and Loss. As the years passed, I had no interaction with Howard, and we became increasingly distant. I had a sense of loss and family disconnection whenever I thought of him. As time went on, I gradually came to the realization that these feelings would likely persist unless something was done about them. As I reflected on all this, I came to see that I had played a role in the disintegration of our relationship. I felt compelled to ask Howard to forgive me for my part in these events.

> "Asking for forgiveness is rarely easy."

Asking for forgiveness is rarely easy, and it is made more difficult when it involves deep hurts in a family, a family business, and a long-term breakdown among several families. As my concerns grew, I turned to Carson, one of my closest friends, to ask if he would be willing to meet with Howard and me to assist us in restoring our relationship.

Carson responded with the wisdom that comes from years of counselling others, saying, "David, if you are not ready to meet with Howard on your own, you are not yet ready to meet."

He was right—I did not need to lean on a friend when meeting my uncle; I needed to prepare my own heart, mind, and words. As a result of Carson's insight and challenge, it took another year before I felt ready to meet Howard.

Meeting for Tea. It was late November 1992, and Christmas was fast approaching when I finally sat down with Howard at the West Vancouver White Spot, located near the foot of the Lions Gate Bridge. He was cordial towards me, as I expected he would be, but I knew that our mutually polite greeting was the easy part. I nervously began to speak, acknowledging that I had been impertinent, immature, and insubordinate. I felt there was no need to go into a lot of detail, as I believed we were both fully aware that I had made a mess of things with my critical attitude and approach. I then apologized for my past behaviour and waited for his response.

Howard was quiet for a time and then flatly replied, "Yes, you were awful." His words stung, although I am quite certain that he had no idea as to their impact.

It was not until many years later that I learned there is a significant difference between apologizing (often a simple "I am sorry") and asking for forgiveness. The vulnerability of the latter takes the acknowledgement of having done wrong to another level. It demands more. An apology does not necessarily require a response, whereas seeking forgiveness is really making an ask (which may be welcomed or not). When I went to meet with Howard, I was apologizing, but, unwittingly, I was hoping for forgiveness.

While the pre-Christmas meeting did not go as planned, Howard did express that he was grateful for it. As a result, he initiated annual get-togethers with our wives, Alison and Shirley. For several years the four of us met for tea just prior to Christmas. These meetings were never long, but the conversations were relatively pleasant, even though we steered away from discussions related to past events.

While these periodic gatherings were never sufficient to fully restore our relationship, they did permit us to reach a measure of "closure" regarding prior events that had been difficult for all of us. They also permitted us to express, at least symbolically, our mutual willingness to avoid future conflict.

Even as I write these words, almost 30 years later, I have discovered afresh my need to think more deeply about what happened between Howard and me. Too often, I had harboured bitterness. If he were still alive, I would need to start over by apologizing again, but this time it would not be for my actions but for my thoughts. Too often I have been guilty of criticizing him, if not publicly at least in my own mind.

It may be a strange thing to say in a chapter on the topic, but to be candid, I must confess that I still have a great deal to learn when it comes to forgiveness.

WHY WE NEED FORGIVENESS IN OUR LIVES

There are two important truths inherent to all people, and they both have a direct impact on our need for forgiveness.

First, all humans are imperfect; it is part of the human condition. That means we all make mistakes, we all hurt others, and we will all be hurt by the mistakes and words of others. Second, all humans have an innate desire to be in relationship with each other.

The result? There is no escaping a life filled with disappointments and wounds from our interactions with others. What differentiates each of us is how we respond to these experiences.

I recently attended a marriage seminar where author and family counsellor Paul David Tripp said, "If you're going to have a [relationship] that lasts any time at all, you will need to learn to forgive, because you're [relating] to an imperfect person and they're bound to let you down."[118] The implications are clear: we all need forgiveness.

We All Get Hurt and Suffer Disappointment

Most of us are unaware of how we respond to disappointments and hurts, but in general our natural reactions stem from our emotions and feelings. Unfortunately, these responses are likely to do further damage to the relationship and, in some circumstances, permanently shut the door to reconciliation. Over the years, I have observed that people tend to employ one of the following three strategies when they are hurt:

- **Gunny-Sacking.** We put our hurts into a backpack so we can carry them around with us and bring them out as a reminder when we need to stoke our sense of being victimized. The problem with this approach is that it does not take very long before our emotional load can become heavy and overwhelming.
- **Cutting Off Relationships.** We do this as an attempt to create distance through silence or withdrawal. This can destroy relationships that might have been restored or lead us to withholding our emotions in relationship to others.
- **Getting Even.** We seek to hurt the other person to repay them for the hurt that they have caused. This may feel good for a while, but in the end, this approach simply recirculates the hurt.

> *Forgiveness is hard, but what is even harder is the pain you live with when you don't forgive.*

Unfortunately, none of these options build open, respectful, or enduring relationships. More importantly, none give rise to a cohesive family unit that is capable of resolving hurts and developing and maintaining a positive, collaborative environment for a family business.

What is the alternative? How can we respond to others who have hurt us in a way that maintains—or even strengthens—our relationships?

Quite simply, *we can choose to forgive.* When we are hurt, forgiveness is the only response that preserves relationships and brings healing to our emotions. In fact, the real benefit of forgiveness belongs to us.

Forgiveness Sets Us Free

Bethany Allen from Bridgetown Church spoke of the pain that she felt as a 14-year-old child when her mother walked out the door and never returned. Over the next number of years, she lived with the confusion of all kinds of emotions, from the devastation of abandonment to a struggle with loneliness and a desire to have a mother. Amongst those emotional extremes was a growing sense of resentment towards her mom. The wounds were particularly painful when she celebrated significant events in her life, including her graduation.

Her mother reappeared seven years later, declaring that she wanted to mend the relationship and be a part of her daughter's life. As the young woman thought about her situation, she wrote the following:

> I know forgiveness is hard … But I want to say this. I think (that) what is harder is the pain you live with when you don't forgive. What is harder is the poison that begins to stick in your heart and mind. It hardens you in places you didn't invite it into. What's harder still is the way unforgiveness robs you of your life and your freedom and your joy. [I came to realize that] forgiveness is setting somebody free and realizing that somebody is you. [It] seems the person un-forgiveness most hurts is us. In our attempt to keep them from healing, we usually poison our own hearts far more deeply.

At just 21, this woman was wise beyond her years in recognizing that the pain of unforgiveness is harsh and the one who is hurt most deeply is the one who refuses to forgive. Unforgiveness is an open door to bitterness, a corrosive, soul-destroying emotion that causes us to wish ill towards another person. It traps us into holding on to grudges and negative feelings because we believe that the other person deserves our scorn. In extreme cases, it can cause depression, anger, insomnia, ulcers, and a host of health issues related to our immune and cardiac systems.

To put it in layman's terms, as one of my friends has often said, "Bitterness is like drinking poison and expecting the other person to die!" But they will not, because *bitterness only hurts you.*

Surprisingly, the real benefit of forgiveness belongs to us. It can set our hearts and minds free from the bitterness, resentment, and anger that typically accompany the wounds we have suffered. Knowing that we have done all we can to mitigate the situation, we can be released from the negative emotions and feelings that have swirled around in our mind since the offence occurred.

SOMEONE LETS ME DOWN...

I feel hurt...

ANGER

FORGIVENESS

BITTERNESS

FREEDOM

I GET TO CHOOSE

> *Bitterness is like drinking poison and expecting the other person to die.*

Whenever we are hurt, there is a clear fork in the road, and we get to choose which road to travel—the road that leads to anger and bitterness or the road of forgiveness and emotional freedom.

WHY WE NEED FORGIVENESS IN BUSINESS

As many executives have realized in recent years, forgiveness can be very important in business. As an example, Sir Richard Branson, the founder of Virgin Airlines, speaks of the need to give people a second chance in the workplace. He states,

> Nelson Mandela taught us all the importance of forgiveness and how by forgiving his enemies he managed to unite South Africa. I think that if all of us can find somebody who we've fallen out with and befriend them, we will all be happier for it.
>
> At Virgin we have forgiven people who've stolen from the company, and they've gone on to do great things at Virgin and have never stolen again. We've taken on ex-convicts from prisons and found they've never committed another crime. So forgiving people and giving people a second chance is incredibly important.[119]

We All Make Mistakes

Branson is not the first business innovator to offer his employees a second chance. Six decades ago, another great businessman and innovator, named Thomas J. Watson Sr., showed similar grace to his employees.

Watson was the legendary head of IBM from 1914 to 1956, and it was under his leadership that the company became an international powerhouse. During the Great Depression, he maintained IBM's employment levels in spite of terrible losses, gambling on the prospects of a future economic recovery.[120]

However, as the economy continued to worsen and IBM's competitors were forced to shut down their research and production facilities, Watson pledged that he would not close a single factory or lay off a single worker. He stayed true to his promise by investing what was at the time a remarkable sum of money (one million dollars) in continuing company research and expanding inventories. He stored punch card machines and their spare parts in warehouses and crowded basements so that IBM would be prepared to ship its products to the market as soon as the economy turned around.

Not everyone shared Watson's optimism. As time wore on, investors pulled out, and IBM's board of directors wanted to fire him. Watson eventually realized that he would need to urgently sell much of the surplus inventories if he, and the company, were to survive.

During this time, IBM made a bid for a government contract that was valued at close to one million dollars. It all looked promising until an IBM salesman failed to successfully secure the sale, and IBM lost the deal. Later that day, the sales rep went to Watson's office and placed before him an envelope containing his letter of resignation. When Watson asked what happened, the salesman outlined every step of the deal, highlighted where mistakes had been made, and told him what he could have done differently.

He then tendered his resignation and rose to leave, saying, "Thank you, Mr. Watson, for giving me a chance to explain. I know we needed this deal. I know what it meant to us."

Watson walked over to him, stared him straight in the eye, and placed the envelope back into his hands, saying, "Why would I accept this when I have just invested one million dollars in your education?"[121]

This is not a typical story of Tom Watson and his leadership at IBM. Most articles and books are filled with stories that depict him as a man with a volatile temper rather than a forgiving spirit. But it was also widely known that his temper was reserved for those who failed to think through actions and problems; in this particular situation, the salesman had owned up to his mistakes. He reflected on what he had done wrong and what he should have done to get a better result.

This situation gave birth to a core business principle for IBM that was eventually summarized by the following policy: "*We forgive thoughtful mistakes.*"[122]

This story illustrates the fact that we all need forgiveness in business because we all make mistakes, and the very best corporate leaders understand this. If we refuse to forgive others whenever they make a mistake, we may too easily give up on employees with potential, and we may be tempted to discard valuable human resources at the first sign of imperfection. Making the same mistake repeatedly may be a sign of incompetence, but the occasional mistake is a sign of humanity. Wise leaders understand the need to forgive some mistakes and to help their employees learn from them.

Maintaining Relationships with Customers

The auto industry is well-known for its commitment to consumer research. After all, buying a car is likely the most expensive purchase people will make, aside from buying a home, and a typical consumer does not buy a new car very often. That means each car purchase is a significant event for the consumer, and car dealers are keen to understand the factors that influence customer experiences, satisfaction, and preferences when buying a car.

While at university studying marketing, I was surprised to learn what factors are necessary when selling automobiles if you want to create a highly satisfied customer. Like many, I expected that the most satisfied customers would be those who never have any problems. Yet consumer research indicates that customers who have no problems typically do not score very high in terms of customer satisfaction. Car buyers typically expect that a new car will not have any problems; therefore, if nothing goes wrong, it just indicates that things are as they should be, and the buyer will rate their customer service as "acceptable."

In contrast, customers who have had problems with their cars and then had them resolved in an exemplary way are the most satisfied.

I was able to apply this knowledge while president of Dominion Construction when I encouraged our project management group to view a problem with an unhappy customer as a golden opportunity to create a "really satisfied customer." I reminded them that if we managed to resolve client problems in an exemplary way, then these customers would have a more profound sense of appreciation for our services and potentially become long-term customers and perhaps even offer enthusiastic referrals.

This principle holds true in most cases where a product fails. If it gets fixed quickly and cheerfully, we tend to have a greater appreciation for the customer support services than if we never had to deal with them in the first place.

Remember—in business, we all make mistakes. But if we apologize and seek to make things right, our customers are likely to forgive us. In fact, not only are they likely to forgive; they will potentially become our best advocates.

Making Things Right

During my university days, I worked part-time as a waiter at the Victoria Station restaurant in Vancouver. It no longer exists, but at the time it was part of a large chain of restaurants across North America that featured prime rib, steaks, and one of the first self-serve salad bars. I always aimed to provide exemplary service, but one evening I made a memorable mistake.

My typical routine was to write all meal requests on an order slip and then immediately take it to the kitchen so that our chefs could begin prepping the food while the patrons helped themselves to the salad bar. On this particular night, I took an order from a young couple, ripped the order slip off my pad, and headed to the kitchen. Before I could get there, I was called to assist another waiter, who was overwhelmed and trying to clear a table in a hurry. As I grabbed some plates to assist him, I stuffed the paper with their meal order into my apron and promptly forgot all about it.

As I continued taking orders from other customers, I noticed that the couple who ordered the steaks had finished their salad and were waiting for their meal. I cleared their plates and checked with the kitchen, but their order was nowhere to be seen. I assumed there must be a backlog in the kitchen, and so I continued to serve my other guests.

A little while later I checked the kitchen again. There were no steaks being cooked for my table, and when I asked the chef about the order, he said he had not seen it. That is when I began to panic. The couple was waiting, and I had no idea where their order slip was. When I finally found it in my apron, I took it to the kitchen, apologized to the chef, and asked him to rush the order.

But how could he "rush" two well done steaks, and how could I possibly explain my blatant error to my customers?

Just then, a street merchant came through the restaurant, selling roses. I leapt at the opportunity to purchase some flowers for the young couple; I then found an empty wine bottle, filled it with water, placed two long-stem roses inside, and headed to their table.

The couple was initially taken aback as I owned up to my mistake, apologized profusely for my error, and offered them the flowers. They were very gracious in their response to me and seemed to eventually enjoy their steaks despite the long wait. I had no expectations of receiving much of a gratuity for my services, but later that night, I discovered that they had left me an extremely generous tip. By the time I subtracted the amount it cost me to buy the flowers, I still had a tip of more than 20 percent—more than double the average tip given to servers for an evening meal at our restaurant.

Once again this demonstrates that the most satisfied customers are often those who have experienced a problem and then have had it resolved in a meaningful and thoughtful way. I think it is almost always true that customers are willing to forgive us if we own up to our mistakes and genuinely apologize.

WHY WE NEED FORGIVENESS IN A FAMILY BUSINESS

Common Observations of Behaviour in Business Families

Just like any other organization, a family business involves imperfect people who inevitably let each other down. If we don't forgive family members who have hurt us, we tend to grow cold and distant, and bitterness can begin to develop. Broken relationships between family members cannot be isolated, and they will often spill over into the business, where they can cause great harm to the company.

How Family Dysfunction Can Impact Business Relationships

PAST FAMILY HURTS	can cause	BUSINESS TENSION
UNFORGIVENESS	may cause	IRRATIONAL BEHAVIOUR
DEEP WOUNDS	can	ESCALATE CONFLICT
IGNORED ISSUES	will often	CLOUD PERSPECTIVES
PAST CHALLENGES	may	PREVENT AGREEMENT

The chart at left highlights some of my observations regarding how past experiences can create challenges in a family business; each one is relatively common in business-owning families.

Family Wounds Cut Deep

There are three unique challenges for a family in business that can lead to unresolved past hurts and lingering emotional pain:

1. Family members have lived together for years before they enter the workforce. This provides ample time and opportunity for wounds, hurts, and disappointments to occur.
2. The wounds from those closest to us are often far deeper and more emotionally charged compared with those that stem from interactions with non-family members.
3. Parents and siblings usually have long histories with each other, so there is potential for unresolved emotional baggage to build up and fester over time.

About ten years ago, I met with four siblings and their parents to discuss succession for their family enterprise. We had a good initial discussion but ran into a snag as we began to plan our next meeting. One of the siblings was a full-time teacher, and she stated that she was available to meet anytime, as long as it was on a weekend. Another sibling, who worked long hours during the week and wanted his weekends free to be with his family, said he could meet anytime—as long as it was not on the weekend. As they argued about these options, they quickly became entrenched in their positions.

I soon realized that this had nothing to do with setting a time for the next meeting. Rather, it had everything to do with childhood baggage. I could clearly see that any future meeting to discuss succession would be counterproductive unless they first dealt with their underlying issues. I suggested that they meet with a family therapist, talk it out, forgive each other, and then call me. They took my suggestion as a challenge and did exactly as I suggested. Once all was forgiven, we were able to reconvene and have productive meetings to address their business issues.

> *Without forgiveness, families often struggle to agree on the simplest of business issues.*

As shown in this example, issues from the past can prevent family members from reaching agreement on the simplest of business issues. The longer that family issues are ignored or unaddressed, the greater the distance created between family members. Sometimes the pain has been there for years, growing in intensity to the point where it can colour people's perspectives and cloud their judgment.

The siblings mentioned previously may have been surprised by the successful resolution of their issues, but I have seen similar results in many other families in business. This is why it is particularly important for successors to be alert to unresolved family issues and to seek reparations for past hurts in a timely fashion, so that they will not prevent the family from having productive, meaningful relationships.

Small Hurts Can Completely Destroy Relationships

Most families fail to fully consider the consequences of not resolving the smaller disagreements that inevitably arise between family members. Some may think they simply do not have the time to deal with minor issues or that the offended individuals will get over the issue in time. Families in business may be able to put aside personal differences for a time, but this is only a temporary solution. In due course they need to communicate with each other in order to make decisions regarding the business, so they will be required to talk eventually.

As described in the story of our family business, problems that were not addressed in a timely fashion led to a downward spiral. For example, the small seeds of envy and jealousy that were planted when Grandad named my father the sole leader of Dominion Construction had plenty of fertile soil to grow in over the next four decades. In the end, some issues that began as relatively small concerns eventually grew into monumental problems.

To make matters worse, when Bob finally took over the leadership, Clark was still chairman of the board, and there were times when he challenged Bob's decisions. This was hurtful and embarrassing for Bob, yet neither of them had developed the capacity to talk these things through and make them right. It is unfortunate that these two brothers never developed the capacity to confront disappointments, to truly understand each other, and to offer apologies and forgiveness when needed. Instead, they allowed these issues to drive them apart.

The Consequences of Not Forgiving

These challenges are common and, in many ways, predictable, and they can lead to a disintegration in relationships and to potentially disastrous results for a business-owning family. This is why, as a family in business, it is critical to learn how to apologize and to forgive.

Consider the following two scenarios:

THE PATHWAY OF BITTERNESS	THE ROAD TO FORGIVENESS
1. Someone in your family offends you or hurts you.	1. Someone in your family does something that hurts you.
2. You experience disappointment, frustration, and anger.	2. Your first reaction is to create distance between you and the other person.
3. You decide you will not talk to this person.	**3. BUT you resist the urge to freeze out the offender and seek *dialogue* in order to understand what has happened.**
4. You relationship becomes distant.	4. You ask them to explain things from their vantage point.
5. You dwell on the incident, reliving the offense over and over in your mind.	5. Through discussion you understand what role you may have played in creating the problem, and you apologize, seeking their forgiveness.
6. Each reliving reproduces the emotions, negativity, and pain from the initial incident. Your emotions become heightened as you fixate on them.	6. As you deal with the situation with humility, empathy, and curiosity, the other person is motivated to ask for your perspective on the situation.
7. You start to villainize your offender.	7. Mutual trust is established, and as a result, you establish respectful, open communication.
8. Hostility grows.	8. Rather than drifting apart, you have found common ground and discover that your differing perspectives can make your relationship stronger.
9. Eventually, there is a complete relational breakdown.	9. You both learn and grow from the exchange.
10. If you are in business together, you determine that there is "no way to carry on" as co-owners, and this leads to a buyout by one partner or the entire business being sold—all because of one interaction that was never resolved.	10. You are thankful for each other and the opportunity to collaborate.
11. Your family business has become a source of upset and disappointment.	**RESULT:** Your family business grows in harmony and unity.
12. Your sibling relationships are characterized by anger and bitterness.	
RESULT: You are left wondering how things could have gone so wrong.	

Why We Struggle to Forgive

The kind of dialogue noted on the right side may seem unrealistic or even naive. Yet, if we are honest, we all desire relationships where we can have honest dialogue and interaction without causing deep hurts. After all, these patterns of interaction lead to good decision-making and excellence in governance. In fact, they are the kind of relationships that every family enterprise needs to stand the test of time.

Why We Struggle to Forgive

There are many reasons why it is hard to forgive someone when we have been hurt. I highlight two of the most challenging ones here.

It Denies Our Sense of Justice. In the midst of an interpersonal conflict, we typically believe we are seeing things correctly while the other party is not. When we are injured and believe that we were in the right, it goes against our sense of fairness or justice to offer someone else forgiveness.

Many of us think that forgiveness *lets the other party off the hook for what they have done.* But this misses the point of forgiveness.

If we forgive someone, this does not absolve them of guilt or condone what they have done; nor does it mean that justice will not prevail. It simply means that we are letting go of our desire for retribution. The power of offering forgiveness is that it sets *us* free—more than the person who has hurt us.

> *Forgiveness sets us free.*

When we are truly forgiven, it is also a gift. Being forgiven relieves us of the weight of our wrongs—whatever they may have been. We are freed of a burden by the person who forgives us. Perhaps even more importantly, mutual forgiveness opens the door for both parties to be able to re-establish or rebuild the relationship. Thus, offering forgiveness is extremely relevant in the context of a family enterprise.

We Fear Exposing Ourselves to Greater Emotional Pain. When anger and bitterness go unresolved, they become so embedded in our feelings and our daily thought patterns that they become *familiar* to us. The pain we feel is a known factor, and we have learned to function with that pain being a part of who we are. It is easier to live in the relative comfort of that pain than to take the first steps to apologize and risk experiencing even greater hurt as old wounds are reopened in a discussion of hurts and misunderstandings. We withdraw, clothing ourselves in coldness and hoping that our icy disposition will somehow guard our hearts from greater emotional pain.

But our attempts to avoid the pain are nothing but "a fool's game." As noted scholar and author C. S. Lewis has observed,

> To love at all is to be vulnerable. Love anything, and your heart will be wrung and possibly broken. If you want to make sure of keeping it intact, you must give it to no one, not even an animal. Wrap it carefully round with hobbies and little luxuries; avoid all entanglements;

lock it up safe in the casket or coffin of your selfishness. But in that casket—safe, dark, motionless, airless—it will change. It will not be broken; it will become unbreakable, impenetrable, irredeemable.[123]

WHAT IT TAKES TO FORGIVE

A few years ago, a colleague of mine faced a serious relational breakdown in an important long-standing friendship. In the paragraphs that follow, she explains the situation and how she found the strength to forgive:

I was deeply affected by a series of betrayals from someone whom I had considered a close friend. I found out that this person, whom I had truly loved and cared for, had gone behind my back and attempted to undermine me both professionally and personally. After the initial shock wore off, I experienced

- *Feelings of deep loss—I had trusted this person with my heart and my friendship.*
- *Visceral anger and self-pity—how dare this person do this to me?*
- *Self-doubt and self-criticism—how did I not see this coming?*

With this cocktail of emotions swirling about in my mind, I attempted to carry on with normal life but soon realized that these feelings were not going away. I found myself easily triggered when this person's name was mentioned; I avoided social events and even lost friendships where this person was a part of the circle.

Embarrassed by my naivety and feeling imprisoned by my personal principle "to not speak badly of others," I sought professional help. And it was in these sessions that the concept of forgiveness was first offered as a means of ridding my mind of the toxicity that was lingering from this betrayal.

I began to acclimatize to the concept of forgiveness but still felt that I needed something tangible to really feel like I was doing something. That is when I was introduced to **The Love Box.** I was given three simple instructions:

1. Go out and buy a box (I found one that has the word *love* on it); place a pen and some small pieces of notepaper beside the box.

2. Every day, take one of the pieces of paper and write on it the person's name that I want to forgive; then fold it up.
3. Place the piece of paper inside the box and, as I do so, verbally, out loud, wish this person great love, success, fulfillment, relationships, and joy in their life. Then close the box.

I was encouraged to repeat this exercise for 30 days.

The first few days involved gritting my teeth, feeling resentment, and sensing that this was never going to work. But by day seven, I started to experience a release of the power that this person held over me. By my wishing them nothing but goodness, the emotional hold they had over me started to untangle. By day ten, I was genuinely wishing them love and happiness; by day eleven, I felt truly free. I never did complete the thirty days. It was unnecessary, because I was already free!

There was something about physically writing their name, verbalizing my hopes for them, and placing their name in the box that made what felt like a philosophical concept—forgiveness—become a real and tangible action in which I could actively engage.

Forgiveness is not about the person who has committed the offence. It is about the person who has been hurt. Wishing love and happiness for the one who hurt me allowed me to reclaim control over my emotions.

> "The weak can never forgive. Forgiveness is the attribute of the strong." [124]

THE ART OF AN APOLOGY

Receiving an Apology

As important as it is for people to forgive, it is also vital to know how to acknowledge an apology when it is offered.

In my experience, the most typical responses to an apology are "It's okay" or "It doesn't matter." These reactions may be rooted in kindness or a desire to not dwell on the past, but they are not adequate in terms of forgiveness. By minimizing the offence or the act of apologizing itself, we send the message that a sincere expression of remorse is unimportant or meaningless to us.

For this reason, after we offer an apology, we are wise to also ask, "Will you forgive me?"

This question allows those who have been hurt to consider whether or not they are truly willing to set the matter aside and extend forgiveness. If the answer is yes, the words "I forgive you" can bring emotional healing to the one who was hurt as well as to the offender, giving them both hope that the relationship will move past whatever the incident or challenge may have been.

Giving a Personal Apology

Not all apologies are equal. Some are heartfelt and sincere; others can be little more than lip service. When Alison and I were first married, apologies were frequently required as we were forced to adjust while sharing our lives (and our living space). At first we sought to make things right as soon as possible; apologies and forgiveness were readily offered and accepted.

It is a good habit to take care of things right away, and I am glad that we developed it early in our relationship. But the problem with such easy forgiveness is that we rarely took adequate time for introspection, understanding what was wrong, and then taking responsibility for our actions. As a result, we seldom understood how we had hurt each other and consequently failed to make the necessary changes that could have moved our relationship forward on a more positive path.

Both Alison and I grew up in families where apologies were required by our parents whenever we misbehaved. We had to say we were sorry

HOW TO APOLOGIZE

I am not an expert in offering apologies, but I often wince when I observe apologies where people say, "*If* I've hurt you, I'm sorry" or "I'm sorry *that you feel badly about this.*"

Both of these apologies are, quite frankly, not. There is no indication that the person is taking responsibility for what they have done wrong. Rather, these statements are couched in what some would call "weasel words." By apologizing **IF I hurt you**, we are implying that **WE** really did nothing wrong and **any resulting problems stem from YOUR feelings, not my actions**. This statement avoids taking responsibility for my own actions or for my role in the relational breakdown. Such apologies are rarely helpful in restoring relationships.

When I was younger, I learned a very helpful three-step process for apologizing. It includes the following simple steps:

1. Apologize for your actions (take responsibility for causing harm).
2. Ask for forgiveness (request that the other party agree to let the issue go).
3. Wait until you receive confirmation that the other party is willing to forgive you.

when we did wrong, but, in many instances, we did not understand the consequences of our actions; nor did we end up changing that behaviour. A quick apology usually got us out of the doghouse, but it did nothing to help us to realize what we had done wrong and how we could do better. This often left us without true feelings of remorse, and we both brought into our marriage this habit of offering *half apologies*.

Our shallow apologies kept us from communicating to each other in a way that could heal, restore, enhance, and grow our relationship. The three helpful suggestions listed on the previous page could have assisted us in learning how to make a proper apology.

I have discovered that this simple three-step *"recipe for restoring relationships"* is both life-giving and practical, partly because of its simplicity.

Making a Corporate Apology

In the business environment, there is a growing list of corporate leaders who, like Richard Branson cited at the beginning of this chapter, understand the importance of forgiveness as well as the need to apologize. Some have made major mistakes and have been required to step up and make public apologies. A few of them have hit the mark and won back the public's favour.[125] These corporate circumstances include an example of an apology that was well done and, at least in some circles, well received. It relates to an iconic Canadian franchise.

I was a fan of The Toronto Maple Leafs as a young boy, and I have vivid memories of them winning the Stanley Cup when I was just 11 years old. Unfortunately, the team has not won the Stanley Cup since, and it's been over 50 years! The hockey team has again become an exciting one to watch in the past decade, but success has been a long time coming. The 2011–2012 season was particularly brutal, and the Leafs lost 15 of their final 17 games. The coach was fired, and shortly after the general manager was sent packing. But the fans were still angry.

In an unprecedented step, the Maple Leafs took out a full-page ad in Toronto's daily papers to apologize to fans, saying, in part, "We have fallen short of everyone's expectations, and for that we are sorry. We take full responsibility for how this team performs on the ice, and we make no excuses."[126] The letter also stated that the club would put "all of the resources at our disposal" to create a competitive NHL team.

Obviously, there was a public relations dimension to this action. Nonetheless, the public letter hit all the hallmarks of a true and sincere apology: it acknowledged the problem, offered an apology to fans, stated there were no excuses, and made a commitment to make changes to improve the team.

As we all know, an apology doesn't fix everything, and now, many years later, the Leafs still haven't won another Stanley Cup. However, regardless of the motives or the team's won/loss record, this is still a good example of what a good corporate apology looks like.

DEAR YOUNGER ME ...

I have learned a lot about the freedom of forgiveness from my eldest sister, Helen. Several years ago, she had a falling out with another family member. It lasted for several years and gradually impacted the entire family as many family gatherings were cancelled or just did not happen because of the tension between them. Both of them were hurting, but it was also difficult for the rest of us, who were swept up in the wake of their emotional upset.

Over time, they reconciled, their relationship was restored, and our family was grateful to be able to move past this unfortunate incident. When we next got together as a family, I asked Helen how she had been able to "fix things."

She said that many years earlier she had been inspired when reading about Corrie ten Boom's experience with forgiveness. Confronted by the ultimate test after WWII, Corrie found herself face to face with one of her former Nazi prison guards. When he reached out his hand and asked her to forgive him, she could not do it. But knowing that she must, she prayed and asked for God's help. Miraculously, the strength she needed was supplied; she took his hand in hers, and with tears in her eyes, forgave her tormentor. (To read this dramatic story, as told in Corrie's own words, see the appendix.)

Helen then explained to me that on a much smaller scale, she had struggled to let go of her resentments and hurt. Although she knew in her head that holding on to the resentment was hurting herself more than the other person, she felt justified and had a hard time letting it go. It wasn't until she became willing to give it to God and open her heart that she experienced the joy and freedom of forgiveness. That, together with Nelson Mandela's example of being able to forgive those who had incarcerated him for 27 years, gave her the courage to forgive too.

Her decision was the key that restored the relationship, and their reconciliation had a positive ripple effect throughout our family, as we were once again able to gather together to celebrate holidays and special events.

We like to think of family squabbles as private or personal matters. However, even minor squabbles have the potential to impact the entire family when there is a family enterprise. Unfortunately, in some circles conventional wisdom states, "Love means never having to say you are sorry." This idea was popularized in 1970 by the movie *Love Story*, but my experience with genuine love is exactly the opposite. Only those who truly love each other and care about their relationships are prepared to say they are sorry. They are the ones willing to take the courageous steps necessary to apologize or ask for forgiveness.

> "If Mandela can forgive being jailed for 27 years, I can let go of my hurts too."

These are some of the reasons why it is vital for successors and all members of a family enterprise to learn how to seek and offer the gift of forgiveness. We all make mistakes, and so forgiveness is the only way we can build relationships that last.

> ### THE BOTTOM LINE
> Forgiveness will lighten your spirit and preserve your family relationships.
>
> *David*

CHAPTER 6
Gratitude: Discovering the Magic in Every Day

"Gratitude is the recognition that life owes me nothing and all the good I have is a gift."[127]

When our son, Jon, was in his teens, he was like most healthy young adults who struggle to individuate from their parents and find their own path in life. It was a difficult passage for him to navigate (as it was for us, as his parents), and he often seemed unhappy. Fortunately, his outlook on life began to shift when he spent a few days in Mexico and had a brief glimpse into how the rest of the world lives.

When Jon was in Grade 11, Alison and I decided that our entire family would benefit from joining a mission group to build a house for a needy family in Tijuana, Mexico. So we piled into the family van, drove to Tijuana, and spent five hot, sweaty, exhausting days building a small two-bedroom home. Despite the heat and the physical labour, it was extremely rewarding to see the build completed in just under a week.

During that time, Alison and I noticed something else that we had not expected—Jon was truly enjoying himself. Like most teenagers, he had not been particularly eager to work under the authority of others. But as the hours passed, he developed a close connection with the foreman and, apparently, discovered that he enjoyed swinging a hammer and working with a skill saw. He was (and still is) a strong, athletic young man, and it was gratifying to watch as he found satisfaction in using his physical abilities to help others.

After the house was completed, we began our long drive home to Canada. Jon sat silently in the back row of the van, as if he was trying to get as far away from his parents as possible. When we crossed the border into California, it was not long before we pulled over at an In-N-Out Burger to get our first taste of American food in several days. Once we were fed and back on the road, Jon blurted out, "You know what's wrong with this family, Dad?"

His question certainly caught our attention, and, almost simultaneously, Alison, our three daughters, and I all swivelled our heads to look at Jon at the back of the van. Frankly, in that moment, I did not want to know Jon's thoughts on what he felt was wrong with our family—but I knew I was about to find out.

His assessment? "Not enough gratitude … Thanks for the burger, Dad!"

A New Perspective. Alison and I were thrilled to hear Jon's comments and to see the change in perspective that our working vacation seemed to have initiated. When we got home, many of our ongoing arguments about rules and material things seemed to lose their intensity and importance. For example, prior to Mexico, Jon was convinced that he had to have brand-new stereo speakers for his car; now they seemed insignificant. This new-found appreciation even extended to the first-class education he was receiving. Earlier, he had considered academics to be a frustrating and meaningless challenge; by the time he graduated, he had come to see it for what it was—a privilege.

Jon was still a normal teenager; the difference was that he had begun to view his life through a lens of gratitude. Once he saw people struggling for the basic necessities of life, it began to dawn on him how fortunate he was to live in relatively privileged circumstances and in a country like Canada.

Jon's experience was so impactful that I have since returned to Mexico for similar house-building projects nearly a dozen times. Typically I am accompanied by young people, in the hope that they too will begin to view their lives with a sense of gratitude. Jon has joined me on several occasions, and I am looking forward to him bringing his own children, perhaps as early as next year.[128]

A good friend of mine who works with wealthy entrepreneurs across Canada has often asked them how they are going to ensure that their children cultivate a sense of gratitude rather than a spirit of entitlement. Not surprisingly, almost all of them respond with a similar strategy—stating that they have made it a priority to take their kids on trips to underdeveloped countries so they can see first-hand how difficult it is for some people to simply eke out a living.

WHERE IS OUR GRATITUDE?

We live in a culture where many pursue happiness by accumulating things.

Yet there are a lot of people who, at some point in their lives, have started to wonder why having more "stuff" does not satisfy. Nonetheless, there remains an inner thirst for more, and, thanks to the power of advertising and marketing, Western society continues to be fuelled by the belief that more things make for a better life. In some cases, a few things can make a major difference. However, as the old adage goes, "money cannot buy happiness," and constantly acquiring more things often ruins our appreciation for what we have. It is hard to savour and enjoy what we have if we are always clamouring for more.

Why do we fail to appreciate all that we have?

Here are some of the most important reasons:

Habituation

Gratitude is missing, for the most part, because *we have too much stuff*. This First-World problem has even been given a name—*habituation*. Journalist Annalisa Barbieri writes that habituation is a process that dictates that the more possessions you have, the less likely you are to appreciate them.[129]

After all, when you already have *everything*, how can you appreciate anything more?

People may experience a fleeting moment of happiness after participating *in retail therapy* (as it is often referred to), but this feeling quickly fades, and once again we are left wanting.

> *We lack gratitude because we have too much stuff.*

According to Barbieri, having too many tangibles (e.g., TV, smartphones, cars) only "makes you want more because the thrill of acquisition is short lived." As a result of the emotional letdown that follows making a purchase and the habituation that makes us less appreciative of what we have, "we are locked in a never ending cycle of dissatisfaction."[130]

Entitlement

Similarly, someone who has always gotten what they wanted tends to develop an attitude of expectation rather than a sense of appreciation, and it is not long before these expectations develop into deep-rooted feelings of entitlement.

Entitlement says, "life owes me something" or "I deserve this."[131] In her *New York Times* best-selling book *The Gratitude Diaries*, author Janice Kaplan quotes a Yale professor who has observed that many teenagers have not only the *expectation* that their parents will give them what they want but the belief that their parents *are obligated* to do so. They have a spirit that "fights gratitude" and encourages them to view their privileges and/or gifts as nothing special. As Kaplan notes, looking at privilege as something that is owed to you is "not a mindset that creates a grateful disposition."[132]

Self-Absorption

Those who grow up in affluent homes are also at risk of becoming self-absorbed, and without a broader perspective, a sense of gratitude does not develop. If a person has been isolated from the common challenges or hardships of ordinary life and virtually everything they want has been provided for them, they can come to believe that the world revolves around them.

This environment is a breeding ground for self-absorption and self-importance, both of which are polar opposites to gratitude. According to the Greater Good Science Centre at the University of California Berkeley, ungrateful people tend to be characterized by arrogance, vanity, an excessive sense of self-importance, and an "unquenchable" need for admiration and approval; in short, "they expect special favors and feel no need to pay back or pay forward."[133]

A genuine problem for inheritors and successors who are self-absorbed is that they tend to see themselves as more important than other people. Sadly, I must confess that this was true about me. As a result of this attitude, successors may develop very little appreciation for the contributions of others, whether they be in their personal or professional lives.

In the end, the adage that "a person completely wrapped up in themselves makes a pretty small package" is probably quite true.

Ruined by Wealth

In his best-selling book *David and Goliath*, Malcolm Gladwell relates a conversation he had with "one of the most powerful people in Hollywood," who said that young people raised in affluent families are often "ruined by wealth." Because they have too much money at their disposal and are not required to earn the money, some fail to understand where the money comes from. In addition, receiving money without needing to work for it often leads individuals to lose their ambition, any sense of pride, and, most disturbingly, "their sense of self-worth."[134]

In contrast, many successful entrepreneurs have built their businesses from nothing, through a combination of hard work, frugality, and creativity. They are often the kind of people who began working at a young age by delivering newspapers, so they have a greater understanding of the value of a dollar than someone who has never had to work for anything. When nothing comes easy and sacrifices have been great, the typical response to success is a profound sense of appreciation and gratitude.

But even when hard work produces gratitude in one generation, it is typical for the succeeding generation to have a much easier road. Gladwell makes this point clear by writing, "Children of multimillionaires in Hollywood do not rake the leaves of their neighbors in Beverly Hills."[135]

In fact, those who have produced great successes often want to give their children an easier life than they have experienced. But such attempts to make things easier often result in parents doing for their offspring what they are capable of doing for themselves.

Unfortunately, by trying to protect kids from the need to struggle, parents can cause permanent harm. It is not unlike what happens when a butterfly fails to develop its wings. As a butterfly struggles to push its way through the tiny opening of the cocoon, this exertion pushes fluid out of its body and into its wings. "Without the struggle, the butterfly would never, ever fly."[136]

HOW CAN WE CULTIVATE GRATITUDE?

It is important for each of us to ask what we can do to cultivate gratitude in our lives. If you were raised in privileged circumstances (as I was), then it is even more important that you consider the following ideas.

Change Our Perspective

As noted at the beginning of this chapter, we saw how our son, Jon, adjusted his perspective after he saw how some people are forced to live without the daily necessities of life. His sense of gratitude did not come by taking stock of all that he had and realizing that he should be grateful. Rather, it came about through a thoughtful reflection on his circumstances *in relation to those who had less.*

The problem in developing gratitude is that most of us compare what we have to the possessions of those who have more than we do. We choose to focus on those who have a bigger house, faster car, or nicer watch, even though these comparisons typically produce envy and jealousy. In contrast, when we take a moment to consider those who have less, we can begin to develop a sense of gratitude. This is a deliberate choice. Who do we compare ourselves to?

Change Our Experience

Malcolm Gladwell further explains that not everyone he met in Hollywood lacks gratitude. One man he interviewed credits his own genuine sense of appreciation to a snow-clearing business that he developed as a teen in Minneapolis.[137] Once he started clearing driveways and sidewalks around his home, he began to make the connection between hard work and the money it produced. Interestingly, his services were in such demand that he began to contract other kids to work with him—he soon had a payroll of eight other kids! He later worked in the family scrap-metal business and ran a laundry service while he was in college.

All of these enterprises taught him to recognize the value of money and served him well when he went on to a highly successful career in Hollywood. He told Gladwell, "Any fool can spend money. But to earn it and save it and defer gratification—then you learn to value it differently."[138]

When I was a teenager, I worked as a construction labourer during the summers. Carrying concrete bricks, mixing concrete, and working as a carpenter's helper taught me a lot about the value of hard work. Similarly, working as a waiter while attending university helped me to understand the value of a dollar. If a successor in a family enterprise never gets their hands dirty, it can be difficult to appreciate what they have. If you or one of your children have not yet had the opportunity to work at a blue collar job in your company, maybe it is time to become an "undercover boss" to learn what it feels like to really work.

Change Our View of Capital

Dr. Lee Hausner is a psychologist who spent 35 years counselling young people in the Beverly Hills Unified School District. During that time, she discovered a great deal about how wealth impacts young people, and in her highly acclaimed book *Children of Paradise*, she describes how overindulging our children can destroy their initiative and gratitude.[139]

For example, parents sometimes think they are being "loving" when helping their kids complete elementary school science projects or write high school papers. But Hausner writes that parents who do the tasks that their children could easily accomplish on their own are actively undermining their ability to develop into self-confident, high-functioning adults. Sadly, Hausner says that this kind of "love" only delays the natural process of maturation and creates an artificial dependency.

> Love refuses to do for others what they can do for themselves.

For these reasons, training the next generation to be self-reliant is important and starts early in life with little things, like taking responsibility for making their beds or cleaning their rooms. In time, they are able to help in the kitchen and take out the garbage. Step by step, their capacity for responsibility grows. But if they do not learn to take responsibility for the little things, they will find it very difficult to take responsibility as adults.

Hausner outlines a brilliant way of visualizing the capacity each person has and explains that we all have four potential sources of wealth. She refers to them as financial, intellectual, social, and human capital—our "F.I.S.H. accounts" for short. She suggests that one of our primary roles as parents is to prepare, teach, and encourage our kids to develop their own sources of capital.[140]

I believe this can be done by encouraging our offspring to become competent in performing specific tasks for each area. For example,

Financial Capital: Kids need to learn how to earn a living, manage their finances, and live within a budget. *By earning an income, saving money, and investing it wisely, young people can learn how to create and grow their own financial capital.*

Intellectual Capital: Kids should be encouraged to become lifelong learners so that their knowledge and experience are always expanding. *By getting a formal education, attending workshops, listening to podcasts, and becoming habitual readers, etc., individuals are able to grow their own intellectual capital.*

Social Capital: We need to teach our children about developing healthy relationships and positive social networks and the importance of contributing to their communities. *By donating their time and financial resources to help others and by building a strong network of relationships, young people are able to grow their own social capital.*

Human Capital: We must cultivate their ability to work and to do so with discipline, reliability, and skill. *By obtaining a job, keeping it, and learning to work, the next generation can develop skills and experience that grow their human capital.*

Hausner advises members of the elder generation to use their wealth as a means of stimulating their kids to develop their own F.I.S.H. accounts—instead of drowning their kids in money, as all too many successful people do. In other words, parents are wise to see their capital as a tool that can be accessed to assist or amplify their child's personal growth, rather than to replace or retard it. The simplest example of this would be education; wise families choose to support their children financially by providing educational opportunities to help them grow their intellectual and human capital.

Change Our View of History

We all know that a strong work ethic, passion, and insight each play a critical role in determining the extent of a person's achievement. But in and of themselves, they are not enough. Research increasingly suggests that there also appears to be some element of luck or timing associated with success. Some people are just fortunate to be in the right place at the right time or to live at a unique time in history. For example, my granddad and his sons worked hard, but they also rode a wave of economic expansion that continued to surge forward throughout most of their careers.

Born at the Right Time of Year. In the book *Outliers*, author Malcolm Gladwell explains that individual achievement is often a result of "being in the right place at the right time."[141] To illustrate this point, he points out that the vast majority of NHL hockey players were born in January, February, and March.

Those who are born early in the year are older and bigger than their peers when each new cohort of boys begins to skate and play hockey. As the players continue to grow, this group of boys maintains their advantage in terms of size and maturity, and this affords them the privilege of more ice time and better opportunities. The accumulation of these benefits allows them to rise to the top of their class and makes it more likely that they will make it to the NHL.

> *Everyone's success is partly dependent on where and when they were born.*

All of these advantages accrue just because some have the good fortune to be born early in the year.

Born at the Right Time in History. Gladwell uncovered a similar pattern when he examined the list of the 75 wealthiest people in history, including such notables as John D. Rockefeller, Andrew Carnegie, Fredrick Weyerhaeuser, and J. P. Morgan. Astonishingly, 20 percent of those on this "top 75" list were born in the United States between the years 1831 and 1840. These individuals may have been hardworking, intelligent, and creative, but they were also born at the right time. Gladwell explains it this way:

> In the 1860s and 1870s, the American economy went through perhaps the greatest transformation in its history. This is when the railroads were built and when Wall Street emerged. It was when industrial manufacturing started in earnest. It was when all the rules by which the traditional economy had functioned were broken and remade. What this list says is that it really matters how old you were when that transformation happened. If you were born in the late 1840s you missed it. You were too young to take advantage of that moment. If you were born in the 1820s you are too old: your mindset was shaped by the pre-Civil War paradigm. But there was a particular, narrow nine-year window that was just perfect for seeing the potential that the future held. All of the … men and women on the list … had vision and talent. But they were also given an extraordinary opportunity, in the same way that hockey and soccer players born in January, February, and March are given an extraordinary opportunity.[142]

Born in the Right Place. As acclaimed author Tim Keller points out, there is great significance to not only being born at the right time—but also being born in the right place. When speaking to an affluent audience in New York, Keller reminded them that hard work alone does not always translate into success. He put it rather bluntly when he stated, "If, instead of being born wherever you were born, you were born on a mountain in outer Mongolia, I don't care how hard you … worked you'd still be poor … if you're born on a mountain in

Tibet in the 13th century, you'd be poor … You never would have gotten in the schools you wanted to get into. They don't take people from Tibet … they didn't have schools."[143]

Born Into Opportunity. Microsoft founder Bill Gates attended Lakeside School, a private school in Seattle, and he acknowledges that this unique opportunity was a key factor that allowed him to become one of the founders of Microsoft. While he was there, generous donors provided a computer terminal for the school, and young Bill was able to learn a great deal about computers—and their potential—years before other schools could even imagine owning a computer. In a 2005 speech at his alma mater, Gates said the following:

> Lakeside was one of the best things that ever happened to me … I can directly trace the founding of Microsoft back to my earliest days here. When I came here as a 7th grader in the late 1960s … faculty members … worked together to get a computer terminal on the campus … Instead of teaching us about computers in the conventional sense, Lakeside just unleashed us … They could have hired an outside computer expert to do the scheduling system. Teachers could have insisted that they teach classes on computing, simply because they were the teachers and we were the students. But they didn't.

As a result, Gates claims, "If there had been no Lakeside, there would have been no Microsoft."[144]

Grateful for Our Destiny. History makes it clear that access to opportunity, being born in the right place, and being born at the right time all have more to do with our success than we like to admit. Consequently, if we want to cultivate gratitude, perhaps the best place to start is by recognizing that we did not choose our date of birth or our country of origin. Even if no other reason exists, we should begin each day by being thankful that we had the good fortune to be born into a country of peace and at a time of relative affluence.

THE BENEFITS OF GRATITUDE IN BUSINESS

For Customers

According to *Harvard Business Review*, "acquiring a new customer is anywhere from five to 25 times more expensive than retaining an existing one … increasing customer retention rates by 5% increases profits by 25% to 95%."[145] As these statistics demonstrate, there are huge benefits to cultivating loyal customers.

When I was at a Marriott hotel recently, within a 24-hour period three separate employees thanked me for my loyalty. I genuinely felt valued and appreciated. This definitely enhanced my experience, but their gratitude, when expressed, also made me want to remain a loyal customer.

In fact, simply verbally expressing gratitude to your clients is one of the most powerful ways to stimulate their loyalty. In addition, a tasteful gift at year-end, client appreciation events, and educational workshops are suitable ways of letting your customers know that they are appreciated and their business is not being taken for granted. Such expressions of gratitude also serve to humanize our commercial interactions.

For Employees

Increased Productivity. In a similar way, employees like to be noticed and to be thanked. According to a survey by Glassdoor, "four in five (81%) employees report they're motivated to work harder when their boss shows appreciation for their work."[146]

Enhanced Motivation. Research shows that appreciated employees are more successful. For example, a University of Pennsylvania study found that when leaders expressed gratitude to fundraising callers, their success rate rose significantly. Their conclusion? Gratitude can be a very effective motivator.[147]

Better Employee Retention. Showing appreciation to your colleagues increases employee loyalty. A recent employee survey found "53 percent of employees admit they would stay longer at their company if they felt more appreciation from their boss."[148]

Improved Company Culture. Starbucks founder Howard Shultz created a loyal and dedicated workforce, in part by providing industry-leading employee benefits. This strategy was one way that the company communicated to their employees that they were valued and appreciated. In a similar way, Chip Wilson, founder of Lululemon Athletica, conveyed appreciation to the company's young, often part-time, employees by offering them extensive career training and personal development opportunities.

Both of these global juggernauts have created powerful work cultures where their employees feel valued and tend to work together more effectively. In addition, Shultz has noted that employees who feel "taken care of" and appreciated do a better job of taking care of their customers.

BENEFITS FOR A FAMILY ENTERPRISE AND SUCCESSORS

One of the most common criticisms of successors is that they display a sense of entitlement. I know this all too well because I think I was like that as a young man. Happily, it is clear that gratitude can be a powerful antidote to entitlement. In addition, there are many other potential benefits for family enterprise successors who are able to develop a spirit of gratitude.

Gratitude Changes Us at the Core

Tony Dungy, winner of two Super Bowls and former coach of the Indianapolis Colts, once remarked that "what's in the well comes up in the bucket." In other words, that which is at our core is revealed whenever we are forced to dig deep. Consequently, if we hold a sense of entitlement in our hearts, entitlement tends to spill over into everything we do and all of our relationships. On the other hand, if we are grateful at our core, then gratitude pours out and positively impacts our personal and professional relationships.

In my experience, successors who cultivate gratitude stand out from the rest of the crowd; gratitude transforms their thinking and produces a positive attitude that is readily apparent to others. More importantly, a heart of gratitude inevitably helps an individual to develop many of the other powerful traits and virtues discussed in this book, such as humility, empathy, and forgiveness. In sum, a heart of gratitude may eventually spark a complete transformation of character.

> Gratitude impacts all of our relationships.

Enhances Business Relationships

Gratitude has a positive impact on all of our relationships. The following relational benefits accrue for a successor when they arrive at work with a grateful attitude. In general, they are

- Less likely to complain, because of their positive attitude and spirit,
- More open to feedback; more willing to accept criticism and coaching,
- More motivated to work; more productive and efficient,
- Willing to be supportive and helpful towards their peers and subordinates, and
- More collaborative in dealing with the senior management.

Who would not enjoy being around successors who do not complain, are open to feedback, are motivated, and are willing to collaborate?

Improves Intergenerational Communication

One of the toughest challenges virtually all families in business face is how to establish strong, respectful communication patterns between generations. Most often, this challenge is rooted in the younger generation's desire to have more responsibility and to have it before the elder generation is prepared to offer it. These desires are sometimes communicated through an air of entitlement or by clamouring for more authority. In contrast, the elder generation may properly expect, deserve, and hope to see hearts of gratitude.

Wise successors are alert to these dynamics and resolve to develop and communicate a spirit of gratitude. This can be a catalyst for changing their priorities and their style of interacting with others. When successors are willing to shift their focus away from what they don't have to *gratitude for what they do have*, relationships between the generations can be transformed and sweetened in an instant.

Changes How We See Ourselves and Others

As seen with my son, Jon, at the beginning of this chapter, gratitude is like a new lens through which to view the world and our part in it. If you are a successor and are able to see yourself as fortunate rather than entitled, other changes ensue:

- You see your work as an opportunity, rather than a birthright.
- You see others as team members, rather than pawns to be used or manipulated.

Helps Us Be More Appreciative

There are times when we are tempted to view our success as something that we have accomplished on our own. Members of the elder generation in a family enterprise, who have built a business, have a greater tendency to see things this way. Yet even the most successful high achievers, when they look at their life through a lens of gratitude, notice that there were some people (or situations) who significantly helped them along the way and to whom they owe a debt of gratitude.

When founders and entrepreneurs have a spirit of gratitude, they no longer see themselves as a "self-made" man or woman but rather as someone who was fortunate to be born at this place and in this time of history. When life is viewed in this way, they are more appreciative of what others have done to contribute to their success, and ultimately they are able to hold on to their success more lightly, recognizing it as the gift that it truly is.

As the illustration on the following page depicts, if we cultivate a spirit of gratitude in our lives, it helps us to see life differently, and there are many gifts that come from this:

CULTIVATING GRATITUDE

If we would like to be more grateful, how can we cultivate this? One way to develop gratitude is to be more purposeful regarding how we think and speak about ourselves, others, and our possessions. Here are a few thoughts to encourage you to look at life through a lens of gratitude:

1. **Be Grateful for Others.** Consider what others have done to contribute to your success and you will naturally become more grateful. Take the time to thank them.
2. **Abandon Criticism.** Take note of what others have done right, rather than looking for ways to criticize them.
3. **View Life as a Gift.** Acknowledge that you could never deserve all that you have; this recognition plants seeds of gratitude in your heart.
4. **Stop Thinking About Those Who Have More.** If you focus on people who have more than you do, your heart is likely to be tempted by jealousy. However, if you remember those who have less than you do, you are likely to see your blessings more clearly.

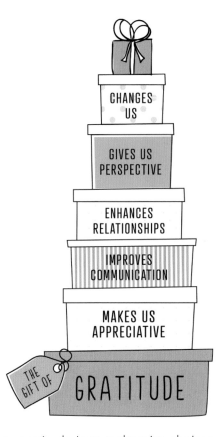

CHANGES US

GIVES US PERSPECTIVE

ENHANCES RELATIONSHIPS

IMPROVES COMMUNICATION

MAKES US APPRECIATIVE

THE GIFT OF GRATITUDE

> *We can change our attitude by changing what we say to ourselves.*

In essence, one way to cultivate gratitude is to make wise choices in terms of what we focus on, how we think, how we view ourselves, and how we talk to ourselves about our life and our interactions with others.

We Can Never Earn All That We Have

I recall speaking one afternoon with a thoughtful young woman who had been born into a successful business-owning family. She was very aware of all that her parents had accomplished and the opportunities that lay before her as a potential successor. To her credit, she did not take her good fortune for granted, but she still felt that she needed *to do something* to earn all that had been given to her. She asked me to help her build a strategy so that she could *earn her inheritance*.

> We will never deserve what we have, so the best response is to say "Thanks."

At first, she was taken aback when I told her that a gift is a gift, and so, by definition, it cannot be earned. The analogy may not be perfect, but I asked her if she could ever have earned the presents that were given to her as a little girl at Christmas. As she shook her head, I reminded her that the best thing a child can do when offered a gift from their parents is to simply say "Thanks."

Successors will never be able to earn the opportunity to own or manage a family enterprise; and the first step in developing an attitude of gratitude is to give up trying to earn it.

As Elizabeth Gilbert, author of the memoir *Eat, Pray, Love*, wisely notes,

> We must all give up trying to pay back the people in this world who sustain our lives. In the end … it's wiser to surrender before the miraculous scope of human generosity and to just keep saying thank you, forever and sincerely, for as long as we have voices.[149]

The Discipline of Expressing Gratitude

A colleague of mine has a simple strategy for cultivating gratitude in his own life. Before he goes to bed each night, he reflects on his day and writes a handful of thank-you notes. *He has done this every night for years.* This daily habit forces him to consider all that he has to be grateful for in his own life and ensures that he communicates his gratitude to others. Reflecting on all he has received and sharing his gratitude with others is an effective and practical way of cultivating gratitude. Beyond that, it has also become a way of blessing others.

Just as he ends his days with gratitude, my sister Helen begins her days with thankfulness. Sitting in her favourite chair with a cup of coffee, she goes through some inspirational readings and then lists in her journal at least three things for which she is thankful.

Similarly, my friend Marina starts every day by having coffee with her husband and daughter. At the end of this special time, they pray together. Marina always thanks God for something specific about her husband and daughter and some blessing in her life, such as her home or simply for a beautiful sunny day. This practice gives Marina the opportunity to vocalize her appreciation to her family and ensures that her day begins with a positive moment of gratitude.

As a child I was trained to say "please" and "thank you." Now, as a grandparent, I am insistent that our grandchildren learn these habits too.

Expressing gratitude *out loud to others* shapes the attitude of our hearts and minds and is a simple act that can transform relationships.

How I Discovered Gratitude

The year 2011 was most remarkable for me as a troika of books helped me to discover a deeper sense of gratitude. The first was *One Thousand Gifts* by Ann Voskamp, a woman whose life was permanently altered when, as a toddler, she witnessed a horrific accident that claimed the life of her baby sister. Ann was stricken by an abiding grief and sadness that stayed with her for decades, even as she married and gave birth to five children of her own. Things only began to change when an insightful friend sent her an email daring her to "write a list of a thousand things [you] love."[150]

> Begin each day by listing three things you are thankful for.

In the beginning, the idea seemed absurd, and Ann found it difficult to think of anything to put on the list. She began her gratitude list with small things that made her thankful, such as "Jam piled high on the toast" and "Cry of [a] blue jay from high in the spruce."[151] As her gratitude list grew, her heart was being trained to see the beauty and joy that were available to her each and every day. By the time her list reached 1,000, her heart had been completely renovated. She has not forgotten her pain, but she has built a new life that is marked by gratitude.

As she shared her journey, I began to see the power in her experience, and it was not long before I started my own list. Now, each morning, before beginning my day, I take time to reflect and express my gratitude in my journal. Sometimes it can be for something as minor as a cup of green tea on a cold morning; at other times, my thoughts are more profound. However, this has become a habit that serves as a daily reminder to express gratitude for all that I have.

The same year, I was given a copy of the book *Unbroken*, by Laura Hillenbrand.[152] It is an astonishing biography that tells the story of former Olympian Louie Zamporini, who endured a catastrophic plane crash and subsequent internment in Japanese prison camps during World War II. It is not a book about gratitude, but as I followed the horrific challenges Zamporini faced during his life, I could not help but reflect on my own life and my good fortune. In contrast with his experience, how could I not be thankful?

No matter how many contemporary challenges I might face, they could never compare to the trials that he endured and, ultimately, conquered.

I developed a similar compulsion to be more grateful while reading the life story of Armando Valladares. He spent over 20 years behind bars in Fidel Castro's Cuba, where he was subjected to horrific conditions, harsh labour, and torture. At the hands of cruel captors, he lost some of the best years of his life, beginning in his early 20s and stretching into his 40s. With humility and courage, he survived outrageous hardship and later served the United States as an ambassador to the Human Rights Commission of the United Nations.[153]

Sadly, the pages of history are filled with individuals who have overcome more than anyone should have to bear. Ann Voskamp, Louis Zamporini, and Armando Valladares have served as my teachers, and they have inspired me to discover my own need for gratitude.

DEAR YOUNGER ME ...

I know that I would have been a very different person as a younger executive if I had cultivated more gratitude. To be fair, my parents taught me the importance of always saying thank you and to be respectful towards others. However, I viewed their instructions primarily as lessons in good manners, and although I recognized how truly fortunate I was, somehow this did not translate into the profound sense of gratitude I have more recently come to experience.

Oscar-winning actor Denzel Washington offered an exhortation to gratitude when he addressed the graduates at Dillard University in 2015. He told them about the day when he realized he was finally making it as an actor. He was so proud that he went home to tell his mother "Ma ... I'm being so big and I'll be able to take care of everybody and I can do this and I can do that."

His mother was less than impressed by his boasts and abruptly stopped him, saying, "All right. Stop it right there." She then told her son of all the ways that she and others had prayed for him over the years and "how many times she splashed [him] with holy water to save [his] sorry behind." "Oh, you did it all by yourself, I'll tell you what you can do by yourself: Go outside and get a mop and a bucket and wash them windows—you can do that by yourself, superstar."

In other words, Washington told the graduates, "Everything that you think you see in me. Everything that I've accomplished, everything that you think I have—and I have a few things. Everything that I have is by the grace of God. Understand that. It's a gift."

His final exhortation captures the intent of this chapter on gratitude far better than I ever could: "I pray that you put your slippers way under the bed tonight, so that when you wake up in the morning you have to get on your knees to reach them. And while you're down there, say thank you for grace, thank you for mercy, thank you for understanding, thank you for wisdom, thank you for parents, thank you for love, thank you for kindness, thank you for humility, thank you for peace, thank you for prosperity ... that's how I live my life, that's why [I am where I am today]."[154]

Recently, I decided to adopt Washington's trick of putting a pair of slippers under the bed, and this helped serve as a reminder to "get on my knees" first thing in the morning and to express my gratitude through prayer.

I should have spent plenty of time on my knees as a young man; I had so much to be grateful for. If only, when I was younger, I had worn slippers …

THE BOTTOM LINE

List three things you are thankful for each day...
Gratitude won't just change your day;
it'll change your life!

David

CHAPTER 7
Critical Thinking: Assessing Options Rather Than Criticizing Others

"Believe what you like, but don't believe everything you read."[155]

Starting a New Business During the Depression. My grandfather Charles witnessed the ups and downs of building cycles while he led Dominion Construction, so he was familiar with the frustration of establishing a competent team during boom times only to be forced to dismantle the group during lean years. During the 1920s, he decided to set aside as much cash as possible for a rainy-day fund, and he encouraged company superintendents and project managers to do the same. After all, Granddad reasoned, these were the key employees who made it possible for the business to develop its sterling reputation for completing projects on time, on budget, and with enviable quality.

By 1930, the company and its leaders had sufficient funds to establish the New Building Finance Company, an entity that would allow Dominion to self-finance the construction of new buildings. Given the horrific financial downturn that occurred around that time, this advance planning proved providential.

Critical Thinking Leads to a New Way of Doing Business. In 1931, Charles was able to use this special fund he had created to make a groundbreaking deal with General Motors (GM) just as the Great Depression was settling over North America, enabling Dominion to retain many of its key employees.

The previous year we had completed a new building for GM in Vancouver. Based on the success of that project, GM had asked Dominion to prepare plans for a similar building in Calgary. Everything looked good until the Depression caused such economic chaos that even the mighty GM was forced to put a hold on all new capital projects, including the one we were about to start.

However, Granddad came up with a creative proposition, whereby Dominion would also finance the construction of the building, and, once it was completed, GM would agree to a long-term lease. The GM executives were enthusiastic about the proposal and readily agreed.

The GM Building, 838 11th Ave. SW, Calgary, Alberta

When Charles returned to his office that day, he advised our then VP of finance, Mr. Tucker, of the arrangements he had just made. Mr. Tucker was conservative to the core and what many today would refer to as a "typical bean counter." As such, he was alarmed by Charles's plan and emphatically declared, "If the largest corporation in the industrial world doesn't have the money for a new building, why in the world would we build it for them?"

Undeterred, Charles responded, "If the largest corporation in the industrial world will sign the lease, why wouldn't we?"

So it was that in the midst of the Depression and while the leaders of other building companies were wringing their hands in despair, Charles launched Dominion into the real estate business. All because he had thought ahead, prepared for what might happen, and used his creativity to come up with an innovative solution. The new GM building at 838 11th Ave. SW in Calgary marked the beginning of our family's long and successful foray into the real estate development industry.

Charles's critical thinking, which led to our first real estate project with General Motors, soon resulted in other opportunities, and this included numerous projects with Canada Safeway. After they had opened their first five stores in Manitoba and as they expanded into British Columbia, Safeway hired Dominion to build 25 stores over a two-year period (opening one new store each and every month!). Beyond this major commitment, Charles saw the potential for Dominion to purchase land that was adjacent to many of the new Safeway stores. In time, each of these properties was redeveloped, enabling the New Building Finance Company to complete numerous shopping centres throughout British Columbia.

Ultimately, financing the development of new real estate projects became one of the cornerstones of Dominion Construction's ongoing success. During the 1950s and '60s, the company also bought industrial land in several major cities (including Vancouver, Calgary, and Edmonton) and sold it at cost to our customers. The land gave us a competitive advantage as we were able to offer our customers a package deal that included design and construction as well as subdivided and serviced industrial land.

Dad Had a Dream, But Not the Money

My dad, Clark, became the leader of Dominion Construction in 1955, and he successfully continued such innovative ventures. For example, his creative negotiating skills and out-of-the-box thinking were critical in obtaining financing to develop the Bentall Centre, our company's widely acclaimed five-tower office complex in downtown Vancouver.

As discussed in chapter 2, the project was conceived as a result of my father's trips to New York City and his fascination with the Rockefeller Center. Having been inspired by its success and beauty, my dad returned to Vancouver with a compelling vision to create a West Coast version of this famous Manhattan landmark. When

The Bentall Centre, Vancouver, BC

he began, few would have guessed that this new venture was destined to become such an iconic destination in the heart of Vancouver's business district.

There was only one problem with his expansive vision—the company lacked the money required to make it a reality. But Dad was not about to let this derail his dream, and he forged ahead by applying his creativity to come up with a novel approach for financing the project. Although more complex and sophisticated financial structures have been employed in the years since, the solution Clark proposed in 1965 precisely reflects the classical definition of critical thinking—"the ability to come up with an entirely new way of doing things."

Dad first needed a financial partner who would share his vision. So he approached Jim Green, a senior executive at Great West Life (GWL), to see if they would be willing to finance Bentall One. They had never done business together before, but Jim was immediately intrigued when Dad told him about the great property that Dominion had purchased at the corner of Burrard and Pender in downtown Vancouver.

Clark then asked if GWL would finance the construction of a 21-storey office tower at this strategic location. More specifically, he asked for a mortgage that would finance 75 percent of the project costs.

When Jim confirmed that GWL was willing to offer this relatively standard loan, Dad then explained that Dominion did not have the money to put up the 25 percent equity that was required. You can probably imagine the look of surprise on Jim's face when he heard this!

This is when Dad suggested a creative proposal to bridge the gap. Since the parcel of land owned by Dominion was valued at approximately 10 percent of the total project costs, Dad suggested that Dominion could sell the property to GWL and they could lease it back to us. This was somewhat unusual, but Jim recognized that the land would likely increase in value over time, so even if we failed to make our debt payments, the risk to GWL would be negligible.

With this arranged, GWL would finance 85 percent of this project, leaving Dominion to come up with the final 15 percent. However, because we didn't have even this amount of equity, Clark used some outside-the-box thinking to propose a joint venture between Dominion and GWL. He suggested that the companies join forces to create a new entity that would own the building jointly. GWL would put up 30 percent of the remaining capital required, and Dominion could put up the remaining 70 percent.

Jim eventually agreed to this rather outrageous series of requests, and a memorable partnership was launched. The new company, known as Bentall Properties, was formed, and this mutually beneficial business relationship lasted almost 50 years.

This is an example of critical thinking at its best. Dad managed to put together the pieces of a complex financial puzzle so he could develop the 21-storey first tower of the Bentall Centre, even though we had very little capital. When all the math was done and the papers were signed, Dominion invested only about 10 percent of the total costs, and yet, if the project went well, we would effectively enjoy 60 percent of the upside.

WHY WE NEED CRITICAL THINKING SKILLS

Critical thinking is currently one of the most sought-after job skills that employers look for in new recruits. According to a survey in the 2016 World Economic Forum, 371 of the world's leading employers (representing more than 13 million employees) forecasted that critical thinking would be the second most important job skill by the year 2020, surpassed only by the ability to solve complex problems.[156]

Not long ago, Jack Ma, China's richest man (with a net worth estimated at $40 billion), as well as the co-founder and former executive chairman of the Alibaba Group, warned business leaders about the need for critical thinking in a society that is increasingly run by technology. In his address to the 2018 World Economic

Forum, he emphasized the need for the next generation to develop uniquely human skills for application in the workplace, or "30 years later we will be in trouble."[157]

Ma believes that critical thinking is one of the key factors that will help keep humans employed when applications for artificial intelligence expand and robotics take over major sectors of the workforce. He states that our current knowledge-based education systems that teach typical workplace skills will not be enough to compete with the increasingly sophisticated applications of artificial intelligence that are rising to prominence globally.

Putting it rather bluntly, he asserted, "We cannot teach our kids to compete with machines who are smarter—we have to teach something unique."[158] As such, Ma contends that society must adopt a new style of education that focuses more on developing the uniquely human aspects of thinking that cannot be

> *Jack Ma believes that critical thinking will help the next generation to compete with A.I. and robots.*

replicated by machines. For example, he recommends a strong focus on understanding abstract concepts (e.g., music and art) and developing human attributes such as values, critical thinking, teamwork, and compassion.

If Ma is correct, the importance of critical thinking goes far beyond developing a trait that is increasingly desirable within the job market or cultivating skills that might benefit a young successor. Critical thinking may well be the single most important ability that sets humans apart from the seemingly limitless artificial intelligence that we are currently creating.

WHAT IS CRITICAL THINKING?

As soon as you begin reading about the topic of critical thinking, you quickly realize that very few people agree on what it actually means. The term has become so common in job postings and is being utilized in so many different contexts that the words are on the verge of becoming meaningless. Some leaders have even avoided trying to define what critical thinking is by simply saying, "You know it when you see it."[159]

Others differentiate it by saying that most thinkers consider the information in front of them and make a decision, while critical thinkers look at the information in front of them and continue to analyze it. They eagerly seek additional knowledge and opinions, and once they have evaluated all the information they can gather on the topic, they make a decision.

One of the simplest definitions states that critical thinking is a skill to analyze problems and seek new solutions using reflection, the input of others, analysis, and questions.[160] By incorporating each of these four elements, critical thinkers are able to come up with creative solutions or new ways of doing things.

Considering all this, critical thinking may be said to comprise the following key elements:

Reflection. Rather than jumping to conclusions or "going with their gut," critical thinkers take additional time to reflect on the information, data, and insights of others before forming an opinion. Such reflection helps them to understand the core issues before they begin looking for solutions. Typically, a better understanding of the underlying challenges can lead to more helpful solutions.

> *Critical thinkers welcome the opinions of others.*

This reflects the same pathway of discovery followed by Albert Einstein. He passionately believed that the process of asking questions was the doorway to discovery, and he once noted, "If I had an hour to solve a problem and my life depended on it, I would spend the first 55 minutes determining the proper question to ask, for once I know the proper question, I could solve the problem in less than five minutes."[161]

Seeking the Input of Others. Critical thinkers welcome the opinions of others and are open to input and comments on their ideas. By obtaining advice and critique from numerous sources, these leaders take advantage of what is essentially a common brain trust, where the ideas of others help to sharpen their reasoning, improve their decision-making, and uncover blind spots in their thinking or logic.

Analysis. Fake news, misinformation, and outright lies are often communicated through trusted sources—so how do we decide what is accurate? Critical thinking. Synthesizing information, dissecting it with logic and arguments, and then coming to a rational conclusion.

Psychologist and McGill University professor Dr. Daniel J. Levitin has brought critical thinking to the forefront of our popular culture through his book *A Field Guide to Lies: Critical Thinking in the Information Age*. He states that we need critical thinking skills now more than ever because of the daily information overload that we experience via the news, the Internet, constant communication on cellphones, and social media.[162] Misinformation has always been around, but the Internet

> *Critical thinking is more important today due to information overload.*

provides a forum where it is now presented alongside or even entwined with real information. From there, it can be quickly propagated through social media, taking its place in our minds and culture—whether it is true or not.

For this reason, we are wise to be more skeptical regarding much of the information we receive. Critical thinking is essential as we consider what expertise and reasoning is behind what we read or hear. That means asking more questions and believing less. As Levitin says, "We're far better off knowing a moderate number of things with certainty than a large number of things that might not be so."[163]

Questioning. Macat.com is an educational website that teaches critical thinking skills. Like Einstein, the specialists at Macat believe that critical thinking is primarily about asking questions that help us to assess the meaning and the significance of claims and arguments. Once we ask the questions and have the information and input of others, we are able to analyze it, determine its validity, and then adapt our thinking and come up with new solutions. Macat even compares this process to evaluating the evidence the same way that a judge and jury would before developing a verdict.

Author and business leader Warren Berger is another cultural influencer who thinks that questions are the most important element in critical thinking. In his best-selling book *A More Beautiful Question*, he refers to insightful questions that open up new possibilities as *beautiful questions*. He encourages readers to return to the unlimited curiosity we felt as children, asking "Why?" and "How?" as much as possible to gain an understanding of the issue before us.[164]

> *Asking questions is the doorway to discovery.*

Berger then suggests that we turn those typical questions upside down and ask "Why not?" and "What if?" These are the four "beautiful questions" (why, how, why not, and what if) that he suggests we employ to stimulate the innovative and critical thinking that will produce new ideas and solutions.

Like Levitin, Berger is also concerned that our society is asking fewer questions and that this may eventually lead to the loss of critical thinking skills. However, in spite of that dour prediction, he discusses the new technologies and innovations that have only come about because someone asked a question that had not previously been asked. He writes,

> Many breakthrough inventions and disruptive business start-ups—everything from the making of the cell phone to the birth of the Internet … began with a person pursuing an insightful question no one else was asking at the time. The questions led to answers that, eventually, led to billion-dollar paydays. It has been said that, in Silicon Valley today, "Questions are the new answers."[165]

In my experience, the best questions are the ones that help us to explore horizons that we may have never considered before. They release us from being captive to the way we have always thought, freeing us up to be more innovative and creative.

THE KEY ELEMENTS OF CRITICAL THINKING

Robert H. Ennis is an emeritus professor at the University of Illinois and a widely respected expert on the subject of critical thinking. He suggests that some people possess characteristics that may make them predisposed to be critical thinkers, and he identifies the following tendencies:

1. They are well-informed and consider the views of others on a given topic.
2. They realize the extent to which their own position is justified by logic and/or evidence.

Ennis also observes that others become critical thinkers by learning and developing specific skills.[166] These include the ability to

• Focus clearly on a particular question and have a willingness to seek clarification when necessary.
• Analyze arguments and their components using logic and by considering the credibility of sources.
• Use both inductive and deductive forms of reasoning.

In practice, all these skills and dispositions are important for successors to cultivate and nurture, especially if they desire to become critical thinkers.

Early in my career, I asked one of my mentors, Dick Meyers, then president and CEO of Dominion Construction, how he made decisions. He gave me one short answer that seems to summarize these points: "Keep collecting information until the decision makes itself." In other words, when we eliminate as much uncertainty as possible and confirm our assumptions, we make wiser choices.

Critical thinkers suspend judgment, collect information, and curb their emotions.

His influence was enormously helpful to me as he urged me to suspend judgment, keep an open mind, and pursue high quality information upon which I could make good decisions. In essence, Dick taught me some of the extremely important elements of critical thinking. The following example illustrates this type of critical thinking in action.

CRITICAL THINKING LEADS TO INNOVATION

A 33-storey office tower, known as 201 Portage, stands proudly at the core of downtown Winnipeg. Originally known as the TD Centre, it boasts 400,000 square feet of office space and a 30-storey curved wall of reflective glass that makes it the most recognizable building on the Winnipeg skyline. Our company completed the building in 1990, but, for a host of complicated reasons, it was an extremely challenging project to get out of the ground.

Dick Thompson, then chairman and CEO of the TD Bank, explained the difficulties ahead when he told me that over the previous 15 years, 10 of the largest real estate developers in Canada had tried to figure out how to develop the bank's property in downtown Winnipeg. In spite of all these efforts, none of them could come up with a workable plan. But Gerry Kendall, our senior vice-president, was convinced that we could find a solution. He asked me to visit Winnipeg to see if we could succeed where so many others had failed.

Define the Problem. When we examined the situation, there were many challenges to overcome. A major obstacle was that the bank's property was too small to accommodate a major tower. The only adjacent property was occupied by CNCP; it was valued at about $2 million, and they were willing to sell. The problem? Their seven-storey building housed critical telecommunications equipment that would need to be relocated if the building was demolished. The estimated cost of moving the equipment was at least $18 million.

The tallest office building in Winnipeg, Manitoba

Another difficulty was the need for a new parking structure. It was determined that building a new underground parking structure would be too expensive and the project would no longer be viable. Finally, the largest and leading commercial developer in Canada at the time, Trizec Corporation, had recently developed a brand-new class "A" 600,000 square foot tower immediately across the street from the site owned by the TD Bank. They had experienced such difficulty in leasing space in the building that they had sealed off the top 10 floors for 10 years, making no attempts to lease it because there was such an oversupply of office space in the Winnipeg market.

Gather Information. As Gerry and I gathered information, we found that there were many prominent corporations seeking new office premises at that time. Potential tenants included the largest law firm in the city, Thomson Dorfman Sweatman, as well as Federal Industries, one of the leading corporations in Manitoba. In total, we identified five companies that were potentially prepared to make pre-commitments to lease in excess of 310,000 square feet of office space. If they all agreed to prelease space, the building could be over 75 percent occupied before we even broke ground. Clearly, this was an opportunity worth considering.

Analyze the Information. As we assessed the situation, we concluded that the tower would be financially viable if we could get preleasing commitments of 300,000 square feet. This would not be easy to do, but it was not impossible. Of course, this would still not resolve the problems related to the size of the property and the parking.

Search for Creative Solutions. After much discussion, debate, and negotiation and many changes to the architectural plans, we had the creative outside-of-the-box solutions that we needed. There were four novel ideas that made our plan work:

- We bought the property on the "other side" of the CNCP building (so we could straddle their existing midrise building).
- We designed a tower that would have half of its foundations on the TD Bank property and the other half on the site that was on the other side of the CNCP building.
- We then "shaved off the front 50 feet" of the CNCP building, keeping all of their equipment intact, and "cocooned" their building inside the new TD Bank Tower.
- We made an agreement with the City of Winnipeg to repurpose an adjacent parking structure for the new building, using a creative public/private financing arrangement.

In the years since, and based on my 40 years' experience working with corporate executives, I've found that if you watch critical thinkers in action, they typically follow a structured process to problem solving similar to what was required to make the TD Centre project a reality. Not surprisingly, they also utilize many of the elements noted earlier by Professor Ennis.

Generally speaking, critical thinkers utilize a structured process to problem solving that incorporates some variation on the following eight elements. (Note that I have explained each by relating them to the TD Centre project described above.)

1. **We Clarified the Problem.** In this case, there were three major problems to overcome:
   - The office market was oversaturated.
   - The site was too small for a major office tower.
   - The market would not support the costs required to build the parking required for a new building.
2. **We Collected Information**. We gathered information to determine if the opportunity was there. Numerous major corporations were seeking new office space, so we focused our efforts on determining which companies would be willing to prelease space.

3. **We Gathered Advice.** To confirm one of our key innovations, we obtained an engineering feasibility study to determine if we could build over and above the CNCP building.

4. **We Discussed Respectfully**. When speaking with my uncle Bob, we acknowledged that the project was a long shot and asked for approval to spend a maximum of $25,000 on preliminary work, pending confirmation of our assumptions.

5. **We Reflected Thoughtfully**. Rather than buying the neighbouring property, we obtained an option on it, deferring any major expenditures until we could complete our feasibility study and secure a joint venture partner.

6. **We Listened Carefully.** We focused on solutions that would help the TD Bank achieve their primary goals, which included having their logo on top of a 30-storey tower to effectively match the prominence of their competitors.

7. **We Debated Tactfully.** When our chief engineer scoffed at the idea of building over and around the CNCP building, we asked him to calculate what could be done and what it would cost. We suspected it would be expensive, but it did not take much analysis to determine that this would be much cheaper than paying $18 million to move CNCP's telecommunications equipment.

8. **We Evaluated Rigorously**. We committed not to proceed until we obtained detailed estimates for all elements of the project, a firm commitment from the city for the new parking facility, and legally binding commitments to prelease the majority of the office space.

> HUMILITY is NECESSARY for CRITICAL THINKING because it allows people to acknowledge the possibility that their thinking may be wrong.
>
> It is an important point for family enterprise leaders and successors who tend to assume that they know what is best for their company and refuse to entertain the thoughts and suggestions of others.
>
> Warren Berger

CRITICAL THINKING IN FAMILY BUSINESS

As this case illustrates, critical thinking can change everything—a nonviable project can suddenly become not only doable but also profitable. Critical thinking is essential for sustainability in family businesses, where decisions can be confused or influenced by emotions, personalities, and family dynamics. To be blunt, leaders of family enterprises simply cannot afford the luxury of having those factors determine business decisions.

Consider the following two examples of what happened when our business allowed family dynamics to override rational decision-making.

A Merger Opportunity

When I first worked in our family company, I brought forward the recommendation that we merge our wholly owned subsidiary, BC Millwork Products, with Artec, an interior contracting and millwork manufacturing company. It was our largest competitor, and the location of our respective manufacturing plants and our complementary strengths made it an ideal acquisition target.

My proposal was greeted with condescension and disinterest by senior management. There was no rational conversation, no explanation, and no discussion; it was just dismissed. I was simply told that our company was not prepared to pursue this opportunity. (Several years later, the logic of my thinking was at least partially vindicated when BC Millwork and Artec were successfully merged.)

I was frustrated that our executive team would make what I judged to be an irrational decision without any analysis or discussion; this seemingly arbitrary response began to erode my confidence in the company's leadership. This problem is not unique, and I have since witnessed similar challenges take place with other family enterprise successors. Sometimes emotions cloud people's thinking or people reject an idea just because it is being championed by someone young or part of the next generation. Unfortunately, when decisions are made on the basis of personal opinion rather than thoughtful analysis, it can be extremely demotivating for the up-and-coming generation, and it can also have a huge and extremely negative impact on interpersonal relationships.

"We Are Doing It My Way." I vividly recall an instance when I was Bob's administrative assistant and we were working together on the strategic plan for the company. At one point, he was reluctant to accept a recommendation I had made; instead, he proposed an alternate course of action that I considered to be suboptimal. Rather than step back and ask how he came to that conclusion, I blurted out my frustration by telling him, "What you are saying doesn't make sense." Bob was visibly distressed. He pushed his chair back from the desk, looked me square in the eye, and said, "I know you are smarter than me, but we are doing it my way."

At the time, I was extremely upset by Bob's reaction, and I viewed it as further evidence that he was not the right person to be leading our company. However, in hindsight, I see how I contributed to the communication problems we were having. In fact, four of the themes that we have talked about so far in this book were all stumbling blocks in that moment: humility, empathy, curiosity, and listening. Unfortunately, I displayed none of them.

In this incident, our actions were influenced more by emotions and family dynamics than critical thinking. As a result, we missed an opportunity to discuss the pros and cons of each other's plans and to rationally explore and perhaps solve the problem together. If either one of us had employed critical thinking instead of criticism, the situation could have been one of collaboration rather than conflict.

Critical Thinking Reduces Emotionality in Decision-Making

In companies that are not family-owned, there are plenty of opportunities for disagreements between members of the leadership team. If the differences cannot be put aside, the most common solution is to remove one or more individuals from the company. Sadly, all too often employees may be fired not because of their incompetence but rather due to an emotional reaction.

> *Instead of thinking critically, I began to criticize and to destroy our relationship.*

However, in a family enterprise, it is not that easy to get rid of employees whom we cannot get along with. Voting someone "off the island" (or out of the family) is not realistic—or healthy. Yet, emotional baggage often comes into play, whether it be between generations or between siblings. Consequently, decisions are all too often influenced by emotion rather than logic.

In contrast, critical thinking allows decisions to be based on rational thought. This is why it is so vitally important for successors to develop critical thinking skills, so they can discern the difference between a challenging situation and a challenging person. When successors have their ideas challenged, they are prudent to defend them logically and rationally. Conversely, they ought to be prepared to respectfully challenge the ideas of others if they have good reason to do so. However, when dealing with a person who is genuinely difficult, the key is to focus on plans, ideas, and facts—not the person.

Critical Thinking Improves Decision-Making

Some entrepreneurial founders or controlling owners make decisions based solely on the fact that they are the majority owner of the business. This "it's my party and I'll dance if I want to" type of leadership means they are not accountable to anyone and their decisions are not required to be based on either facts or sound reasoning. They correctly argue that it is their money and their company, so they can do what they want. No analysis is necessary if they don't want one.

The inclination to lead by intuition or "gut feel" is more common when owners have already had a great deal of success in their careers. If they have not often suffered from the consequences of bad decisions, they may feel justified in continuing to lead however they want. Such freedom can be intoxicating; however, as mentioned in chapter 2 of this section, this approach can eventually lead to results that are not only disappointing but potentially disastrous.

> Critical thinkers distinguish challenging situations from challenging individuals.

Another problem with this type of decision-making authority is the message that it sends to the rising generation. They may come to believe that being in charge is essentially the same as having the freedom to do whatever you want, without having to justify or explain your decisions. Who needs critical thinking skills if you can do what you want?

What makes matters worse in a family enterprise is when differences of opinion arise. After all, if there are no facts or logical arguments to debate, disagreements can become emotional and irrational very quickly. In these circumstances, tensions can soon heat up and boil over.

I have found that such situations are less likely to develop when the controlling owner is accountable to an independent board of directors. They have both a duty and the objectivity to step in, without emotion, and mediate conflicts by getting arguments refocused on the facts, rather than the people. As a result, as a family enterprise advisor, I have seen more and more of my clients embrace the value that accrues from having independent non-family board members (or advisory board members).

Critical Thinking Stimulates Healthy Dialogue

Because critical thinking is focused on asking the right questions, critical thinkers are more concerned with the ongoing search for wise answers than on winning arguments or being seen as right. As a result, critical thinkers are typically eager to engage in dialogue, getting other people's input, while they seek innovative solutions. Because they are emotionally secure in themselves, they are able to focus on ideas rather than getting their ego linked to a particular way of thinking. As a result, they are not easily drawn into win-lose debates.

This kind of leadership is undergirded by some of the key virtues that we have already discussed in this book: curiosity, listening, humility, and empathy. Each of these characteristics enables critical thinkers to rise above their own interests and opinions and to enter into mature discussions focused on what is best for the business at any given time.

By bringing a rational approach to the discussion of business issues, critical thinkers develop the capacity *to dialogue rather than debate*. Leaders and family enterprise successors who have learned the art of critical thinking are able to engage in constructive solution-oriented dialogues, rather than getting bogged down in useless debates.

Here is a summary of the stark contrast between these two approaches:[167]

CRITICAL THINKING VS. CRITICAL SPIRIT

A critical mind can easily give birth to a critical spirit. This realization is one of the touchstones that led me to write this book. As a successor, I had been given the gift of a good mind and had the capacity for critical thinking.

Contrast Between Dialogue & Debate

DIALOGUE	DEBATE
Goal is to understand different perspectives	Goal is to "win" the argument
Work toward mutual understanding	Attempt to prove each other wrong
Accept the experiences of others as valid	Critique the experiences of others as invalid
Open to expanding their views	Resolved to not changing their views
Speak from their own experience	Speak based on assumptions about others

But I failed to develop—and utilize—this capacity because I had developed the unhelpful habit of criticizing others rather than critically assessing their ideas. Had I been unique in my approach, it would have been potentially tragic but not very notable. However, I have since witnessed many other family enterprise successors who display similar counterproductive tendencies. At the root of this problem is a lack of disciplined critical thinking.

Over the past 20 years, I have worked with nearly 100 business families and well over 200 successors. It is not unusual for such successors to allow their critical thinking to be swamped by

> *My capacity for critical thinking was swamped by my critical spirit.*

a critical spirit. When this happens, their potential to contribute to the business is greatly compromised, and the divide between younger and older generations grows deeper. In the best situations, this can lead to a breakdown in communication; in the worst, there can be a complete relational breakdown, as happened in our family.

Passion Can Eclipse Rationality. If you are wondering whether you might be falling into the habit of becoming a critic rather than a critical thinker, pay attention to the volume of your speech when advocating a position. Those with critical thinking skills do not need to speak loudly to have their ideas heard, as their ideas speak for themselves. As Bertrand Russell once noted, the degree of passion displayed is typically a good "measure of the holder's lack of rational [thinking or] conviction."[168]

The Problem with Being Critical. Recently, after I had finished speaking at a family business workshop, a senior executive approached me. During my remarks, I had mentioned how my critical spirit had prevented me from developing my critical thinking skills.

> *Right beside a critical mind lives a critical spirit.*

He said that my statement "hit [him] right between the eyes." He then went on to explain that his critical thinking capacity had propelled him to considerable success in his profession as a financial executive, yet a critical spirit was undermining many of the positives he had created in both his personal and professional life. He stated it this way:

> The idea that right beside a critical mind [or critical thinking] lives a critical spirit very succinctly articulated my condition. This trait that makes me a success in business and in leadership positions often mixes with pride for a nasty cocktail. I jokingly tell my wife that "being right all the time really is a curse"—and she does not see the humour. I am always critiquing what goes on around me, and I'm sure my attention to detail drives others crazy.
>
> I could never really put my affliction into words but knew I suffered from something. I had never connected these dots before. Thanks for allowing me to put a label on my weakness.

As the following illustration depicts, critical thinking may look very similar to a critical spirit, but the implications of each are radically different. Typically, a critical spirit leads to a judgmental attitude, negative thoughts about others, and an iconoclastic view of organizational life. On the other hand, critical thinking is analytical, and it is usually both innovative and creative.

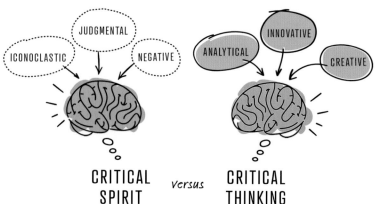

Abandoning a Critical Spirit in My Marriage. In 1986, my wife, Alison, and I were going through a particularly difficult time in our marriage. While reading Dr. Ed Wheat's classic book *Love Life for Every Married Couple*, I discovered the importance of couples never criticizing each other.

This insight struck me deeply because I had, unfortunately, developed a very deep-rooted habit of criticizing Alison, and it had caused significant damage to our relationship. When Dr. Wheat encouraged his readers to take a pledge to never criticize their spouses again, not even behind their backs, I decided to take his advice. Not surprisingly, it took me a long time to eradicate a habit that had been almost 10 years in the making. But gradually, over the years, I have learned to affirm and support my wife, rather than habitually criticize her.

I never told Alison of my pledge to change my attitude and behaviour. Two decades later, we attended a Valentine's Day dinner where we were all invited to share one thing we appreciated about our spouse. Much to my surprise (and delight), Alison said that what she most appreciated was the fact that I never criticize her and that I am always encouraging. It may have taken 20 years to get this affirmation, but I am so grateful that she noticed. If I can learn to do this, given where I was at in our marriage, I believe that anyone can successfully learn to abandon a critical spirit.

Replacing a Critical Spirit with Critical Thinking. There are a number of practical strategies that can be utilized as a safeguard to prevent your critical thinking skills from devolving into criticism. The following are relatively simple, yet profound, skills to develop:

1. **Discipline Your Thinking by Developing Formal Written Recommendations.** During my undergrad studies at business school, we learned a four-point process for analyzing problems. Whenever faced with a challenging case study, we were asked to follow the following four steps and to make formal written recommendations:

   i. Define the problem.
   ii. Identify options.
   iii. Evaluate alternatives.
   iv. Make a recommendation.

   In the 40 years since first learning this technique, I have seen how the discipline involved in this simple process can be applied to virtually any business problem. In addition, it can help any young executive learn how to bring their critical thinking skills to bear in a systematic, rational way.

2. **Submit Your Ideas to the Review and Critique of Other Executives.** When I was CEO of Dominion Construction, we had a management committee that included 11 vice-presidents. Our board of directors, to whom I reported, required me to get the support of our management committee before they would entertain any recommendations at the board level. This protocol ensured that before I could bring any recommendation to the board, I would carefully analyze what I was proposing and test it first with our senior executives. This form of peer review coupled

with formal analyses helped sharpen my thinking and ensured that I had carefully considered the potential consequences of any recommendations before submitting them to the team for review. This process ultimately helped our company to both grow and remain profitable during the 1980s, when many of our competitors were forced out of business as they faced the many challenges in our industry at that time.

3. **Learn to Present Your Ideas Thoughtfully and Respectfully by Serving on Boards.** Earlier in my career, I had the opportunity to be involved in numerous charitable and not-for-profit initiatives. As a result, it has been my privilege to serve on boards of directors for St. George's School, Pearson College, Keats Camps, Young Life, and Hope International. Through these experiences I learned to listen to other people's perspectives, to articulate my own arguments, and to work towards collaborative solutions. Not only were these boards a fulfilling experience, they helped tutor me in the art of critical thinking. In more recent years, as I have served on the boards of Jervis Investments, Big Steel Box Inc., and Lightheart Hospitality. In each of these contexts I have often witnessed the value of critical thinking as a key requirement for making wise decisions.

4. **Invite Feedback on Your Leadership Style Through Regular Performance Reviews.** In my book *Leaving a Legacy*, I explained how immensely valuable it was when, twice a year, our CEO, Dick Myers, would sit me down for a rigorous "no-holds barred" performance evaluation.

Each session began with some affirming feedback, followed by a discussion of what others in the corporation, most particularly our vice-presidents, had said about my management style and performance as president. We would review my objectives, the progress to date, and my goals for the subsequent six months.

This objective forum enabled me to gradually knock off many of the rough edges that had previously impaired my abilities as a leader. I believe that there is no finer gift we can give to members of the rising generation than to provide them with honest, constructive performance evaluations. It is a tool that can help them understand where they are doing well and what they need to do in order to develop as leaders. During this process with our CEO, not only did I learn more about how I should relate to others better, but I was also invited to become more self-aware and less focused on criticizing others.

5. **Submit to the Support and Guidance of Professional Mentors.** When I graduated from university, Paul Schoeber, the general manager of B.C. Millwork Products, became my first mentor. He helped me focus my attention on what we needed to do, rather than on what was wrong.

Subsequently, when I worked in the Shopping Centre Group at Cadillac Fairview, Jim Bullock became the first person to ever encourage me, as a young executive, to *make decisions* (noting that if I did not make any decisions, they would flow upwards in the organization, making me redundant). This clear mandate and implied vote of confidence forced me to greatly accelerate my critical thinking skills.

6. **Obtain and Learn from a 360° Review.** When I worked for our business, 360° performance reviews were not that common. However, in more recent years, they have become more commonplace. One of the great advantages they offer is candid feedback from peers and subordinates in a way that typically augments the perspective offered by a person's superior. A few years ago, I was hired to help coach the third-generation successor of a large family-owned corporation. He and his brother had recently been appointed co-presidents of the company, and he wanted to continue to develop as an executive. In particular, he wanted to have a clear understanding of his strengths and weaknesses (especially since his father and brother had strong opinions about them).

To do this, we conducted eight confidential interviews with senior executives of the firm, including peers, subordinates, and senior executives. By obtaining comprehensive feedback from these individuals, this wise successor was empowered to engage in thoughtful self-evaluation, personal reflection, and professional critique. As a result, he was able to take steps to refine his critical thinking skills and to improve his approach to leadership.

DEAR YOUNGER ME ...

All of the characteristics that we have identified so far are crucial for the repertoire of a family enterprise successor and integrally related to one another. When successors work at cultivating each of these qualities, they discover synergies between them, and these synergies have the potential to radically transform their leadership.

Importantly, critical thinking is vital to help executives integrate all of these characteristics into a professional approach to leadership.

Perhaps even more importantly, critical thinking serves as both a foundation for good decision-making and a safeguard against a critical spirit.

While working with many successors from family companies, I have seen the tremendous potential for critical thinking to have a wide-ranging influence in a person's life and career.

THE BOTTOM LINE

Critical thinking is hard on ideas
but not on people.

David

CHAPTER 8
Patience: Waiting Without Frustration

"The key to everything is patience. You get the chicken by hatching the egg, not by smashing it."

Attributed to Arnold H. Glasow

By the time I had completed my bachelor of commerce degree in urban land economics, I was filled with fresh ideas, the latest theories in management thinking, and an unbridled enthusiasm. I could hardly wait to enter our family business, ascend the management ranks, and presumably take my place as the head of The Bentall Group.

Once I joined the business, I wasted little time in creating what I thought was a very appropriate career plan that would provide me with the necessary experience to be a legitimate successor to Uncle Bob within 10 years. At the time, Bob was 55, and while I did not want to usurp his role, it seemed reasonable to anticipate that he would step down at age 65 and that I would be the one to succeed him. So I carefully prepared a career plan that outlined five alternate scenarios that would help prepare me for the president's office within a 10-year window.

With my plan in hand, I requested a meeting with Dad (then chairman of the board) and Bob. I anticipated that our meeting would focus on setting the priorities for my apprenticeship, but much to my surprise, it quickly turned into a contentious discussion about the proposed time frame. Bob was adamant that I needed 20 years to prepare for the presidency; my father thought that I could be ready in 10—and so the argument began. As it continued, any prospects of a productive discussion rapidly deteriorated.

I decided that it was best for me to leave Bob's office. So I gathered my papers with a sense of resignation. As I headed for the door, I left Bob with one final request: "All I ask is that you consider me as a potential candidate."

As I look back, I realize how different things could have been if only I had been more patient. I could have also been more considerate of Bob's position; after all, he had waited 35 years to become president and was only 3 years into his term as leader when his 23-year-old nephew came forward with a plan to replace him. In all fairness, it is easy to see why he was not pleased to learn of my aspirations.

If I had been willing to accept a 20-year development plan, I might have had the opportunity to lead our family enterprise by the time I turned 43 years of age (still pretty young). This could have allowed me the prospect of serving as president for more than 20 years (assuming retirement at age 65). Waiting for another decade would not have hurt me in any way, and, who knows, during that time we may have been able to work out our relational tensions and preserve our family enterprise.

If only I had not been so short-sighted and so lacking in perspective. If only I had not forced things. *If only I had exercised more patience.*

WHAT KEEPS US FROM BEING PATIENT?

Our Culture Rewards *Instant* Anything

Patience is a willingness to tolerate delays or to even set aside our own agendas and emotions as we wait. But that is not easy when we live in a culture that is geared to a rapid or instantaneous response to almost anything. Amazon delivers packages within days; fast food is available in minutes; Google finds us answers in seconds. Like it or not, we live in a world where waiting is rarely required—and that has made most of us unwilling to be patient.

A recent conversation with a friend illustrates how easily we get frustrated by waiting. He complained that he was not able to get a cup of coffee prior to work because he had to drive his son to school. When I suggested that he could have used a nearby Starbucks drive-through, he replied, "There was a lineup, and I didn't have the patience to wait."

It is interesting how quickly our expectations have changed. It was not long ago that we had to park our cars, go into a café, line up with other people, and then order a takeout coffee to accompany us on our morning drive. Before that, we actually had to take the time to sit down in a restaurant to get coffee. Yet now, as my friend makes clear, even the smallest wait at a drive-through has become too slow for our fast-paced lives.

Remember when we had dial-up connections for the Internet? Or, should I say, do you remember *waiting* for the dial-up connection? Today it is unfathomable for us to wait any longer than a few seconds for our computers to access the information we want. But it was only 20 years ago when Jack Ma, the head of Internet giant Alibaba, had to wait almost half a day for the Internet to download half a page of the *China Pages*, a directory service for the businesses that he had created.

According to Ma,

> The day we got connected to the Web, I invited friends and TV people over to my house … We waited three and a half hours and got half a page … We drank, watched TV and played cards, waiting. But I was so proud. I proved the Internet existed.[169]

Circumstances Are Beyond Our Control

Not getting our way in the midst of circumstances that are beyond our control or not planning for unexpected changes in our circumstances is another surefire way to test our patience—particularly if we are trying to get somewhere on time. For example, if we plan our day around the mistaken expectation that traffic always runs smoothly, parking spots are always available, and flights are always on time, we are soon disappointed. It would be nice if those scenarios were true, but reality is usually very different, and we will continue to be frustrated and impatient unless we come to accept that life may not always unfold as we hope or plan.

People Fail to Live Up to Our Expectations

Unrealistic expectations can influence the amount of patience that we show others. We may quite naturally become impatient if people do not conform to our expectations or behave the way that we think they should. This also holds true for our expectations of ourselves when learning a new skill, trying to process new information, or setting goals for our day. More often than not, our expectations of what we can accomplish in a day fail to line up with the realities of what we actually can get done. Unrealistic expectations are a frequent obstacle to our patience.

Time Is Money

There has always been an added sense of urgency in the workplace, where, everyone knows, "time is money." In the early 1900s, my wife's grandfather Ed Emmons was the general manager at a British Columbia gold mine. Back then, common practice included blasting through the rock with individual sticks of dynamite, and miners were responsible for drilling the holes for the dynamite. There were established quotas for how many holes they had to drill each hour, and if they could not keep pace, they were quickly replaced.

One day, when his men were complaining that 12 holes per hour was unrealistic, Ed loosened his tie, took off his waistcoat, picked up a drill, and promptly completed 20 holes in less than an hour! Unfortunately for his men, this quickly became the new standard.

In business, we have come to value those who can get things done quickly, and a sense of urgency is what fuels many of today's business leaders and entrepreneurs. They call themselves *drivers*; they want results quickly, and this kind of leadership is highly lauded, celebrated, and rewarded. As a consequence, few business leaders are convinced that patience is an important trait in the workplace; in fact, most likely see it as counterproductive to success.

But problems can develop when business leaders become impatient and overly focused on results while ignoring the importance of human input and the processes that are necessary to achieve the desired outcomes. The end result of this scenario? Impatient leaders transfer a sense of urgency to others around them, creating stress for everyone involved.

For example, our daughter Jen experienced tremendous pressure when she worked at a Michelin three-star restaurant in Paris. "Chef" was constantly barking orders, demanding that everyone rush to get meals plated and orders out while they were hot. The guests may have enjoyed a luxurious dining experience, but the chef kept the kitchen staff totally stressed, and they went home every night with their emotions frazzled.

> *Impatient leaders create stress, leading to mental health issues and lower productivity.*

Some leaders exert their authority by shouting, and they probably believe that they have created ideal employees if they are willing to jump at the sound of their boss's voice. But this approach creates tension for employees, and the ripple effects of stress on employee health are well documented. As an example, a 2018 study by the Mental Health Commission of Canada found that "Canadian employees report workplace stress as the primary cause of their mental health problems or illness."[170]

Furthermore, a global study of 22,347 employees across 12 countries notes that workplace stress also has an impact on productivity and absenteeism, stating, "Employees suffering from high stress levels have lower engagement, are less productive and have higher absenteeism levels."[171]

This research reveals a tragic irony about impatient leaders who deliberately enhance the stress felt by their employees—it backfires. There is no increase in productivity from driving people harder. It only results in more sick days and a lack of productivity—the polar opposite of what is desired.

THE BENEFITS OF PATIENCE IN BUSINESS

Patience Empowers Employees

In contrast, patience has a positive impact on a business and can significantly assist management's efforts to empower their employees. Some may say they do not need empowered employees, but consider the following:

> Google, Disney, and Four Seasons … are all well known for going above and beyond to empower their employees. Four Seasons was even awarded Fortune's 2017 "Great Place of Work Legend," as its employees named it employer-of-choice for the twentieth consecutive year …
>
> As more and more leaders come to understand that employee empowerment is paramount to achieving organizational goals, they realize that people are their most strategic asset; all other organizational elements—technology, products, processes—result from the actions of workers. To that end, leaders are increasingly concerned about ensuring that their employees feel truly empowered to contribute to the company's mission and drive value to customers.[172]

Dr. Curtis R. Carlson, CEO of the well-known research group SRI International, notes that there has been a shift in leadership style over the years, and the effective leaders of today empower and collaborate rather than dictate to others. He believes that "we have moved from … leadership by authority and power, to … leadership by consent."[173] This leadership style requires patience.

How do you empower employees through patience? Leaders who want to enlist others, bring them onside, and engage them in their work must first take time to build rapport, develop understanding, and create commitment with their employees—and all of these efforts require patience.

Years ago, Dominion Construction's then president, Dick Meyers, coached me in the value of taking time to provide context and explanations when asking others to perform a task. That is, rather than simply tell them what to do, I should slow down long enough to explain to them the context for the task—why I was asking them to do it and how it fit into the bigger picture. He noted that there are several benefits:

Employees would

• be more motivated because they understood "why" I was making the request,

- be able to problem solve if challenges came up (because they understood the context and end goal), and
- feel more respected and valued as fellow team members.

In essence, leaders can get more done if they are willing to be more patient with their team members.

Patience Gets More Deals Done

I remember as a young executive being warned not to be overly zealous in my pursuit of a particularly exciting new deal. One of my mentors cautioned me by saying that even if I missed this opportunity, it was like missing a bus—there would always be another one. He then added that the real danger in chasing after deals is potentially getting run over by the next bus while chasing after the first one. With these words he encouraged me to be patient for the "right deal" to come along.

This wisdom is echoed by Chris Myers, the co-founder and CEO of BodeTree, a franchise services firm. In a *Forbes Magazine* article, he asserts that, as a general rule, entrepreneurial leaders tend to be impatient and believe that in order to build a business they need to hustle and seize opportunities when they can. Consequently, he notes, impatience and an entrepreneurial mindset seem to go hand in hand. In fact, when discussing the negative impact of impatience on his own career he acknowledges that he had been "particularly guilty of this behavior."[174]

As an illustration, he explains how he and his co-founder lost a major transaction that they were about to consummate with a public technology company. The due diligence process was taking longer than Chris thought it should, and so he gave the other company an ultimatum. This led to the other firm walking away from the deal. Looking back on this experience he says, "I realize that I allowed my impatience to influence my actions, which in turn ultimately scuttled the deal." In other words, his overeagerness to make the deal happen resulted in self-sabotage.

Subsequently, Chris had a chance to try a different approach when BodeTree had an opportunity to acquire another business. This later transaction took seven months from start to finish, and he was again tempted to grow impatient. He recounts the experience: "Every deal dies three times before it closes, and this was no exception. There were a number of instances where it appeared that the deal would fall through, and I know that had I given in to my natural impatience," this deal would have fallen through too.

Fortunately, Chris had learned from his previous experience and was more patient. As a result, the second transaction was successfully completed, and the end result was an agreement that was good for all parties. This experience should serve as a reminder to all of us that "all good things take time."

Patience Fosters Creativity

American author and business consultant Dov Seidman encourages leaders to use patience as a means of extending trust to others. That is, "Think of patience as a way of extending trust to others by allowing them the time to be more thorough, rigorous and creative."[175] This gives others the opportunity to demonstrate their creativity as they take charge.

I experienced this several years ago while planning for a family retreat with our four adult children and their spouses. As the benefactor and instigator of these gatherings, it had always fallen on me to be both the architect and chair for these events. But I began to realize that my leadership prevented other family members from developing any sense of dedication to, or ownership of, these meetings, and as a result they often showed very little enthusiasm or commitment.

That is when I knew that it was time for me to get out of the way and let others take the lead. This not only took patience; it also required me to extend trust.

Our daughter Jen, who has had outstanding management training during her 11 years of working at Lululemon, volunteered to help plan and chair our next meeting. She first asked me about the goal of the meeting, and I said that my hope was "for everyone to enjoy it enough that they would *want* to get together again, rather than always feeling simply obligated to meet." That said, she asked me what topics I wanted us to discuss, and I gave her a list of five, including investments, charitable giving, and vacation planning. Finally, she asked me to write out the main bullet points for each topic.

Then she made one last request—for me to trust her. She developed the agenda on her own terms and in her own time; I was not allowed to see it in advance.

Our family spent a full week in Phoenix, Arizona, and our four-hour family meeting turned out to be truly unforgettable. Rather than sitting around a boardroom table (my style) with a written agenda (my approach), Jen had us all sit around a coffee table in the living room. After serving tea and some healthy homemade snacks, she brought in a giant poster board labelled *Bentall Family Jeopardy*. There were five topics listed across the top, and she had developed six questions for each topic. There was much laughter as we starred in our own TV game show, pitting the girls against the boys!

> *Patience builds trust and fosters creativity.*

This approach was an inspired solution, and our discussions were as productive as they were unique and memorable. As Dov Seidman rightly observed, patience allowed me to step aside, and a more creative approach was the result.

Patience Builds Trust

Since that day I have been emboldened to have our daughters, Christy and Steph, each organize subsequent retreats. Each one has done a much better job than I ever did, and even though family meetings are still not everyone's favourite pastime, we have been blessed to have meaningful get-togethers and fruitful dialogue.

Under Christy's leadership, we have recently completed a successful joint venture project to build three three-bedroom dwellings, all on the same 50-foot lot. Consequently, each of our girls and their families will be able to own a home in Vancouver, in spite of our skyrocketing real estate market.

Last year, Jen took another turn leading our family and superintended a preliminary discussion regarding the vision for our small private foundation.

Stephanie then led us as we discussed our plans for the shared use and maintenance of the summer cottage that we are about to start building on Keats Island. It is a gift to my wife, Alison, but we hope it will also prove to be a magnet for our grandchildren, especially during summer vacations.

As each of these situations illustrate, patience and trust are inextricably linked. Had I not been willing to exercise patience and trust our daughters as they facilitated these occasions in their own way, we would not have experienced such productive and effective meetings. As a result, we were able to make decisions together, we had fun, and we grew closer as a family.

Patience Celebrates Incremental Change

What does patience look like in practice?

Two words: incremental change.

Admittedly, there are some circumstances where a sense of urgency is vitally important, but *family business succession is not one of them.* This is where incremental change can be exceedingly valuable in helping families develop a productive process that moves steadily forward.

I first learned about the wisdom of being patient and adopting an incremental approach to change from Denis Waitley, a research scholar and performance consultant who has been an advisor to many Olympic athletes. He is the best-selling author of books such as *Seeds of Greatness* and *The Winner's Edge*, as well as the audio series *The Psychology of Winning*.

> "Champions 'stair-step' their goals."

Waitley makes the point that "champions stair-step their goals." That is, the athletes who make the most progress are those who take small, incremental steps towards their long-term vision, rather than trying to achieve everything all at once.

For example, consider decathlete Bryan Clay, who won the gold medal at the 2008 Olympics in Beijing. Early in his career, he writes, he was only able to complete the 100-yard dash in 10.8 seconds. In order to win an Olympic gold, he would need to have a time of 10.3. But as he worked to improve, he did not focus on achieving a time of 10.3 seconds; rather, he set intermediate goals of 10.7 seconds, then 10.6, and then 10.5. In the end, this incremental approach won him a world championship, an Olympic gold medal, and the title of best overall athlete in the world.[176]

Similarly, Dick Meyers adopted an incremental approach when helping me transition into the role of CEO at Dominion Construction. Rather than throwing me into the deep end and hoping I could swim, he helped me to wade into the new leadership responsibilities gradually. He created an incremental plan, which was implemented successfully at six-month intervals, subject to my good performance and the board's approval.

His plan is summarized as follows, and as it shows, I initially had just one person reporting directly to me. This person had two staff in the human resources department, so I was ultimately responsible for just three people. Over time, more and more direct reports were added, until I reached the position of CEO and had 11 vice-presidents reporting to me and a total of 150 employees.

TITLE	ADDED RESPONSIBILITLES	DIRECT REPORTS	TOTAL STAFF
Vice-President	Human Resources Department	1	3
Sr. Vice-President	Edmonton and Calgary Branches	3	15
Executive Vice-President	Regina and Winnipeg Branches	5	50
Chief Operating Officer	BC Division and Engineering	8	115
President	California Office	10	130
Chief Executive Officer	Finance and Accounting	20	150

Dick showed great patience and wisdom as he let this transition play out in manageable increments. As a result, I was able to assimilate each new area of responsibility and get to know additional staff in an orderly way. This process also helped me to build self-confidence, just as it helped the board and employees to build their confidence in me.

Patience Helps with Ownership Succession

Similarly, patience can be a great asset in planning both the management and ownership succession in any business. In 2017, Matt Saneholz and Marianela Collado utilized patience as they successfully acquired the full ownership and management of Tobias Financial Advisors from the company's founder, Benjamin Tobias.[177]

Ben is a well-respected 40-year veteran of the financial services industry who wanted a plan that would enable him to transition out of the business within a 10-year time frame. Matt and Marianela were "up-and-comers" in the industry, and they were eager to acquire the business as soon as possible. Unfortunately, not only did they have a shorter timeframe in mind, they also had a different risk tolerance, as well as limited financial resources.

Consequently, it took many years to simply reach an agreement on how and when the business transition would occur. With the help of an independent advisor, the group patiently explored multiple strategies, addressing issues such as ownership, compensation, and growth. As each potential path was modelled, they had an opportunity to examine their goals and their risks associated with each option. They also assessed whether the overall plan was too fast or too slow and whether or not the steps proposed were financially realistic.

"Don't expect to step into a firm and change everything on day one."

It took patience to work through all these questions, particularly while they were simultaneously dealing with their day-to-day responsibilities of managing the business.

However, by being patient and listening to each other and to the company founder, these successors were not only able to achieve their goal of buying the business; they were also able to preserve good relationships with the founding owner. As testament to this, "although he is no longer an owner, Ben continues to participate in the firm and to support the new leaders' vision, but in a manner that allows him to enjoy other priorities in life."[178]

Because they were willing to be patient, Matt and Marianela were able to successfully complete this purchase. In addition, the long-term client relationships Ben had established were preserved, and the business has continued to prosper. Looking back over their experience, Marianela offers sage advice for all successors when she says, "Don't expect to step into a firm and change everything on day one."

Patience Yields Many Benefits

When we are patient, there is a host of positives that accrue to us in due time. Perhaps the three most important benefits for successors are that patience helps us become better leaders, assists us in managing the succession process, and improves our relationships. It takes time for the hourglass to gradually empty, but patience eventually leads to good things.

THE ROLE OF PATIENCE IN A FAMILY ENTERPRISE

Patience Preserves Relationships

The value of patience is particularly significant for family businesses because of that one key word: *family*. For most of us, our family relationships are some of our most important and enduring and therefore ones that deserve special attention. These are the personal connections that we typically want to preserve and protect as a priority. However, the stress of being in business together often threatens these relationships, and anything we can do to mitigate this is worthwhile to consider. Patience is one of those things.

As discussed in chapter 3 of section II, Fisk Johnson and his father, Sam, are members of the family that owns S. C. Johnson and Son Co. They shared their story of succession when visiting Vancouver for one of the largest family business events ever hosted in our city. Their experience was a remarkable illustration of patience. At that time, Sam was still the top executive of the company, and Fisk was the heir apparent, waiting to become the fifth generation of his family to lead the company.

The younger man was asked whether it had been difficult for him to wait for his appointment as the top executive in the family firm. With deference to his father, Fisk explained that it had been a long wait. But he also explained that one of the reasons he had resisted the urge to join the company for many years was because he knew his father was a strong executive leader who was not yet ready to give up the reins of power. So, rather than trying to rush the succession process, Fisk determined that he would continue to pursue more education while he waited.

His experience, including attending university almost until his 30th birthday (and in the process completing six degrees), is one of the most striking examples of a potential successor who was patient while preparing for his future duties in the family business.

When at age 30 Fisk finally joined the family business in 1987, his first role was as a marketing associate. Over the next 17 years, he served in many different positions, before eventually being appointed as CEO in 2004. Ultimately, the management transition from Sam to his son worked out extremely well, even though it required a generous amount of patience on Fisk's part. Can you imagine, after such an extended university experience, still waiting almost 20 more years to be appointed as company CEO? That's a combined total of approximately *3 decades preparing to lead*!

Today, Fisk is the chairman and CEO of S. C. Johnson & Son Inc. and leads one of America's most highly respected corporations. I am certain he believes that it was worth the wait. More importantly, Fisk demonstrated exemplary patience as he waited, and he certainly made his time count while waiting—studying subjects that prepared him well for leadership. He then showed additional patience once he joined the family firm, waiting almost two decades to reach the top job.

This all may seem extreme, but as his story vividly illustrates, there can be many positives if successors are willing to take the time to patiently prepare themselves for leadership.

Fisk's patience was not only a key element in making the succession process work at S. C. Johnson. It was also instrumental in maintaining good relationships between the generations. By delaying his entry into the firm, Sam wisely and studiously avoided creating what might have been a power struggle with his dad.

Patience Assists with Management Succession

Patience on behalf of the successor was key to a successful transition of leadership in Canada's Rosen family. Larry Rosen currently serves as chairman and CEO of Harry Rosen Inc., an upscale men's retailer that has captured approximately 40 percent of the quality menswear market in Canada. When his dad, Harry, turned 69, he retired from active duties and transitioned the role of CEO to Larry.

Larry was the kind of man who wanted to lead, but he did not grasp for leadership; instead he was willing to wait for his turn to come. He began by obtaining a law degree and then an MBA. Afterwards, he practised corporate law in Toronto, before joining the family company full time at the age of 29. When he started working at Harry Rosen, he was immediately assigned to be a buyer—a position on the lowest rung on the company ladder. But Larry did not complain or grow impatient. Instead, he worked hard to earn his credentials. For the next 15 years, Larry learned all aspects of the business from the bottom up, and it was not until he was in his mid-forties that he was finally appointed to the top job. By this time, he had demonstrated the patience, maturity, and experience necessary to gain the confidence of his father and the respect of all the non-family employees.

Without Patience, Succession Can Be Challenging

One family that has faced challenges with succession because of impatience is still grappling with the process. In this situation, the young daughter (then age 25) and her father (almost 50) had very different expectations in terms of the timing of succession. The father indicated that he would like to lead the business until he turned 65. Meanwhile, his daughter expected to become president before her 30th birthday. It does not take a math wizard to recognize the 10-year difference in their expectations.

When I first met with them, the daughter was gainfully employed at another company in another city. She was learning the industry while earning a suitable salary. On numerous occasions I suggested that she stay away from the family firm for at least 5 years, if not 10. I warned both her and her father that working together sooner would inevitably cause tension and strife.

Despite my pleas, both of them were determined to work together; both Mom and Dad wanted their daughter back home, and she could not resist the opportunity to get into the family business and to accelerate the leadership transition. As expected, their relationships have been challenging, and this has resulted in several stressful years for the entire family.

Happily, the daughter is both hardworking and intelligent, and as a result of her leadership there have been radical improvements to the company's financial results. However, the relational cost for the family has been significant, and it has been difficult to witness, as it could have been easily avoided if this woman and her parents had been more patient, letting her gain more experience before coming to work alongside her dad.

The Elder Generation Gets to Decide

Succession in any enterprise can be a tricky process, and it can challenge both careers and friendships. But in a family business, the stakes are so much higher; family relationships and personal finances can be radically impacted if things go wrong. Additional stress is often added when young successors are raised in a familial context that promotes their future involvement from an early age. Such parental anticipation, even if well-intentioned, can create unrealistic expectations. In these circumstances, patience and a willingness to respectfully trust the succession process become critical factors.

Over 30 years ago, you could find a Black's Camera store in 200 retail stores across Canada. Just before the family sold its business in 1985, I ran into a Black family member at a family business event. During our conversation, he mentioned three things that he believed were almost always true in a family business:

1. The elder generation wants the younger generation to succeed and one day lead the business.
2. The younger generation wants to show their elders that they are capable as leaders.

3. The elder generation gets to decide when the younger generation gets their chance to lead.

The first two statements may not always be true; but if the elder generation owns the business, the third statement is a fact. It is their business, so they can do with it as they wish. They can even sell it if they want, so they can certainly determine *when and if* members of the next generation are given authority to run it.

Lots of successors may not like this truism (I know I did not), but there is nothing that we can do to change the situation. As a result, the wisest course of action is to demonstrate patience throughout the succession process. If you are unwilling do that, perhaps the most logical option is to leave. Personally, I tried a combination of arguing, complaining, fussing, fuming, and negotiating, but it was like fighting gravity. It accomplished nothing positive; it undermined my own credibility, destroyed my peace of mind, and thoroughly irritated members of the elder generation.

The best way to reduce such friction and get things back on track with the elder generation is to be patient, work hard, and let them decide when you will get your chance to lead. (Working elsewhere or getting more education are also worthwhile options to consider, especially if working together proves to be really challenging.)

Envisioning Your Future

One way to promote patience, according to current research, is to imagine future outcomes. Visualization can help successors wait, in much the same way that visualizing a cool refreshing swim while working in the hot sun can provide an extra bit of stamina to keep going.[179]

The idea of imagining a vision for the future proved to be very helpful in a recent meeting with six third-generation successors. I was assisting them as they researched and established their career goals. As a starting point, the company had articulated 10 senior executive roles that they anticipated would be required for future leadership. The potential successors were then asked to identify and communicate to the advisory board which of these roles they aspired to hold in the future. The result? Each individual had a clearly imagined future to work towards.

At the same time, we assisted them to create personal development plans that covered education, training, and mentoring initiatives over the next five to ten years. Coupling this exercise with the strategic planning initiative previously completed produced a clear vision for their future roles in the company. The payoff for each of the future owners was that they were able to connect their day-to-day efforts with the future they had visualized. This helped each of them to be *patient in the moment*, while simultaneously pursuing their long-term vision.

> *A clearly imagined future can help create patience.*

Impatient successors do well to follow these steps: clarify the future vision for the company; determine what role(s) you aspire to, and create a concrete plan for developing your skills and experience. Most importantly, each of the initiatives ought to be undertaken with the collaborative input of company leadership. (Without this, there is a significant risk of creating false hopes, rather than creating alignment.)

Advice to Successors

Vision provides a long-term impetus to stay focused, yet every day, in the short term, there are a host of occasions when successors are required to respond with patience. How can family successors begin to cultivate patience when things are not going their way?

It does not have to be complicated, and it is a character trait that most of us learned years ago. I am reminded of a wonderful book written in the 1980s by Robert Fulghum, *All I Really Need to Know I Learned in Kindergarten*. He writes, "Wisdom was not at the top of the graduate-school mountain, but there in the sandpile at Sunday School." These are some of the things he learned:

- Share everything.
- Put things back where you found them.
- Play fair.
- Don't hit people.
- Clean up your own mess.
- Don't take things that aren't yours.
- Say you're sorry when you hurt somebody.

Based on my experiences and Fulghum's insistence that we keep it simple, I have developed a short list of proposals for family enterprise successors who want to develop patience. These are contained in the adjacent list entitled "Wisdom for Successors."

> ### WISDOM FOR SUCCESSORS
>
> 1. Be willing to wait; set aside our own agenda and desires.
> 2. Do not force things; let them mature and develop in due course.
> 3. Stop rushing and grasping for more.
> 4. Learn to bite your tongue, and trust those in charge to make decisions.
> 5. Do not let your emotions get in the way as you wait.

DEAR YOUNGER ME ...

Many family enterprise successors are tempted to force things to happen, rather than to wait for things to happen. They want to be (and be seen as) on the fast track to the top. However, as I have experienced, this approach only serves to fuel their impatience, and this inevitably creates challenges, both at work and at home.

As I reflect, I wish I had realized that there was no need to rush. I was the only one who perceived any sense of hurry. Had I been more patient, my personal life would have likely been much more harmonious. I would have benefited by seeing myself more like an apprentice, someone who over time would be able to earn my credentials.

With more patience, I could have focused on learning from those older and more experienced than me. Instead, I sabotaged my own career by my ill-fated attempts to leapfrog over others in my haste to reach the corner office.

THE BOTTOM LINE

All good things take time...
so, until your dreams come true,
patience will help you enjoy the wait.

David

CHAPTER 9
Contentment: The Pathway to Poise and Focus

"He who is not contented with what he has, would not be contented with what he would like to have."

Attributed to Socrates

The reality of turning 60 years old prompted me to reflect deeply about my life, and eventually this led me to the realization that over the past six decades I have seldom been content.

There were so many occasions when I could have stopped for a moment to soak in the remarkable life that I have been given, but instead I chose to focus on the next goal or objective. It recently occurred to me that I had done this so many times that it became a habit; it was my natural way of responding to both the big and little events in my life. You could say that I was actively "wishing my life away" by always longing for something better, something else, or something in the future.

When I was a child, I wanted to be more grown up. When I entered high school, I longed for my 16th birthday and a driver's licence. After that, I set my eyes on purchasing my first car and being free from the discipline and supervision of living at home. When I had all that, I yearned for the day when I would finish university, get married, and join the company. Certainly then I would be content (or so I thought).

But contentment never came. Instead, I became preoccupied with career goals, and whenever I would achieve one, I simply shifted my focus to the next. My ultimate goal was to become president of our company, and I often told myself that once I had the top job, I would be able to truly enjoy my life. *Then life would be different.*

But it was not. When I became president and CEO of Dominion Construction, my attention turned towards paying down debt and growing our sales. It seemed as though I lived my life like some people read books; they are so obsessed with getting to the next chapter, madly flipping pages, that they barely notice the words.

My wife, Alison (left), with our daughter Jennifer

This realization created a desire within me to change everything about my life.

I decided that I would share this seismic shift in my thinking with Alison and our daughter Jennifer over dinner one night. Jen had recently moved home after a number of years living on her own, and we were about to enjoy one of her fabulous creations for dinner. She is a graduate of the Cordon Bleu culinary school in France, one of the foremost culinary institutes in the world, and, as I have often joked, "If one of the kids had to move home, it might as well be the gourmet chef!"

That night, I announced that I wanted to "change everything about my life." I had come to the place where I yearned for things to be different, and I wanted to learn to savour the moment. Because they both know me so well, I said that I hoped they would be able to provide support and accountability to me in this new quest.

Their reactions were not quite what I had hoped for. Alison's first response was to raise an eyebrow and give me a puzzled look; Jennifer simply stated that she thought I was being slightly overdramatic. It was a tough start—but I pressed on knowing that both were well aware of my lifelong tendency to miss out on the beauty of the present. As I explained my recent insights to them, they agreed that my focus on tomorrow was stealing my opportunities to experience each day and that this was robbing me of contentment. We all agreed that I should make it a personal goal to *become more present*, and as a result I could actively begin cultivating a spirit of contentment.

WHAT KEEPS US FROM BEING CONTENT?

Dissatisfaction with the Status Quo

Dr. John R. W. Stott was the honorary chaplain to the queen of England and had an outstanding—and diverse—resumé, including many years serving as an Anglican priest. He was also a scholar and writer who published over 50 books during his illustrious career. No wonder that in 2005 he was named as one of *Time* magazine's 100 most influential people in the world.

When I was in my 20s, he came to Vancouver to give a series of public lectures. Afterwards, he accepted an invitation from my parents to spend a week on our family boat, cruising the coastal waters of British Columbia. On several occasions, John and I were able to sit together on the upper deck, and I was thrilled to have one-on-one time with such a brilliant thinker. Reflecting on my career ambitions, I asked John what I would need to do in order to become a successful leader.

His reply was both surprising and enlightening. Succinctly put, he said that the foundation for effective leadership is a "healthy dissatisfaction with the status quo." In other words, the animating spirit of a leader is a recognition that things ought to be different. As I pondered this, I realized that many men (Gandhi, Churchill, and Martin Luther King Jr., for example) became great leaders because their dissatisfaction with the status quo prompted them to passionately pursue change.

I privately made this mantra my own when I joined our family firm. As I have previously written, I was not satisfied with

Dr. John R. W. Stott

the way things were being done, and my leadership aspirations were focused on bringing about substantial change. Unfortunately, my attempt to apply Dr. Stott's advice resulted in me developing a spirit of defiance, creating havoc around the office, and openly criticizing almost everything.

> *The foundation of all leadership is a "healthy dissatisfaction with the status quo."*

At the time, I thought I was demonstrating leadership. However, I can see that I had radicalized John's notion of leadership as having a blatant dissatisfaction with everything, and I was using this erroneous interpretation as a means of justifying my actions. This was definitely an unhelpful starting place for my career.

With the benefit of hindsight, I understand that rejecting the status quo does not necessarily mean wiping the entire slate clean and starting from scratch. After all, there is usually much that is worth preserving in almost every organization, and wise leaders retain the positives when they are reimagining the future of an enterprise.

Perhaps more importantly, I can see how my amplified dissatisfaction with the status quo had begun to infect every aspect of my life. I have been richly blessed, yet rather than enjoy the life I have been given, I have often allowed my discontent to overwhelm my perspective. It often seems to me that everything around me is in need of fixing.

It was only when our company was wrestled from my father's control and ultimately sold that I began to see my attitude more clearly. In the aftermath of that traumatic event, I was compelled to take stock, and in doing so I realized that there were many things for which I should be thankful.

Pieter Van der Linde, winner of national body building championships in both South Africa and Canada

I realized that I could choose a path that resulted in me no longer missing out on the joy and contentment in my current circumstances. In fact, over time I could learn to see each moment as precious and worth savouring. As I spoke with my family and enjoyed the sumptuous meal prepared by Jen, I noticed that in more recent years I had started to be more present and consequently to be more content with my life.

Preoccupation with the Future

Most people would agree that goal setting is an important and essential skill for any aspiring leader. However, like any strength that is taken to an extreme, it can become unhelpful. Just as I had pushed the idea of "a healthy dissatisfaction" to an extreme, I had also allowed my goal-orientation to overshadow almost every area of my life.

This became particularly obvious in my training as a competitive water skier. During the offseason, I train regularly in the gym, and yet I am rarely content with my progress. While it may be helpful to always want to lift more or do more, there are many different ways of approaching the process.

One afternoon, while I was preparing to do a series of step-ups, I asked my trainer, champion body builder Pieter Van der Linde, how many reps he wanted me to do. Surprisingly, he told me to not think about the number but to focus on each rep. This rocked my world! I had always counted my reps, and I had always been focused on achieving a specified goal for each exercise. To me, achieving such goals was my motivation to keep going.

But Pieter explained that I would be able to do more reps and do them better if I focused on each rep, one at a time. As any high-level athlete knows, focus is critical to performance, but until that day I didn't realize that I could significantly improve my results in the gym if I learned to focus on one step at a time, rather than focus on the end result.

I soon realized that this same principle was affecting the pleasure that I felt when water-skiing. For almost 25 years, I thought of my day-to-day training like climbing a mountain, with successful tournaments as the mountain peaks. But my world-renowned water ski coach, Chet Raley, was convinced otherwise. He felt that the main event (and potentially the real joy for me) could best be experienced during practice, as I worked to improve my technique each time I was out on the water. According to him, tournaments were simply there to help us evaluate our progress and were best seen as interruptions to our training schedule.

> *Being present every moment is the key to contentment.*

I never quite bought into his theory until recently, when he and I trained together for 10 days in Florida and then travelled together to attend a two-day competition in Mississippi. The lengthy training stint had me on a high, and I felt great about my progress, as I had worked to perfect my craft, run by run. When I got to the tournament, I found it to be rather disappointing, and in sharp contrast to the previous several days, I did not ski very well. I spent most of the two days waiting for my turn to ski, and I longed to be back at Chet's lake, practicing and enjoying the opportunity to learn.

The juxtaposition of a great 10 days of training and 2 days of waiting for my turn showed me that my greatest joy was in training, not competing. In short, I was starting to discover, as an athlete, that being present, enjoying each moment, is the doorway to contentment.

This may not seem like a big shift, but it amounted to a monumental change in my perspective on life. Rather than blurring the present by looking towards my goals, I began to focus on the moment and to savour and appreciate each day more.

This past season, I made an unusual decision to not attend any water ski tournaments during the summer. At first, I felt lost, like a ship without a rudder. However, as I adjusted my approach, I began to look at each day as a gift and each opportunity to be at the lake as a privilege. Eventually, I was able to return to that feeling of childlike joy that I had experienced decades ago when I first learned to ski.

FOCUSING ON WHAT OTHERS HAVE

My lack of contentment has impacted how I sometimes view my personal financial situation. This was startlingly underlined quite recently when I found myself seated at a boardroom table having lunch with a group of successful and well-known businessmen. I was enjoying it immensely until my mind began to focus on the fact that I was the only non-billionaire at the table. Although my own net worth is not inconsequential, it was difficult to realize how modest my net worth was by comparison. Although I recognized that I lack for nothing, I began to feel very inadequate, even sorry for myself.

I am very fortunate to live in a beautiful home, and we are the owners of a remarkable boat that has brought great pleasure to our family over the years. More importantly, I am blessed to be part of a wonderful, loving family. Yet, in that one moment, I felt very hard done by and very much like a failure. A flood of discontent undermined the pleasure that I had initially felt in having lunch with a group of good friends and inspiring individuals.

> *It isn't what you have that makes you happy; it's what you think about it.*

As I drove home that afternoon, I recalled a quote by Dale Carnegie, a motivational speaker and the author of *How to Win Friends and Influence People*. Carnegie died long ago, but some of his ideas and principles still have a considerable influence today. One of his most notable quotes is "It isn't what you have or who you are or where you are or what you are doing that makes you happy or unhappy. It is what you think about it."[180] As I reflected on my experience, I realized that I had simply *chosen* to be discontent that day.

This classic beauty, named the Lazee Gal, *has been enjoyed by our family for almost 45 years.*

How Much Is Enough? At one point, John D. Rockefeller, founder of the Standard Oil Company, was known as the world's richest man. He became America's first billionaire in the early 1900s, and when his net worth is considered in terms of today's dollars, he is thought to be the richest person in modern history. Yet, when a reporter asked him, "How much money is enough?" he surprisingly responded, "Just a little bit more."

Sadly, it appears that the wealthiest man in history never learned the secret of contentment. A century later, this sentiment remains predominant in our society, and we all seem to need "just a little bit more."

A 2018 Leger poll conducted on behalf of the financial services group Edward Jones asked almost 1,500 Canadians "how much individual pre-tax income would make them feel 'financially comfortable' … The verdict came in at [a] cool $250,000."[181] While this might make people feel more comfortable, I doubt that it would provide them with contentment. According to author Malcolm Gladwell, "scholars who research happiness suggest that more money stops making people happier at a family income of around $75,000 a year."[182] This suggests that satisfaction remains elusive—especially as our income increases.

Statistics show that an income of just $32,400 a year would put you into the top 10 percent of the population globally. To reach the top 1 percent in wealth, you only need to acquire a net worth of $770,000, counting the equity in your home and the value of your investments (less any debt).[183] By these measures, I must admit that I am in the top 1 percent in the world in wealth, and therefore 99 percent of the world's population might happily trade places with me.

Why, then, am I, and so many like me, not more content?

I believe it is because contentment is never found in either our possessions or our circumstances, and because this is where we are often looking, we are searching in vain. In other words, the problem is not what we have but how we are looking at things. Since realizing this, whenever I am tempted to feel a lack of contentment, I find it comforting to go back to the facts about wealth. (I am truly fortunate, by any measure, and if I ever forget this, someone should forcefully remind me of the facts!) Thankfully, as I learn to reorder my thinking and my perspective, I find myself cultivating a greater sense of contentment.

Remarkably, many of the world's poorest people have been found to be just as happy as many of the world's wealthiest. For example, when those on the Forbes 400 richest people list were surveyed, researchers found that their satisfaction was rated at exactly the same level as the Masai people of Kenya and the Inuit people of northern Greenland—groups that lack electricity and running water.[184]

CONTENTMENT AND JOY

The truth is, *we can experience contentment in spite of our circumstances.* Performance coach and author Jim Murphy asserts that most of us are, at least at some level, simply seeking to be happy. But Murphy says we should have another goal in mind. He refers to the pursuit of happiness as "a fool's game" because it is a temporary feeling that is based on our circumstances. For that reason, Murphy urges people to pursue contentment—a feeling that he equates with joy and has much more staying power than happiness because it is not dependent on our circumstances.[185]

So what are our circumstances? Obviously, our lives include a host of variables, including our jobs, families, marriages, and possessions. In addition, there is one of the most significant—and commonly overlooked—

factors: our health. In his book *You Gotta Keep Dancin'*, motivational speaker Tim Hansel chronicles the intense back pain he faces each day as a result of a horrific fall he suffered while mountain climbing.[186]

Several vertebrae in his back were shattered, but for a long time he continued to hope for a medical miracle, and he decided to put any measure of joy or happiness aside until his body healed. But after attending a host of medical experts, he realized that nothing could be done to remedy his situation. His back was stable, but he would always experience pain, and the doctors told him that how he dealt with that pain on a daily basis was now up to him.

> *There are only two ways of living, either as a victim or as a gallant fighter.*

Hearing this prognosis, Hansel faced a dramatic fork in the road; he could either spend the rest of his life feeling frustrated, angry, and trapped by his pain and living "as a victim," or he could choose to live "as a gallant fighter."[187] It was essentially a choice between a life of discontent and a life of contentment and joy.

He resolved that day that he would not allow the pain to steal his joy.

Tim's decision had an immediate impact on his relationship with his two preschool-aged sons. Prior to his injury, he often shared joyful times wrestling on the floor with his boys; after the injury, that special time together was gone. That is, until Tim came to terms with the fact that he was going to be in pain anyway, so he might as well enjoy the time with his sons.

Tim made a decision to be content and to choose joy in spite of the pain.

DEFINING CONTENTMENT

Contentment is not a word that is often used in the corporate world, and very few would ever imagine that the concept could be useful in business, let alone in a family business. Why on earth would we encourage successors to adopt an attitude of contentment? After all, we frequently hear of wealthy inheritors who are either spoiled or undermotivated. Most of us assume that this would only lead to greater complacency, further undermining any drive to work hard.

Contentment Is Not Complacency

But being content is not the same as being complacent; nor does it mean a person is lacking in passion or drive. It also does not mean putting on a false happy face or suppressing real issues and conflicts. In other words, it is not a synonym for suffering in silence.[188]

Instead, contentment should be understood as a rich state of acceptance and appreciation of one's situation, in spite of difficulties and unresolved goals or even when dealing with complex emotions. In other words, contentment can coexist with a drive for achievement. In some ways, it involves remaining patient and calm and not giving

> Contentment does not require complacency or a lack of passion.

in to frustration while waiting for things to change. In essence, contentment, when properly understood, can be present in an environment where there are many issues or concerns that still require resolution.

Contentment is a foundational element that can assist in achieving excellence. Many of the most gifted and accomplished athletes illustrate this principle by remaining focused and poised in the heat of competition. A deep sense of contentment offers them stability and rationality, and they are not panicked by a *need to make the next shot*. Instead, they are content in knowing that the key to winning is to be well-prepared and to give each circumstance their very best. This approach serves to calm their minds and enables them to perform well under pressure. A similar attitude of contentment can be a great asset for aspiring business executives, especially when tensions mount.

What Is Contentment?

Merriam Webster's dictionary offers the word *satisfaction* as a synonym for contentment; it also describes it as a feeling of well-being. Satisfaction is vitally important for optimum performance at work; it enables an individual to focus on their job and to apply their energy to the tasks that need to be done. If we are not content in our work, we find it hard to remain focused. As a simple example, if we are always looking over the fence into our neighbour's yard, believing that the "grass is greener" over there, we are not likely to do a very good job of mowing our own lawn.

> When we are not content, we find it hard to focus.

CONTENTMENT IN BUSINESS

So how is contentment relevant in business? There are four significant ways that contentment benefits executives.

Contentment Helps Us to Focus

I recall consulting with an extremely intelligent and talented executive who worked at a major ski resort and was struggling with contentment. His creativity and dedication had already earned him significant management responsibilities, but he was constantly frustrated by a malaise that engulfed his co-workers. Much of it stemmed from decisions made by other executives, either senior to him or in other departments. In general, he found their actions (and inaction) distracting, and this situation often caused him to lose his own focus.

When we talked about potential solutions, he suggested that he would be able to fix many of the problems in the firm if he could simply get others to understand how their decisions were creating havoc in other departments.

In addition, he felt that he could improve things if he had more authority and could deal with the problems that he had identified. I concurred with his assessment. However, we both agreed that until he was given a larger mandate, he had no control over what other members of the management team did or did not do.

As his mentor, I suggested that he stop presumptively agitating for change and cease lobbying his superiors for more authority. Instead, I urged him to remain content in his current role and to excel in discharging his current responsibilities. I counselled him to simultaneously give up his futile attempts to manage factors that were out of his control. I argued that if he could demonstrate competence by remaining focused on his role, he would, in due course, likely be asked to help solve some of the other organizational challenges.

> When he became content, he became more focused, effective, and productive.

That is exactly what happened.

Once he decided to be content where he was and stopped trying to do other people's jobs for them, he became more focused, effective, and productive. In addition, he was able to sleep better at night, and this further enhanced his ability to focus. Before too long, the company executives took notice, and he was promoted to a much larger role.

Contentment Is Foundational for Growth

Most of us likely consider discontent to be a powerful motivator for change in our lives. It may be in some ways, but discontent is a largely negative emotion; it saps our energy and robs us of our ability to focus and achieve. For these reasons, I have realized that accepting my circumstances and being content with my current reality serve to create a more powerful foundation for growth and change.

Being content is one of the keys to staying present and focused, both of which are essential building blocks to achieving our best. Some of us may be motivated by a strong desire to impress. Others of us may be animated by a need to avoid looking foolish. Ironically, both of these extremes can become attachments that enslave us. Instead, in order to perform well, we are wiser to find ways to break free from our attachments.

This helps us move away from tension and toward freedom and optimum performance. As Jim Murphy puts it, "Often what hurts us the most is the fear of failing, which is neither present nor balanced."[189]

Being content with who we are and with whatever circumstances we are in helps us avoid the twin challenges to peak performance—namely, worrying about past results and obsessing about the future. In other words, if we are discontent, constantly upset by our failings, and preoccupied by what we have not yet done, we undermine our ability to execute. Instead, if we cultivate a deep-rooted sense of contentment, we accept our circumstances, assess what to do next, and move decisively forward, one step at a time.

> Contentment is essentially "accepting reality."

By way of example, some individuals are afraid of stepping on a weigh scale because they fear what it will say. They reason that it's better to not know how much they weigh because it would only be discouraging. Paradoxically, those who possess a sense of deep contentment look reality in the eye, learn from the facts, and then build a plan for improvement. Ironically, those who lack this kind of inner peace and contentment may find it too scary to make the changes they long for, whether it be in their fitness levels or anywhere else in their lives.

Contentment Develops Composure

Similarly, contentment helps us to forge a path that leads towards composure. Rather than emotional driv-enness (either *amped up* or *worn down*), contentment leads us to stability and cool headedness under pressure. This approach is exemplified by some of the best professional athletes, who thrive under pressure, not because they do not have a drive to win but because they remain in the moment and play *within themselves*.

Tennis greats, including Roger Federer, Novak Djokovic, and Raphael Nadal, typically exhibit this type of composure, and it is one of the hallmarks of their success. More recently, basketball star Kawhi Leonard led the Toronto Raptors to the best season in franchise history, inspiring his team with a great sense of confidence and composure—true marks of a champion.

Leonard's individual drive and will to win are ferocious, but one of his most remarkable attributes is his lack of emotion on the court. He rarely criticizes himself, his teammates, or even the referees.

> True champions are simultaneously content, composed, and confident.

He is fuelled by a combination of determination and drive, and yet he also plays with a sense of freedom and contentment. I believe he understands that as long as he gives 100 percent, he can be content with whatever results. Consequently, there is no need for anger if he misses a shot and no prideful boasting when he drains a three-pointer.

This approach is one that all family enterprise successors are wise to adopt: simultaneously being content, composed, and confident.

Contentment Enables Employees to Accept Reality

In his article "Leading with Contentment," Timothy O'Keeffe observes that our culture seems to have an unhealthy obsession with trying to create happiness in the workplace, rather than cultivating contentment. He argues that contentment is a more worthy goal because it "is a middle ground that can lead to the delicate balance of achieving business results, while retaining and nurturing talent."[190]

Happiness can be an emotional extreme, and this may not contribute to better results for a business.[191] It is unrealistic to expect employees to always be happy at work. Sometimes work is difficult, and sometimes our jobs require grit and determination to get them done. Accepting the good with the bad involves maturity and perspective, and an attitude of contentment can help us to develop a balanced approach to both. As a result, contentment is essentially "*accepting the reality of the situation,*"[192] and the wisest, most content employees are able to be grateful for their circumstances rather than wistfully daydreaming about how things could be better.

Contentment Equips Us to Face Challenges

Managers who are constantly waiting for the markets to go up or down are never satisfied in their work. This lack of contentment makes things worse by creating tension, fear, and anxiety, all of which undermine performance.

However, those who cultivate a deep inner contentment are able to meet success and failure and treat both as imposters.[193] As a result, they foster one of the secrets to managing with poise.

Paradoxically, a sense of personal contentment is one of the inner qualities that enables us to reach for the stars. When we establish an attitude of contentment, it enables us, as leaders, to develop inner harmony, thereby releasing us to act in freedom and with maturity, resulting in poise and composure, especially when under pressure.

We might easily assume that a quality like contentment, or even a powerful emotion such as joy, is some-

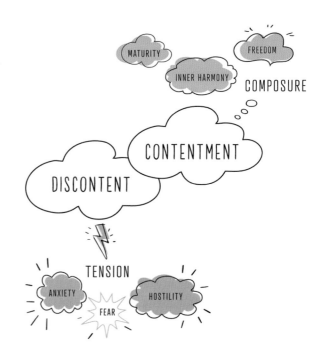

thing that happens to us. However, as we have discussed, our level of contentment is actually determined by our perspective and our choice about how we view our circumstances. Theologian Miroslav Volf resists speaking of joy as *merely* a feeling, instead emphasizing that it constitutes an *active response*,[194] a particular posture toward both positive and negative aspects of one's circumstances that may be cultivated and even practiced. I argue that contentment may be understood in a similar way. Both begin with a decision to embrace our situation and to respond wisely to it. Consequently, as we grow in our ability to accept our circumstances, we can then develop the capacity to find contentment, and maybe even joy, in the midst of our challenges.

CONTENTMENT IN FAMILY ENTERPRISE

Simply put, patience reorients our time frames, gratitude reframes our perspective, and contentment restores our equilibrium. Together, these three traits are a powerful antidote to some of the challenges faced by successors, including entitlement and frustration.

Rather than being buffeted by circumstances, when we possess these qualities we are able to bring stability and rationality to our interactions. This kind of mature approach is invaluable in a family enterprise, where all too often emotions are permitted to rule the day.

Discontentment Destroys Relationships

When I first joined our family business, I set a goal of only working in any given role for a short period of time. My first job was at our millwork operation, and it was proposed that I work there for two years; yet I wanted to learn and contribute as much as I could and then move on within one year.

Twelve months later, I was promoted to a role at head office, and again I was asked to commit to my new role for at least two years. But after a year I took on a new role in Alberta. Clearly exasperated, my uncle Bob reminded me that in my first two positions I had refused to be content with my assignments. He then asked me to commit to my next position for at least five years. In my mind, I was determined to "get in and out" within two years—and I did precisely that. Part of this was due to my impatience and immaturity, but it was also a reflection of the fact that I was never content to work at what was in front of me. This deep discontentment mixed with my critical spirit became a toxic combination that undermined any potential for me to build a mutually satisfying working relationship with Bob.

Contentment Reduces Conflict

Everyone who has seen a dramatic movie or read a novel knows that where there is discontent, there is eventually conflict. This rule is particularly relevant in a family enterprise where intergenerational and sibling relationships are at play, and that is why it is so important to cultivate contentment in a family firm.

An example of this is when one member of the family feels that they have not received what they judge to be their fair share, whether that be financial or otherwise. Trying to determine what is fair in the context of a family enterprise can stir up powerful emotions, and the potential for damaged relationships can be significant and long-lasting.

A number of years ago, my family discovered that, in spite of our father's best intentions, there were considerable financial inequities between the four members of my generation (my brother, my two sisters, and me). We met as siblings and decided that we should, as my brother, Chuck, put it, "rectify any inequities from the past," and we all agreed to a financial review of the gifts given to us by our dad over the previous five years. Reaching agreement on what we thought was "fair" took us almost five years of regular discussions and required the assistance of our VP of finance and an independent facilitator.

Once we had confirmed the nature and extent of the inequalities, we agreed to make retroactive adjustments. For me, this meant going to the bank, taking out a fresh mortgage on our home, and distributing the cash to my siblings. I did not relish this idea, but I also knew it was the right thing to do. The key to contentment, in this situation, was to let go of a desire to have more, or to have the same as someone else. By choosing to *be content* with my lot in life, I was able to voluntarily borrow money and pay it to my siblings.

Our family circumstances were not unique. Several years later, I worked with another family whose situation was remarkably similar. In their case, the eldest had received substantially more money than his younger siblings. As this became more of an issue between him and the rest of the family, he volunteered to repay the excess to his four siblings, and this enabled them to achieve an equitable settlement.

There are two important dynamics in their story. First, before the eldest child decided to voluntarily return some of his money, he resolved that he would be *content* following the proposed redistributions. If he either was going to harbour resentment or had been seeking to maximize his wealth at any cost, he would not have chosen to pay this money to his siblings. Second, he was rewarded with a profound sense of relief by giving back to his siblings and taking steps to improve their relationships. At the end of our meeting, he thanked his siblings for giving him *the opportunity* to pay the money back, saying, "Knowing that I had received more than the rest of you has been bothering me for years! *Thank you for allowing me* to make things right."

Being Content With "Good Enough"

As you can see from these examples, conflict can be reduced or even eliminated when family members are prepared to focus on being content with what they each have. Unfortunately, the search for fairness is often a dead end because fair *does not necessarily mean equal, and equal does not always mean fair*. As a result, in the context of a family enterprise it is sometimes extremely difficult to resolve what fairness or equality looks like. In such situations, being content with "good enough" may be all that is possible.

> *An attitude of contentment helps eliminate family conflict.*

For another of my clients, this meant developing a plan that was not necessarily equal but was still found to be acceptable. This particular family operated in a remote location off the British Columbia coast. All five family members/owners wanted to meet at their place of business at least once per year for a family meeting and their annual shareholders' meeting. Of the five siblings, one lived on-site, one was about two hours' away by car, and two had to make a journey of approximately five hours. However, the fifth sibling was a teacher in the Middle East, and attending annual meetings would require a journey of several days, at great cost. As a result, the estimated travel costs for the five siblings were $0, $40, $200, $200, and $5,000, respectively.

Obviously, it would not be equal for the company to pay each person's travel costs; nor would it be fair to pay everyone an equal amount (say, $1,000). This would be a windfall for some while still leaving significant hardship for the sibling living on the other side of the world. If this were just a once in a lifetime meeting, I think the family might have agreed to simply pay everyone's costs. However, given that they were planning to meet annually, the travel costs would, over time, be fairly significant.

After much discussion, they all agreed that a fair resolution did not exist and, rather than seeking fairness, they agreed to settle on a solution that was considered to be *good enough*. So they agreed to pay everyone's travel costs to attend regular shareholders' meetings—but not every year. Instead, they agreed to pay travel costs for the sibling in the Middle East every three years, and in the intervening years, he would participate by Skype. The resulting plan was neither fair nor equal, but it was acceptable and workable, and each sibling was *content* with that.

Passing Contentment onto Succeeding Generations

In North America, $30 trillion in financial and non-financial assets is expected to pass from the baby boomers to their heirs over the next 20 to 40 years.[195] But money is not the only thing that can be transferred between generations; perhaps the most important thing to be transmitted to the next generation is an understanding of the family's core values. Contentment can be one of these values.

My parents happily arriving at my dad's 75th birthday party

To illustrate, if the elder generation has cultivated a spirit of contentment and actively demonstrated it to their children, it is quite likely that similar attitudes will follow in the rising generation. However, as Malcolm Gladwell notes, if parents are going to be successful in transmitting values to their offspring, they must "know how to articulate them, and know how to make them plausible."[196]

My parents were masterful at this, showing us what a heart of contentment looked like in practice. They did this through both what they said and how they lived. For example, my dad would often talk about how fortunate we were and how hard Granddad had worked to give us a good start in life. Dad also recognized and acknowledged that it was our employees and clients who made it possible for our business to prosper. As a result, he was fiercely loyal to our staff and to the companies that had been clients over the years. As an example, Scott Paper had been a client for decades, and Dad insisted that Mom never buy any other brand of tissues—just Scotties. Kleenex usually had a broader selection of colours, but Dad encouraged us to be content with Scotties.

In spite of their financial resources, my parents were neither proud nor ostentatious—never showing off their wealth or grasping for more. Similarly, Granddad's life was marked by both generosity and frugality. Famously, the very first decision he made when he bought Dominion Construction in 1912 was to sell the company Cadillac. He decided he would be content with a Ford.

Both my parents and grandparents were generous with their financial resources. This included helping the next generation get a good start in life, but it also extended to helping others in our community and around the world. Unlike Dickens's Scrooge, they were content, and that enabled them to be generous towards others. (After all, if you are not content with what you have, how can you give anything away?)

DEAR YOUNGER ME …

As I look back on my life I see that I lacked for very little, and in terms of finances I had every reason to be content. However, I now realize that in my career and my constant pursuit of various goals, for many years I lacked a sense of contentment in who I was and what I was doing in spite of all the great opportunities I was afforded. Unfortunately, this fostered a drive and an impetuousness that undermined almost everything I had hoped to achieve. Rather than being poised, I became frenetic. Rather than being content, my life was marked by dissatisfaction, especially in my career.

In recent years, I have come to understand that contentment, when properly understood and judiciously cultivated, is a great asset. I have realized how powerful it can be for all family enterprise successors. It can help an individual to abandon an attitude of discontent and instead stimulate them to face reality with a posture of agreeability and composure.

Looking back, I regret that I was not more content earlier in my life. I had so much to be grateful for, and yet I was consumed by a desire for more. This is why I feel so strongly about the importance of contentment. It is why I advocate that aspiring executives, especially those who are family enterprise successors, develop this quality in their own lives. It can enable them to be more present (both as leaders and in their homes), and it can help them become more satisfied with their circumstances.

Contentment can also enable them to focus more effectively on their current roles and responsibilities. This kind of attitude inevitably leads to poise under fire, minimizes conflict, and improves relationships.

THE BOTTOM LINE

Contentment is not just a state of mind; it's a strategy for building better relationships and achieving better performance.

David

SECTION IV
Wisdom from Successors

It has been my privilege to meet and work with many family enterprise successors over the years. I want to now introduce you to some of these individuals.

Each of the successors profiled in the following pages possesses many of the nine qualities from section III. Their stories are both instructive and inspiring.

They are all great examples and potential role models for their peers and colleagues. None of them are perfect, as they would readily confess, but that does not mean that they cannot inspire and encourage others by the success that they have enjoyed.

In describing their experiences, I endeavor to illustrate what humility, empathy, and gratitude (and the other six traits) look like in real life and business. I hope their experiences will encourage other successors to cultivate these same virtues in their personal and professional lives.

ADRIAN FLUEVOG (FLUEVOG SHOES)

"HUMILITY IS MORE THAN JUST A NICE IDEA"

Fluevog shoes are unique, inspired, and instantly recognizable. As a result, their distinct art-deco-inspired designs have caught the attention of movie stars, celebrities, and fashion trendsetters in New York and Hollywood. Beyoncé. Lady Gaga. Madonna. They all wear them, and the Fluevog name is synonymous with fashion footwear around the world. There are Fluevog retail stores in every major city in Canada and more than a dozen in the USA, including in New York, Los Angeles, Boston, Washington, DC, and New Orleans. Fluevog's first European outlet was recently opened in Amsterdam.

John Fluevog began designing shoes in Vancouver almost 50 years ago. His son, Adrian, became CEO in 2017 and is the second-generation leader of the family business. In his younger years, Adrian watched as his father became increasingly famous, successful, and influential. He also observed that his father never allowed the adulation and success to go his head; John never became arrogant or proud. Adrian believes that his father's humility is one of the keys to the company's success.

I recently spoke with Adrian about the connections between business and humility; his following insights are quite compelling.

Humility in Leadership Inspires Mutual Respect

Adrian believes that humility in leadership serves to establish *a bond of mutual respect* between leaders and their employees. As he has consistently treated his employees with respect, their respect for him has

Adrian Fluevog, 2nd generation CEO of Fluevog Shoes

grown, and Adrian notes that building and maintaining that bond have resulted in (at least) two key advantages for his company.

INNOVATION

Once a foundation of mutual respect has been created, people become willing to share their thoughts and ideas more openly, whether it be in formal or informal lines of communication. It also opens the door for employees to point out problems and opportunities that they see (and that the company ought to be addressing). This is where the true value of humility begins to emerge—it fosters open dialogue and the sharing of ideas that can, eventually, lead to innovation. Ultimately, as discussed in chapter 2 of section III, greater innovation can result in a competitive advantage.

Adrian has seen this principle at work in his company. As the CEO, he constantly feels pressure to come up with new concepts and eye-catching designs for the upcoming season. His humble leadership has inspired a trusting and respectful relationship with his employees, and in turn they have openly (and regularly) shared with him their ideas for design and business. This constant influx of ideas is one reason that creativity and fresh designs are the hallmarks of Fluevog shoes.

On their own, Adrian and his father, John, each has plenty of design ideas. The point is that they are wise enough and humble enough to ask for (and encourage) input from those around them.

Loyalty

Adrian has followed in his father's footsteps by recognizing that the company's employees are essential to Fluevog's success. His humble style of leadership has allowed him to develop valued relationships with his employees; he treats them as equals and is continuously looking for ways to demonstrate his appreciation to them. When people feel valued, they are happier in their jobs and typically enjoy coming to work. This helps to create an organizational culture where people support one another and want to work together. When you have employees who are valued and happy and enjoy coming to work, employee loyalty blossoms.

Humility Is More Than a Nice Idea

In today's world, employees are becoming more transient, and retaining talent is a genuine challenge for many companies. Consequently, human resource experts have been developing creative strategies to improve employee retention. Better benefits, Friday night beer-and-pizza nights, and bigger bonuses can play a significant role in improving company loyalty and employee retention.

But the least expensive and most reliable way to generate loyalty is to let employees know that they are valued. This starts at the top with humility in leadership.

Astonishingly, being a humble leader is not just a "nice idea." As Adrian Fluevog has discovered, it can generate innovation, establish a competitive advantage, and even enhance the employees' loyalty and dedication.

Who would have thought that humility could be such a powerful asset in the toolkit of a leader?

LAURA KUSISTO (KENROC BUILDING SUPPLIES)

"CURIOSITY CREATES A CAREER"

Laura Kusisto was born and raised in Regina, where she grew up as a third-generation successor in a family of entrepreneurs. However, now far from home, she and her husband, Adam, reside in New York, where Laura is a senior journalist with the prestigious *Wall Street Journal*.

Laura strongly believes that curiosity is at the root of everything she has accomplished in both her academic and professional lives. Along the way, it is also the spirit that resulted in her living and working in Israel for a year, while seeking to understand some of the most intractable challenges of our times.

Quoting Diane Sawyer, a long-time and widely revered ABC reporter, Laura emphasizes that "a good journalist … [follows their] curiosity like cats." It is no wonder that she has excelled in this field.

Curiosity Led to an Education and a Career

From a young age, curiosity is what fuelled Laura's desire to learn and in time this led her to the University of Toronto to do a master's degree in English literature. Upon graduation, she wanted to test the waters and explore journalism as a career. It seemed to be a natural choice, as it would complement her desire for knowledge and her propensity to ask questions. Eventually she headed to the Big Apple to study at Columbia University and subsequently earned a master's degree in journalism.

At the outset, she was just asking questions and exploring opportunities. Eventually, however, she found a job with *The Wall Street Journal*, and for the past eight years, she has been employed as a senior writer covering housing and the economy.

Curiosity has been a great asset for Laura, particularly in her career as a journalist. In fact, you could say that she is primarily being paid to be curious since her job involves asking questions, collecting information, and then reporting on what she has discovered.

Curious About the Family Business

More than 50 years ago, Laura's grandfather Ken Sexton established a drywall distribution business in Regina, Saskatchewan. Over the years, the business expanded into tools, building supplies, and trucking. Ken, the man whom Laura affectionately refers to as Papa, passed away just recently, but he left his mark of success on the company he founded. Kenroc Inc. is a thriving national enterprise where Laura's father, Brian, served as CEO up until February 2020. The company employs over 300 people and boasts 20 branches across Canada.

As part of their succession planning process, Laura and her two sisters (Jill and Megan) have been given the opportunity to become partners in the business, and they may eventually succeed their father as co-owners of the enterprise. Aside from brief stints during summer holidays, none of the women had been involved in the family business until a few years ago, when they were each invited to join the company's advisory board as part of a strategy to prepare them for their future responsibilities regarding the family business.

Curiosity Equips Successors for Their Roles

Much to her surprise, Laura has come to realize that playing a role in stewarding the family business is more about asking questions than knowing all the answers. As such, her curious nature has been an enormous benefit as she has settled into an advisory role in an industry that was largely unknown to her.

Laura writes the following:

> I never imagined myself working in any capacity in our family's Western Canadian building supplies logistics business. It was simply not the sort of thing that appealed to a young woman in her twenties who wanted to be a newspaper correspondent in the Middle East. However, since my dad told my two sisters and me that our grandfather is leaving us his business, I have had to learn to be curious about gypsum pricing and truck driver wages and income statements.
>
> I've also had to learn to be curious about my father and grandfather. What made them so good at what they did? How can I emulate my father's sense of fairness, his calm under

pressure, his methodical approach to business? How can I take risks when needed, like my grandfather, to grow the business and channel some of his passion for it?

As Laura's comments illustrate, there are times when her natural sense of curiosity may not be enough. Because the drywall business was unknown territory for her, she needed to develop new skills and gain sufficient understanding to know the most important questions that she needed to ask. As an added bonus, her curiosity has been invaluable in her interactions with senior management as she has endeavoured to understand and support them in their respective roles.

Curiosity Improves Sibling Relationships

Initially, the three sisters had fears that working together or co-owning a business could have a detrimental impact on their relationships and, by extension, their families. Each of the sisters is unique, and it is obvious that they have different gifts and interests. For example, Jill is trained as a social worker, Megan is a full-time homemaker, and Laura works in the heart of Manhattan. As one might anticipate, they do not always agree.

I have had the privilege of advising the Kusisto family for over five years, and much to everyone's surprise, our regular family council meetings have brought the sisters a greater understanding of each other and instilled in them a greater confidence in their collective abilities to navigate the waters ahead.

It has been gratifying for me to see these women find common ground as we have gone through the process of continuity planning. Although the sisters are, in some ways, quite different from one another, Laura realizes that they can do more than just get along; they have discovered that their varied perspectives can be complementary and therefore beneficial.

Megan, Jillian, and Laura Kusisto, 3rd generation successors of their family-owned company

In the end, it is fitting that curiosity—asking questions and understanding each other's hopes and dreams—has strengthened their family bonds.

Curiosity Creates the Future

While travelling home to Regina for a family business meeting, Laura read an essay in the *New Yorker* by Nathan Heller. In it he reflects on his experience of returning home after his first semester at Harvard University.

His grandfather asked him, "So what kind of business do you want to go into?"

Heller knew that building a business had been his grandfather's dream. But as a young English major, the world seemed so much bigger than business, and he soon came to realize that his father's and grandfather's dreams were not his. As he poignantly summarized, "Our children and our children's children will leave our dreams behind."

The sisters have not yet decided if they are willing to take on the dreams of their father and grandfather. For now, Laura is exploring what a future partnership with her sisters might look like. She is learning about her family business and getting to know her father and sisters in a whole new light. As a bonus, Laura is getting to know herself better and beginning to uncover her own dreams for the future.

As Laura and her sisters continue to allow curiosity to lead them in exploring their options, they are coming to value the dreams of their forebears, perhaps in a way they never imagined.

ANDREW WILLIAMS (NORTH PRARIE DEVELOPMENTS)

"LISTENING MAKES A LEADER"

More than 33 years ago, John and Bernice Williams bought a home, did a few renovations, and sold it for a profit. Today we would call it a "flip," but for John and Bernice it was the beginning of an amazing journey. Since then, the Williams family has built more than 3,000 homes and established itself as one of the leading private real estate developers in Saskatchewan. The substantial enterprise is known as North Prairie Developments, and part of its success can be attributed to a willingness to *listen*.

When they started their business, John and Bernice did not have any professional training in real estate. Consequently, they built their company the old-fashioned way, by hard work and determination. As the company grew, they listened carefully to the advice of others, including customers, employees, and professional advisors.

Similarly, their son, Andrew, has grown as a leader by observing his parents and following their example in being willing to listen to others. He notes, "My mom and dad were open to being guided by their marketing, legal, and financial experts." Andrew says that his dad's ability to listen has been further cultivated through time spent with colleagues that he both enjoys and respects. Sometimes he watches a hockey or football game with friends, but John is known as a person who listens thoughtfully to their input on a host of subjects and, as a result, has learned much from his friends and confidants.

A Blunt Employee Speaks the Truth

Andrew has recently been appointed president and is a respected leader of the family-owned enterprise. However, like me, there was a time when he was convinced that he had all the answers and was far more likely to do the talking than the listening! He admits he was a bit brash, and it was not long before he realized that his "know it all" approach was not endearing himself to anyone at the company.

Andrew Williams, 2nd generation CEO of North Prairie Developments Ltd

He recalls one exchange that he had with a long-time employee:

> I was visiting one of our new house builds and stopped to have a cup of coffee with one of our senior superintendents. Within a few minutes, the conversation turned towards my plans for the future, and our veteran employee asked what my ambitions were. When I explained that I hoped to one day run the business, he responded with characteristic bluntness, saying, "If you ever become the leader, I'm quitting."

This exchange was significant for Andrew, and it led him to do some serious soul-searching. As he thought about it, he realized that he was going to be in big trouble if all the senior staff felt that way and were prepared to leave when he became CEO. He knew then that his future prospects were in doubt unless he changed the way that he interacted with others at the company.

Andrew had grown up watching his mother and father develop a successful business by listening to the wisdom of others; that day, he resolved to become more like them and to become a better listener. Over the next five years, prior to joining the business, he began to ask questions and listen to others. That learning continued during the subsequent ten years while at the family business and as he worked towards his goal of becoming CEO.

It took him a while to get over his belief that he had all the answers and to discard the mistaken notion that he needed to have all the answers. But as he developed more listening skills, he became more of a collaborator. He worked hard, and his dedication was rewarded. After a decade in his family business, he was named company CEO. Happily, no one quit when he was appointed!

Another Lesson to Learn

Andrew had much to learn when he became the top executive at the company. He writes, "When I came into the top leadership role, I came in with the approach that I

was the one and only person that should make decisions and that I needed to demonstrate that I could make decisions on my own."

Andrew was well aware that the company had gained much success by focusing on creative niche projects, and with this in mind, he began looking for ways to innovate.

> My first innovative idea was to put economical elevators into affordable single-family two-storey homes. My rationale, at the time, was that we had a large baby boomer demographic coming through the market that would eventually want to move into bungalow (single floor) houses.
>
> However, when our economy was booming, land prices skyrocketed, and developers adapted by creating narrow lots that could no longer fit the traditional bungalow model. Simultaneously, multi-family land values shot up in price, and this made it unaffordable to develop bungalows in a condo setting. My "brilliant idea" was to create a new two-storey model, add an elevator, and market it as the "new bungalow."

In response, Andrew's team developed a strong marketing plan, which resulted in many prospective purchasers visiting their show homes, and the *Vancouver Sun* even published an article on their innovative approach. Andrew was convinced he had a winner.

A full month passed, and the company had no sales. The baby boomers loved the concept, but they did not like the perception that was created by the prospect of living in a home with an elevator while they were still in good health.

But Andrew did not want to give up on his innovation and says, "I continued to push my idea. Rather than sitting down with our team or speaking with potential customers, I put my blinders on and threw more marketing dollars at the project. A year later, we still had no sales!"

Good Leaders Are Good Listeners

Andrew admits that it was a mistake to "ignore the feedback I was being given" and that his approach to the project was wrong. He learned a lot from this experience and says,

It was an expensive lesson, but a valuable one. If I had simply taken the time to listen to the market and to my team, we could have discounted the product, made a small margin, and moved on. Instead I took the approach that I was right, and the market would come. As a result of my stubbornness, we lost quite a bit of money chasing my "brilliant idea."

The one positive from this mistake was that I decided to reshape my approach to decision-making. I now realize that, like my mom and dad, good leaders are good listeners!

MICHELLE JONES-RUPPEL (WEST COAST AUTO GROUP)

"EMPATHY IN A MAN'S WORLD"

If you had to choose one word to characterize a woman who has broken through the glass ceiling in the male-dominated automobile industry, I doubt that *empathy* would be at the top of your list.

Some women might feel guarded or even have the need to exert excessive control or authority in what is essentially a "man's world," but Michelle Jones-Ruppel has chosen to master her situation in part through empathy.

Michelle is a highly respected executive in British Columbia's car industry and a co-owner of the West Coast Auto Group, a family enterprise that encompasses six dealerships in the Greater Vancouver area. Throughout her career, she has demonstrated empathy to co-workers, employees, clients, and family members. In doing so, Michelle has broken through one more stereotype—that of the hard-nosed executive (male or female) pushing employees to reach targets in a sales-related industry.

She understands that some people are not accustomed to accepting direction, guidance, or leadership from a woman. But rather than grow angry or frustrated with such attitudes, Michelle chooses to empathize with them.

"It's not their fault," she says. "It may be how they were raised. Or, for some, all they have ever known or experienced in this industry is having a man in charge."

With remarkable insight, she adds, "I'm the one who decided that I wanted to work in a male-dominated industry, and so I'm the one who's created the challenge."

However, now that she has proven herself, she is fully accepted by the men, and, she jokes, "They treat me like one of the guys." In fact, Michelle says, "some of the guys even confide in me if they are facing a bit of a rough patch."

Michelle Jones-Ruppel, dealer principal of West Coast Auto Group

Showing Empathy to the Elder Generation

Empathy has been a particularly valuable asset as Michelle and her brother, Scott, have transitioned into management at the family firm. It has been almost 50 years since their dad, Ron, founded the business, and naturally one of his greatest pleasures in life has been to see it grow and prosper. But once a founder has invested so much hard work over so many decades, it can be difficult to let go and let others take the lead, even at an age when most people are retired or, at the very least, slowing down.

Despite the pull to stay, Ron has done an exemplary job in preparing for management succession, and he transitioned authority to Michelle and Scott several years ago. But even the most robust preparations could not overcome the feelings of loyalty that many employees had for Ron. Those who had worked for decades with Ron sometimes found it difficult to adjust.

To help make the transition of loyalty easier, Ron graciously relinquished his office and moved to another building, away from the day-to-day operations of the dealerships. This helped the staff to develop new patterns of relating to Michelle and working together.

These changes have afforded Ron more time to invest in his golf game, his charitable endeavours, and his real estate portfolio. But he still has a need to feel included, and Michelle fully understands this. Consequently, she has made a point of keeping him well-informed during this transition. There are times when Ron goes to Palm Springs for several weeks, but even when he is away, Ron is always eager to talk with his daughter about the business.

Michelle notes that she is "happy to chat with him anytime" and that she consistently makes an effort to "keep him up-to-date on things." Occasionally when he is in town, and perhaps for old time's sake, he visits the sales floor to say hi to some of the long-term team members.

Some young successors without the maturity and empathy of Michelle might resent their dad for dropping in to visit or for wanting to know how things are going. But Michelle has displayed great empathy and respect for her father; she has never tried to push him out of the operations, and she still welcomes his advice on decisions. She is always willing to meet him for lunch or coffee to gain his input, and she does not object when he is out on the showroom floor chatting with former employees. Instead, she is willing to let Ron find his own rhythm as he has moved more fully into retirement.

All of these efforts require great love, great empathy, and, on occasion, a willingness to subordinate her own desires to those of her father. But through it all, Michelle has been a loving, supportive daughter, showing patience and empathy as Ron has created his own path and as he has stepped away from the business.

Partnering with Her Brother

Michelle says she "loved cars from a young age"; she knew that she wanted to sell them, and she knew that she wanted to be involved in running the family enterprise. When she started to show an interest in and a capacity for the business, her parents welcomed her presence at the company. Michelle and Scott are the only siblings in the Jones family, and their mom and dad have always made it clear that if they both wanted an opportunity to work in the family business, they would both be given an opportunity to do so. Consequently, after many years working with Ron and learning the business, they became co-owners of the six dealerships in 2000.

As is common in the world of family business and, frankly, with any siblings, it has not always been easy for Scott and Michelle to share the decision-making. (Think of young siblings learning to share their toys in the sandbox, only now the stakes are much higher!)

It is even more challenging when the two siblings are equal partners. How do you make decisions if you cannot come to an agreement?

To resolve this issue, and to give them each authority and autonomy, the family divided the day-to-day leadership of the West Coast Auto Group between the two of them. The group is comprised of six dealerships; Michelle has responsibility for Ford, Lincoln, and Nissan, while Scott manages Mazda, Kia, and Toyota.

As equal owners, Michelle and Scott meet regularly to keep communication lines open and to take advantage of the synergies that exist between their respective operations. By collaborating, they remain highly focused on doing what they can to ensure mutual success. As Michelle says, "Scott is my partner, and so my success is his success, and vice versa."

Conclusion

Michelle readily admits that she is not a perfect sister or a perfect daughter. But she has seen her empathy grow as she keeps her focus on others and makes it her goal to love those around her (her mom and dad, her brother, her husband, their two daughters, and those with whom she works).

In contrast, as Daniel Goleman notes, "Self-absorption in all its forms kills empathy … When we focus on ourselves, our world contracts as our problems and preoccupations loom large. But when we focus on others, our world expands."[197]

It is therefore no wonder that Michelle's world has expanded. She is an individual who seeks to remain outward focused when meeting people throughout her day and to take the time to imagine what it would be like to be in their shoes. As she has discovered, this makes it far easier to show to others both grace and empathy. This she does.

SHAUN PLOTKIN (PLOTKIN HEALTH)

"FORGIVENESS IS A WILLINGNESS TO LET GO"

There are four Plotkin brothers who have executive oversight at their family business. Shaun, the oldest, is a lawyer and the president of Plotkin Health. Each of his three younger brothers have MBA degrees and act as executive VPs in charge of various divisions of the company. Behind the scenes is the founder of the family firm, their recently retired (yet still very involved) father, Dr. Colin Plotkin.

In addition to being highly educated and intelligent, each of the Plotkin men comes equipped with determination, an entrepreneurial drive, and a strong set of opinions. In a family business, this combination of dynamic personalities can be a "perfect storm" of disagreements and relational challenges that potentially derails a business.

Shaun readily acknowledges the difficulties in getting all four siblings to find common ground and says, "Sometimes we argue strenuously, going at it 'toe-to-toe' with one another."

Sometimes feelings get hurt and egos are bruised during these clashes. I recall on more than one occasion, as their advisor, leaving a Plotkin family council meeting feeling convinced that the four siblings were unlikely to sustain a long-term working relationship.

Glenn, Darren, Shaun, and Ricci Plotkin, co-owners and members of the 2nd generation leadership team at Plotkin Health

Yet, as Shaun says, "we were determined to make our partnership work in spite of our differences." As a testament to that commitment and their determination to succeed, they kept coming back to the table, making an ongoing effort to make things work and asking for guidance and support.

Keeping Short Accounts

Thankfully, their never-say-die attitude and will to succeed help to unite them as they continue to grow in their effort to figure out how to work together productively.

The key to maintaining unity? Forgiveness.

As Shaun explains, "The best way to [forgive] has been to keep short accounts. If I have had a fight with one of my brothers over the weekend, we need to get past it when we come to the office on Monday morning. Rather than carrying grudges or sulking about a disagreement, we needed to learn to let it go, and then move forward."

In other words, Shaun and his siblings have learned to forgive one another—both for the sake of family harmony and for the sake of the business. They have now worked together for many years and, during that time, had plenty of occasions when one or another brother has been disappointed by one or another brother. Yet their ability to forgive and move forward has enabled their family business to succeed where so many have failed.

The Beginnings of a Family Enterprise

Plotkin Health was founded by Shaun's father, Dr. Colin Plotkin, who led the company to remarkable growth and great success. He and his wife, Cheryl, brought their family to Canada from South Africa in 1993, hoping that they could provide a better life for their boys. When government regulations did not allow Colin to practice medicine here, he combined his medical training and his entrepreneurial drive to create an innovative and highly specialized enterprise that expedites the settlement of international medical claims.

Plotkin Health works on behalf of health insurance payers that provide medical coverage to people entering the United States. Their systems include a fanatic discipline regarding email response times and an extremely customer-centric culture. While assisting major insurance companies, the company has established a sterling reputation as one of North America's industry leaders.

Conflict Between Generations

Colin led the family firm for almost 25 years, with his sons joining him as each of them completed his university education. In 2018, Shaun was named president and Colin retired, retaining the title of chairman emeritus.

Forgiveness and empathy have both played a significant role in easing the succession transition, and it has had to come from both the elder and the younger generations.

There have been occasions when a contest of wills has arisen between the two generations, particularly as the Plotkin brothers assumed greater responsibility for leadership of the family business and both generations were working in the office.

For example, Colin could be quite stubborn when the boys would present him with new ideas and suggestions for a different way of doing things. They would explain to their long-suffering father that such changes were needed if the company was to adapt to the changing business culture in which it operates.

In the same way, Colin would remind the boys that he was still in charge. He often told his sons that they were intelligent and hardworking and would one day own the company, but today it was run by him, and until he retired, he would be responsible for all the major decisions.

In other words, they would need to do things his way, whether they liked it or not—and Colin had no problem making this very clear to his sons.

Shaun Plotkin, president of Plotkin Health

Forgiveness Helps to Bridge the Generation Gap

Naturally, this would lead to frustration, and at times sharp words were spoken. But Colin showed great patience, wisdom, and forbearance. He recognized that his sons were still growing and maturing, and he was willing to forgive them for their presumptive attitudes. Instead, he kept his focus on their future potential.

Similarly, Shaun and his brothers have had to learn to forgive their father for sometimes being unwilling to consider their ideas and for his demands for obedience and respect for his authority.

Over the past few years, they have also come to understand and empathize with their father. Shaun says, "As Colin got older, we recognized how hard it was for him to relinquish power and authority to us, especially since he had devoted most of his life to building the business. It was his baby. And so we were willing to look past his autocratic tendencies and his controlling style and to forgive him. After all, he's imperfect (just like we all are). He has also earned our respect and loyalty given all that he has done for us."

Forgiveness in Action

It is interesting to note that the phrases "I am sorry" and "Will you forgive me?" are not frequently used in the Plotkin family. However, in their own way, all four brothers and their father have become experts at forgiving. They have done this in three powerful ways:

i) By developing a willingness to let go,
ii) By cultivating a spirit of flexibility, and
iii) By their dedication to not harbouring grudges.

ERIK BRINKMAN (BRINKMAN REFORESTATION)

"FINDING GRATITUDE IN THE AMAZON"

Erik Brinkman is a tree-planting legend. He began his planting career at the age of 15 and made his mark the very first day by planting 1,600 trees. When compared to the average first day of about 300 trees planted, it was clear that he was a natural, and he quickly became known as one of the fastest tree planters to ever swing a spade. His personal best was 5,500 trees in one day, and by the time he was 25, he had planted more than 1.5 million trees.

You might say that he comes by his gift honestly; Erik is the middle child in the Brinkman family, who own and operate the largest tree-planting company in Canada, Brinkman & Associates Reforestation Ltd. Since its inception, the company has planted 1.5 billion trees, primarily in British Columbia, Alberta, and Ontario. It has also diversified into other ecosystem restoration businesses, with 1,500 employees operating in five countries.

As a teenager, Erik spent his summers working in the communal tree-planting field camps, surrounded by men and women who were typically much older than him. He stuck out and, from day one, was labelled "the boss's son," and it was assumed he was there because of favouritism, rather than skill.

Erik plants his one millionth tree, Rocky Mountains, BC, 2003.

Erik responded with a determination to show his fellow planters that he deserved to be there. As Erik recalls, "I took to planting as if my life and reputation depended on it, measuring my worth by the number and quality of the trees I could plant in a day."

Explaining further, he notes, "Tree planting is a physically and mentally demanding job, which makes it impossible to fake excellence. You either can do it well or you can't, and for me this became a badge of authenticity that I could wear as a shield against any accusations of nepotism."

A Great Worker with a Bad Attitude

While Erik proved he could keep up with anyone based on skill and hard work, his boasting, youth, and lack of maturity led to a different kind of entitlement, which manifested as arrogance instead of laziness. Erik admits, "I felt invincible. I believed that I couldn't be fired from the family business and had a hard-earned confidence that I could outperform anyone else at the job. As a result, I was a highly productive worker and a moneymaker for the company, but also a headache for management."

For example, in response to any rebuke from his supervisors or foremen, Erik would simply plant away, believing he was immune to following the rules. His trademark was to laugh and hold up a warning finger, saying, "One phone call!"—implying that one call to his dad was all it would take to get his field boss fired.

He would make such remarks in a joking tone, and his friends would always laugh. At the time, Erik thought it was a good way to make light of his position of privilege. But as he looks back now, he says, "I don't remember my supervisors thinking it was funny."

Erik Brinkman, horsing around with 4 of the Alvarado children, Ecuador, 2003

The Amazon Offers a New Perspective

After working as a tree planter for seven years, Erik had the opportunity to travel to Ecuador. There, he was far removed from his father's protective umbrella, and the Brinkman name meant nothing. He was seen as a foreigner and viewed with skepticism.

Erik befriended a Quechua Indigenous medicine man, César Ricardo Alvarado, who lived with his family deep in the Amazon jungle. Erik says, "César offered to take me on as his apprentice for a year, during which time I would live in his community to study, but not as a researcher—rather as a fully-immersed participant in the local culture."

It turned out to be an extraordinary year: Erik learned to speak Spanish, studied traditional Quechua medicinal plants and their cultivation, worked with a local agroforestry company, and joined forces with a local apiculturist to collect and sell honey from wild killer bee colonies.

It was exciting and stimulating for Erik, and it led to new insights as he came to view the industrial world through their eyes. Erik noted, "The community I lived with struggled immensely to navigate the impact of industry, especially mining, deforestation, and oil exploration, encroaching on their traditional territory."

He says he witnessed an entirely new reality where "People experienced extreme suffering, living entirely within the crucible of humanity's impact on nature."

Erik's understanding of the value of work also changed, as he saw that Ecuadorians needed economic activity to put food on the table for their children. Work was no longer a game, as it had been for him in North America—here, work was survival.

The more he reflected on his good fortune—growing up in Canada, being part of a successful family-owned business with loving and supportive parents—the more he realized what a profound blessing it was. Erik began to realize that "all this was nothing that I deserved, nor could ever deserve. It was simply a gift."

As this understanding grew, *Erik began to discover the importance of working to contribute rather than working to impress.*

Coming Home to Contribute

When Erik returned to Canada and his family firm, these revelations continued to change him. The prideful know-it-all successor began transforming into a grateful hardworking apprentice, willing to learn and eager to contribute.

Over the next 10 years, Erik worked in roles of increasing responsibility, leading planters in a supervisory capacity and project-managing major reforestation contracts. He learned to take responsibility for the safety and well-being of his employees and accepted the mentorship of senior supervisors, district managers, and board members. From there, he took a position in the head office and found a new mentor in Sergio Gallego, one of the senior business analysts at Brinkman. Under Sergio's tutelage, Erik began to look at the company holistically, no longer focusing on the next tree to plant or the next contract to procure. In this light, he saw

BRINKMAN & ASSOCIATES REFORESTATION LTD.

the company as a mission, and he began to appreciate its vision, as well as the culture and ecosystem that linked hundreds of employees.

Sergio reinforced some of the lessons Erik had learned in the jungle and helped him realize the significance of serving the organization and working productively to create change. He encouraged Erik to go beyond criticism to take responsibility for the development of new strategies that would improve operations.

In response, Erik rolled up his sleeves, studied process improvement strategies, and developed proposals for productivity enhancement. He found new ways to bring value to the business by uncovering opportunities for financial improvements and updating management practices.

Sergio's mentoring was invaluable in teaching Erik how to serve the company—with a keen eye on the future. Inspired by Sergio, Erik decided to expand his business education, and as he explains, "I recently enrolled in an executive MBA program to help me gain the skills that I need to steer the family business through its next phase of development."

With the support of his mentor, Erik is becoming a constructive agent of change within Brinkman. Taking a tip from his mom's political experience, he reflects, "It's much easier to be a member of the opposition than it is to be in government. When you are not in power, you can always find something to criticize; but when you are in power, you need to make decisions and live with the results, in spite of the criticism that inevitably comes."

Gratitude Leads to Success

Erik grew up in the shadows of both his father, Dirk, and his mother, Joyce. The couple incorporated Brinkman in 1979 and took the company to incredible levels of success in a new industry. They were both successful, well-known entrepreneurs, and in 2001 Joyce began a political career that continues to this day. She previously served as the environment minister in British Columbia's provincial government, and since 2008 she has served as an elected official both in the federal Opposition and as a member of the Government of Canada. The Honourable Joyce Murray currently serves as president of the Treasury Board and minister of digital government.

Erik Brinkman (right) with his father, Dirk, CEO of Brinkman & Associates Reforestation Ltd.

With such accomplished parents, it is no wonder Erik always felt he had something to prove. The opportunities provided by the family business, along with the work ethic woven into the tree-planting culture, gave him a sense of determination to show everyone that he could be the best, without any special treatment. However, had it not been for his life-changing experiences in the Amazon, he might have never seen his position in the company for what it is: a privilege, and not a right. By spending such a pivotal time away from the family business, Erik developed a passion to serve the company with a "heart full of gratitude."

BREANNE RAMSAY (BRITT LAND & ENGAGEMENT)

"HARD ON ISSUES / SOFT ON PEOPLE"

Land development in Canada typically involves a time-consuming battle with red tape, politics, legalities, stakeholders, and activists. Nowhere is this truer than in our western and northern provinces, where a spectacular panorama of beauty covers soil that is rich in natural resources. Given our culture's current state  of heightened sensitivity towards sustainability, it takes a very skilled and talented leader to bring together diverse groups with varying interests; it takes even more skill to find a way to make that collaboration successful.

This is where Breanne Ramsay and her team truly shine. As the young CFO of Britt Land and Engagement, she navigates her clients through the maze of bureaucracy and compromise that is associated with any effort to bring about positive change.

Considering Every Angle

What has made her so successful? There is a host of reasons, but one essential element is Breanne's ability to think critically. She is highly skilled in gathering information, considering it from every angle, and then developing an innovative approach to solving a problem.

Critical thinking seems obligatory for someone in Breanne's position, where she must assess the potential impact of new industrial developments, unravel regulatory environments, and help clients navigate a landscape of dynamic and often unpredictable stakeholders. Each step forward is enormously complicated, yet Breanne and her team of professionals have established a sterling reputation for getting the job done.

Establishing Collaboration

Another prerequisite to their success is knowing how to establish collaboration amongst stakeholders with widely divergent interests. It is a challenge to find common ground—and then use it to establish a constructive process amongst environmental groups, Indigenous peoples, project proponents, and regulatory/legal authorities. From start to finish, this is complicated, expensive, and time-consuming. Yet it is in this context that Breanne and her partners excel through critical thinking.

Brittney Ramsay (president and CEO), Dayna Morgan (COO), Breanne Ramsay (CFO) (left to right)

As an example, Britt Land and Engagement was recently successful in helping an oil and gas company obtain support from both environmental and Indigenous groups for what was initially viewed as a rather controversial project. They accomplished this by listening to all groups, exploring multiple options, and ultimately recommending an innovative solution that accommodated everyone's needs. The agreement required a major redesign of the project, but in the end, the changes may even provide a more profitable outcome for the project sponsors.

Hard on Issues; Soft on People

At Britt Land, they have very high expectations of their employees. But they also have a philosophy of "working together," and Breanne has used her collaborative skills to help create a cohesive people-oriented culture within the company. Britt Land says its employees are "the lifeblood of our company," and its leaders make the well-being of their employees a priority. The company has even adopted a slogan to reflect this: "Here at Britt Land, *we are hard on issues, but soft on people.*"

In return, the payback is often huge. There is a sense of solidarity and care as they stand "shoulder to shoulder," solving the complex problems of their clients. According to Breanne, "We know if we put our people first, they will, in turn, go the extra mile."

Collaboration and Critical Thinking

Breanne was not yet 30 years old when she took on a senior role in her family company. However, as they say, times are changing, and potential successors are often assuming senior roles at younger ages. Today, Breanne works closely with her sister, Britt, the company CEO. Together with their COO, Dayna Morgan, the women lead and co-own Britt Land and Engagement. As a team, they bring their critical thinking skills to each new assignment, looking at every angle and working collaboratively to support and serve their clients.

ELLISHA MOTT (MOTT ELECTRIC)

"PATIENCE IS A DELIBERATE CHOICE"

Ellisha Mott is a woman who makes things happen. She is young, highly educated, accomplished, and committed to leading the way for women in the male-dominated construction industry. She is a vice-president and fourth-generation member of the family firm Mott Electric, one of the oldest and largest electrical contracting companies in Western Canada.

When someone has a resumé as impressive as Ellisha's by the age of 30, it is easy to presume that patience might not be her most obvious personality trait—and Ellisha would likely agree. She used to always be in a hurry to make her mark in life and says, "I was in a fiercely competitive race to grow up. Each time I would reach a personal milestone, I would barely pause to enjoy the achievement, partly because I was already focused on my next goal."

Ellisha's mom, Lissa, is referred to as the CEO (chief emotional officer) of the family. She often tried to use the powers of her "CEO position" to encourage Ellisha to be more patient. She would remind her of some of the great fables (such as *The Grasshopper and the Ant* or *The Tortoise and the Hare*) that illustrate the benefits of this virtue. However, like many children, Ellisha largely ignored her mother's advice and forged ahead, determined to live life at full throttle.

Ellisha Mott, 4th generation successor and vice-president, Mott Electric

Impatient Attitudes and Business Do Not Mix

This attitude may have helped Ellisha in completing her education and pursuing her career in business, but it did not serve her well when she first joined Mott Electric, especially when she found herself at the bottom of the organizational chart.

CONNECT WITH CONFIDENCE

SINCE 1930

MOTT ELECTRIC

Given her last name, Ellisha was well-known throughout the company as the founder's great-granddaughter. Anxious to dispel any rumours of favouritism or that her gender made her less competent, she was eager to prove herself. Naturally, her impatience easily rose to the surface as she pushed to succeed.

She says, "Every time I had to wait in line or was caught in a conversation that went on too long, I would battle internally with frustration. I would sometimes rap my nails on my desk, whispering to myself … *patience, patience, patience*. Yet, things seemed to always take too long. It was as if the world was just not keeping up!"

Over time, Ellisha came to recognize that this was not a wise approach, and as she entered management positions, she came to realize "that my eagerness to get ahead was actually holding me back." The family business would not tolerate an impatient leader for long!

Patience Is a Choice

More importantly, she began to understand *"that patience is not just a fleeting state of mind, but a conscious choice, something that takes deliberate, cognitive effort every single day."*

Patience does not come easily. Many successors (my younger self included) have had or will have to deal with this issue at some point in their careers, and, according to Ellisha, earlier is probably better because of its value in dealing with others in a family business.

She offers this newly found wisdom by saying, "Now I recognize the tremendous value of patience in all interpersonal interactions, and the extreme strife that can develop when it is absent. Rather than wrestling with forces beyond my control, I choose to believe that there is a greater purpose behind my wait, behind my delayed gratification, and behind my parents or my boss telling me … not yet."

Patience Is Action

Patience has given Ellisha an unexpected, yet refreshing, sense of emotional freedom. In the past, she often associated waiting with anxiety, simply because she considered it to be a mark of passivity or resignation. In her mind, patience was the equivalent of doing nothing.

That idea has since been abandoned. As she made the daily choice to be patient, she discovered that being patient is an active state that involves making a deliberate choice.

The choice to wait.

Learning Patience on the Farm

Ellisha's father, Dan, is president of the family firm, but that does not keep him from exploring his other interests, such as running the family ranch. Ranching is Dan's passion, and more than 20 years ago he acquired a few hundred acres near Aspen Grove, British Columbia. That land has become home to a working cattle ranch, and each year their herd of Black Angus cattle gives birth to over 100 calves.

Dan sees the ranch as a break from the office and city life, as well as a place that offers unique opportunities to develop life skills. On one memorable occasion, as the family joked about the complexity of family business, he quipped, "I realized that we could all get therapy, or we could get cows."

Ellisha notes that working on the ranch has provided opportunities for her to see the merits of being patient. During calving season, for example, she has seen that patience during labour is the best way to ensure a successful birth.

This holds true when the calf is born without complications or intervention as well as when the birth is difficult and requires a helping hand. Illustrating the importance of being patient during the birthing process, Ellisha notes that trying to prematurely grasp or pull the calf from the womb can result in broken limbs and other injuries, to the calf or mother.

Ellisha Mott, with her dad, Dan Mott, president and CEO of Mott Electric

Patience While Waiting for "Your Turn"

As Ellisha thinks about it, she recognizes that life has its own natural rhythm, and too often, whether it be on the ranch or in business, we try to force things. This has direct application for her as she seeks to give birth to her own leadership in the family company. Her experiences on the ranch have shown her how risky it can be to force change or to grasp for authority.

Consequently, she is developing more patience while she is waiting for her industry, her colleagues, and even her father to be ready for her to become the leader of the company. In the meantime, her demonstration of patience as the "heir apparent" is earning her the respect and admiration of those in her family and at Mott Electric.

She summarizes her thoughts on the subject of patience by saying, "I am grateful for my growing understanding of patience because it is imperative to the succession process and, moreover, to my psychological serenity. That is why I am constantly reminding myself: You will get what you want when you need it; be patient; it will be worth the wait."

MEILI COON (TRILOGY EXCURSIONS)

"PURSUING YOUR PASSION LEADS TO CONTENTMENT"

Imagine yourself in the Hawaiian Islands, where you marvel at the exotic vegetation, sandy beaches, and glorious mountain ranges. Above you, the sky is a brilliant blue, and all around you are the azure waters of the Pacific Ocean. As the sun rises on this particular day, you step onto the deck of a magnificent 65-foot catamaran, where you are greeted by the smell of freshly baked cinnamon buns, and the friendly staff welcome you with hot coffee, hot chocolate, and freshly squeezed orange juice.

As the sun steadily climbs into the cloudless sky, you sail to Molokini for a spectacular snorkelling experience under the watchful eye of the experienced crew. After spending an unforgettable morning splashing in the water, you recline on the foredeck for the leisurely sail home. En

Trilogy's catamarans, under full sail

route, you are treated to BBQ chicken, corn on the cob, and tropical libations. This is exactly what my family and I experienced a number of years ago during one of our most memorable family vacations.

Outstanding Hospitality

Welcome to Trilogy Excursions—Maui's leading on-water tourist attraction—offering visitors the ocean excursion of their dreams, whether it be the opportunity to snorkel with schools of exotic fish or to watch whales, dolphins, and other sea creatures in their natural habitat or to have a romantic evening dinner cruise. You can leave all your worries behind because the company is an industry leader in safety, environmental stewardship, and Hawaiian hospitality. For all these reasons and more, Trilogy has repeatedly been voted one of the premier tourist experiences in the Hawaiian Islands.

MeiLi Autumn Coon, founder and president of MeiLi Autumn Beauty

This enterprise is now owned and operated by the third-generation members of the Coon family. It was founded 46 years ago, when two Coon brothers headed to Hawaii as part of an epic family sailing trip around the world. Maui was supposed to be a pit stop to replenish their supplies, but it turned into a love affair with the land, its people, and two island girls. The boys had found their home. They planted roots, established families, and co-founded a business that allows them to share miraculous ocean adventures with the island's visitors.

Almost all of the second- and third-generation Coon family members work at Trilogy, enjoying the idyllic environment as they continue to build their successful, award-winning family business.

It is difficult to imagine that this is not the perfect picture of contentment for everyone, but there is one Coon family member who has found her sense of contentment by following a different path.

A Different Passion But the Same Spirit of Adventure

MeiLi Coon is a gifted aesthetician and makeup artist. These are her passions, and she has chosen to follow them rather than to work in the family business. It may seem like a far cry from ocean excursions and adventures, but her determination to forge her own way on an unknown path reflects the same spirit that inspired her dad and uncle when they set out for the South Pacific almost 50 years ago.

In 2014, MeiLi founded her own bridal services business, MeiLi Autumn Beauty. Today the business is thriving, and she is happy in her chosen career. More importantly, she has found contentment in pursuing her own dreams.

Three Secrets to Contentment

MeiLi has given a lot of thought to what constitutes contentment. With great wisdom and insight, she offers the three attitudes that she says have been crucial in cultivating a heart of contentment.

1. **Cultivate Gratitude.** MeiLi actively stimulates a sense of gratitude each day by reminding herself that the vast majority of the people in the world would happily switch places with her, especially if it meant living in the Hawaiian Islands, with its natural beauty, temperate climate, and magnificent culture. *As the sun rises each morning, MeiLi's heart beats with gratitude.*

2. **Stay Present**. MeiLi has developed the habit of being present each day and enjoying life as it comes. To her, that means she is not focused on the past or past regrets; nor is she looking to the future to bring her satisfaction and contentment. Instead, she lives in the present, experiencing life as the beautiful gift that it is. Her ability to remain focused and present also contributes to her capabilities as a great makeup artist, uniquely enabling her to do an exemplary job for each and every patron.

3. **Avoid Comparison.** MeiLi knows that there are always people who have more authority, more responsibility, and more financial resources than she does. At the same time, she realizes that there are always those who have far less. MeiLi has learned that contentment is not rooted in comparison or in acquiring more things. She does not focus on her bank account or waste time comparing herself to her siblings or cousins who work in the family business. She says, "I am content because I have a job that gives me the freedom I want to spend time daily with my precious little daughter, and I continue to earn enough to pay the bills and to afford my own little apartment."

She also takes time to remind herself that she is "living [her] dreams, one day at a time" and "Regardless of what you have, it is always enough."

The Temptation to Do More

MeiLi has a bright future, as she continues to work hard, grow her business, and extend her reputation as a highly respected artist. But she is also very aware of the constant pressure to do more when you run your

own business. She says, "There is literally no end to the potential for creating new streams of revenue, potential for growth, new marketing strategies, and better systems. It never ends."

In the face of this, MeiLi knows that she is, once again, confronted with a choice to be content, emphatically stating, "Either we find alignment with our business and enjoy the journey or we can let it become an obsessive force that robs us of our joy."

With great insight she notes, "If you are not content with where you are at with your business, *at this very moment*, then in six months or five years, when you hit those benchmarks, make that goal, or see the bank statement with those extra 0s, it will never be enough. If you live for the next horizon, you will find yourself always reaching for the next thing, and you will miss out on celebrating the steps that get you there."

MeiLi acknowledges that it is good to have lofty goals for the future of your company, but she also points out, "We will not have a feeling of victory when we stand on the peak of whatever mountain we've been climbing if we've grumbled the whole way while getting there."

Recognizing the need to enjoy the journey is why she regularly asks herself the following three questions:

Is this fun?
Are you enjoying it?
Would you do it if you weren't getting paid?

If she cannot truthfully answer these questions with a yes, then she knows it is time for her to change her path in life.

MeiLi summarizes her thoughts on contentment this way: "If you can have joy in the beginning (the rush of launching), joy in the execution (establishing well-oiled systems), and joy in the accomplishment, then you will have mastered not just the art of business, but you will have cultivated the art of living well and being content. You will naturally exude a spirit of gratitude and contentment, which will, in turn, make your victories that much more rewarding."

SECTION V
Exemplary Leaders & Role Models

Einstein was insatiably curious; Nelson Mandela was forgiving beyond all expectations; Benjamin Franklin pursued humility with great dedication. These leaders were exemplary in many ways.

For our purposes, let's examine how each of these well-known historic figures exemplify one of the traits we've discussed.

As such, each may serve as a role model for family enterprise successors. While none of them are without flaws, as history attests, they can be a source of inspiration and guidance for anyone wanting to develop these characteristics.

By following in the footsteps of these exemplars, a family enterprise successor is able to create a leadership style that helps ensure both their personal and professional success.

BENJAMIN FRANKLIN

CHOOSING TO CULTIVATE HUMILITY

Benjamin Franklin was one of those extraordinary people who seem to succeed at whatever they do. He was, at various times in his life, an author, a scholar, a physicist, an inventor, the first postmaster general of the United States, a governor of Pennsylvania, and one of America's founding fathers. There are few people who can claim such a varied and distinguished resumé.

Beyond all of these successes, Franklin serves as a remarkable example of an individual who was dedicated to developing the virtues related to personal character.

At the young age of 20, when most of his achievements were still before him, he found himself frustrated by a lack of productivity in his life and set out on a project that he called "moral perfection."[198] His insatiable desire for self-improvement led him on a path to rigorous self-examination where he ruthlessly assessed his own shortcomings. He composed a list of 12 virtues or areas of his life that he felt needed improvement and then sought the advice of a friend, asking him to look at the list. *His friend bluntly told him that the list was incomplete because he had failed to mention pride.* Apparently, Franklin had a reputation of being arrogant in relating to others and dismissive of their thoughts during conversations.

Reaching for Humility

Franklin admitted that sacrificing his pride would not be an easy task. It would be a lifelong battle, and even if he should conquer it, he reasoned, the accomplishment itself would only serve to fill him with greater pride.

> Franklin had a reputation of being arrogant.

In the record of his life, published after his death as *The Autobiography of Benjamin Franklin*, he writes, "In reality, there is, perhaps, no one of our natural passions so hard to subdue as pride. Disguise it, struggle with it,

Benjamin Franklin, born in Boston, Massachusetts, Jan. 17, 1706

beat it down, stifle it, mortify it as much as one pleases, it is still alive and will every now and then peep out and show itself … for, even if I could conceive that I had completely overcome it, I should probably be proud of my humility."[199]

However, as a result of his friend's honest feedback, Franklin added humility to the list of 12 virtues he was seeking to cultivate. As a part of his quest for moral perfection, he created an 18th century version of "a little black book" and used it to monitor his progress. He recorded daily self-assessments that noted how often he failed or succeeded in his attempts to develop each of the 13 virtues he was striving to attain. Using this dedicated strategy, he began developing the characteristics that were consistent with the kind of person he wanted to become.

He made earnest attempts to control his pride, particularly in his interactions with others. He writes, "When another asserted something that I thought an error, I denied myself the pleasure of contradicting him abruptly … observing that in certain cases or circumstances his opinion would be right."[200]

Notably, as he controlled his penchant for contradiction, he found that his conversations were much more pleasant and, perhaps most significantly, that his own opinions found "a readier reception and less contradiction."[201]

Putting Franklin's Conviction to the Test

I first heard Benjamin Franklin's story on an audiobook while my wife, Alison, and I were driving on the Florida Turnpike, and I vividly recall my astonishment at Franklin's determination to not disagree—even when he thought the other speaker was wrong. His new approach to conversation was effective and, I had to admit, compellingly attractive.

> "I decided to deny myself the privilege of ever disagreeing with anyone."

I decided I would like to become more like him in discussions with others and told Alison that I would now strive to "deny myself the privilege of ever disagreeing with anyone."

That evening, we found ourselves heading to dinner with another couple. We were planning to eat at one of the hotel's restaurants, which was located on the second floor. However, after an earlier attempt to get to that particular restaurant, I knew that it was only possible to access it from the ground floor. When we got in the elevator, one of our friends pushed the button for the second floor, apparently believing that we could access the restaurant from there. Knowing this was impossible, I started to explain that we needed to go to the ground floor. That is, until a gentle nudge from my wife reminded me of my desire to "never disagree."

I was virtually certain that our friend was wrong, but what would it profit me to argue?

So, I admitted that I could be mistaken, and much to my surprise, he responded in kind, saying, "I could be wrong too; let's go down to the ground floor." I will never forget that moment; I had denied myself the opportunity to disagree, and a pleasing solution immediately presented itself.

> "My list of virtues contained at first but twelve, but a quaker friend having kindly informed me that I was generally thought proud, that my pride showed itself frequently in conversation, that I was not content with being in the right when discussing any point, but was overbearing and rather insolent … endeavouring to cure myself, if I could, of this vice or folly among the rest … I added humility to my list."[202]

ALBERT EINSTEIN

INSATIABLE CURIOSITY

The name Albert Einstein is legendary and virtually synonymous with superior intelligence.

As a world-renowned scientist, he is revered in scholarly circles for his contributions to theoretical physics, even as his distinctive appearance has made him an icon in popular culture. Although he died more than 50 years ago, photographs depicting him with his wild, unkempt hair have come to symbolize what it means to be a scientist. He is at once considered to be somewhat wild and the epitome of brilliance.

Einstein is most commonly known for creating the algebraic formula $E=mc^2$ and as the genius who developed the theory of relativity. However, in spite of all his scientific discoveries, Einstein did not see himself as unique or especially gifted. With great self-awareness and characteristic modesty, he once famously quipped, *"I have no special talent. I am only passionately curious."*[203]

> "I have no special talent. I am only passionately curious."

Einstein believed that curiosity was the key to knowledge and that the process of asking questions was the doorway to discovery. He purportedly once noted, "If I had an hour to solve a problem and my life depended on the solution, I would spend the first 55 minutes determining the proper question to ask, for once I know the proper question, I could solve the problem in less than five minutes."

Driven to Ask Questions

Note that Einstein's problem-solving genius was rooted in asking the right questions and his desire to determine the crux of the problem. He was inclined to ask, "What is the basic problem or question that needs to be answered?" For many of us, it can be surprising to discover that the real issue that needs to be resolved

Albert Einstein, 1879–1955
"If you can't explain it simply, you don't understand it well enough."

is not always the one that is first presented to us. That is why we should endeavour to cultivate our curiosity and our ability to ask the questions that will help us get to the heart of the matter.

Einstein's curiosity was insatiable; he was driven to ask questions, not because he wanted answers but because he wanted to explore new horizons. It was his indefatigable search for fresh ideas that led him to his remarkable discoveries.

During his lifetime, Einstein made numerous references to the inadequacy of intelligence on its own. On one occasion, he famously observed, "Imagination is more important than knowledge. Knowledge is limited. Imagination encircles the world." In his view, both imagination and curiosity are superior traits that are needed to transform mere intelligence into an intellect that can make a difference.

Einstein certainly had a superior intellect, but he believed that all of his achievements resulted more from his curiosity than from his intelligence, and he told others, *"The important thing is to not stop questioning."*

"The important thing is to not stop questioning."

GANDHI

LEADING BY LISTENING

Mohandas Karamchand Gandhi was a devout religious man who wore simple clothing, ate simple foods, and, for the most part, spoke in a soft voice. Yet he was one of the greatest political activists of the 20th century, and his non-violent approach to change still serves as an inspiration to those fighting for civil rights in countries around the world.

Gandhi was born in British-occupied India in 1869, and he devoted most of his life to leading India in its quest for independence. He studied law in London and later made his way to South Africa, where he gained some prominence for defending his fellow Indians from bureaucratic oppression. This no doubt influenced his antipathy towards colonialism, and when he returned to India in 1915, he began his remarkable lifelong journey to bring about change through non-violent civil disobedience.

> Gandhi's remarkable leadership was rooted in listening.

Much of what he accomplished was started by simply listening.

Leaders Are Listeners

We typically think of prominent political leaders as being master orators who carefully use their words to inspire and persuade. Eventually, as his prominence grew, Gandhi also became a gifted communicator and an inspiring leader, but he first became a leader of the Indian independence movement by listening.

At a time when there were plenty of shrill voices and activists demanding that the British leave India, Gandhi developed credibility primarily by *listening* to the needs and concerns of his fellow countrymen and serving as their legal advocate. In this way, he came to be trusted and to enjoy tremendous influence amongst his country-

Gandhi, 1869-1948
Born in British-occupied India, he devoted most of his life
to leading India in its quest for independence.

men, including peasants, farmers, and labourers. Similarly, he gained the attention of the authorities for his willingness to work within the British legal system.

Gandhi was allegedly able to listen even to his enemies instead of getting angry. This was remarkable, and such magnanimity was perhaps one of his greatest weapons in his successful quest to bring about the liberation of India.

> *Listening to his enemies was one of Gandhi's greatest weapons in the liberation of India.*

Listening to Those Who Oppose Us

After the highly controversial and non-violent revolution had begun, Gandhi faced fierce opposition, and his opponents would often write him to decry his approach. Desai, one of his loyal aids, "feared that the vengeful letters would only distract Gandhi from his mission of nonviolence and decided to shield his leader from all the negativity. He hid the bad letters and quietly answered them himself."

But it did not take long for Gandhi to realize that something was amiss, and he told Desai, "I seem to be getting only nice letters lately. Where are the critical ones?" Desai admitted that he had kept the hate mail from Gandhi. We can all learn from Gandhi's response to the situation: "I need the negative letters. My critics are my best friends—they show me what I have still to learn."

What a liberating insight! Rather than reject criticism, Gandhi chose to embrace it and learn from it. His detractors became his tutors.

Rather than simply becoming a self-righteous advocate and a crusader for his own cause, Gandhi was open to listening—always seeking to hear more, know more, and understand more.

Gandhi's approach has since inspired leaders of civil rights movement such as Martin Luther King Jr. and Nelson Mandela. It has inspired both world leaders and those in the lowliest of places. It is of little wonder that it also holds great potential to inform and assist family business successors today.

Successors as Agents of Change

> Rather than reject criticism, Gandhi embraced it and learned from it.

Family enterprise successors often want to be catalysts for change. I know, because I was once a young executive who tried to change our family business by constantly advocating for radical change. I believed that those who led our business at that time ought to have been much more open to new ideas.

So I became an agitator for change, but not in the way that Gandhi did. I did not ask questions or cultivate my listening skills, and I certainly did not seek to understand the perspective of those in charge. I was demanding and critical and sought a result that worked for me instead of a solution that worked for the good of all the stakeholders. In the end, this resulted in me being removed from the business, and, as a consequence, I forfeited my opportunity to have any influence at all.

Wise successors are those who resist the temptation to become self-righteous advocates or crusaders for their own pet projects. Like Gandhi, they recognize that their most important asset is their ability to listen. Wise successors ask questions and then truly listen to the answers in an effort to understand what is best for all the stakeholders. Then they can become an educated agent of change who can champion solutions that are in the best interests of everyone.

Gandhi listened to the people of India, and he heard their cry for change. But that is only half of the story, because Gandhi also listened to the British authorities. By listening to both sides, Gandhi was instrumental in finding a path forward that honoured and respected both sides.

As has been noted in earlier chapters, listening can become an extremely powerful tool when it is coupled with humility and empathy. In fact, these other two qualities not only amplify the impact of a good listener; they are foundational to an individual who wants to improve their listening skills. If a person then adds curiosity to the mix, they have the potential to turbocharge the impact they make. (See diagram on page 152.)

MOTHER TERESA

CHANGING THE WORLD WITH EMPATHY

Countless people know the name Mother Teresa. Perhaps most would recognize her face, especially when surrounded by her trademark blue-and-white habit. Many would know that she helped the poor in India and was canonized a saint by the Roman Catholic Church. But very few would be able to say much about the remarkable humanitarian work that has been accomplished by this diminutive saint.

I first read about Mother Teresa when attending university, and I was inspired by the depth of her character and the many rare qualities that truly set her apart as a human being. As a young man who sought to understand leadership in its various forms (including athletics and business), I was both amazed and inspired by her leadership skills.

Leadership? This tiny woman who was barely five feet tall and lived most of her life caring for the poor in the slums of Calcutta?

By today's standards, she was by no means a typical leader. There were no Twitter followers, book tours, or marketing campaigns. But she was a great leader nonetheless. She was a woman who saw what needed to change and then created solutions to facilitate that change. As we might say about most effective leaders, "She took the bull by the horns and did what had to be done."

> Mother Teresa dispensed love and empathy wherever she went.

As a young nun, she believed that God had called her to leave the convent, live amongst the poor, and serve them. She went into the streets of Calcutta by herself, and from then on, from dawn to dusk for the rest of her life, she dispensed love and empathy to everyone she met.

*Mother Teresa, wearing her trademark
blue-and-white habit
"Spread love everywhere you go. Let no one ever
come to you without leaving happier."*

It was not long before others began following her, wanting to work alongside this amazing woman. In time, even the prime minister of India heard about what she was doing. In 1950, the Vatican gave her permission to organize those who were helping her into a congregation, known as the Missionaries of Charity. She then started a school and founded the Home for the Dying Destitutes. During her lifetime, she saw this charity grow to a congregation of 4,500 nuns, each of them following Mother Teresa's example by taking vows of chastity, poverty, obedience, and "wholehearted free service to the poorest of the poor."

Over the years, these women also managed homes for those dying from HIV/AIDS, leprosy, and tuberculosis. There were soup kitchens, dispensaries, mobile clinics, orphanages, and schools.

All of this came about because Mother Teresa saw the need and acted with empathy to do something about it. She once said, "Our poor do not need pity and sympathy … they need love and compassion." She added, "I can sincerely tell you they give us much more than we give them."

Her example may seem too much for us to aspire to in our ordinary lives. Yet the challenge that she set for herself and all others is very simple and very doable:

Let no one ever come to you without leaving better and happier. Be the living expression of God's kindness: kindness in your face, kindness in your eyes, kindness in your smile.

Moved by Empathy

Empathy is the virtue at the heart of all that Mother Teresa did during her lifetime. She recognized that she did not have much to offer those dying in the streets of Calcutta's slums. In fact, in the beginning, she realized that she had neither medicine nor medical training, and there were no hospitals that would admit the lowest in the Indian caste system—those destined to live in the gutters.

> *Empathy moved Mother Teresa to cradle the poor and dying in her arms and to pray for them.*

Most of us would have simply passed these people by, thinking there was nothing we could do because the problem was either too big or unsolvable. But love moved this young woman to touch each of these impoverished souls. With great empathy, she cradled them in her arms and prayed for them. Her genuine love and compassion flowed into their lives, and many died knowing that at least one person had loved them and cared for them during their final hours.

It was her one-on-one ministry that captivated people everywhere. Eventually, it was images of her empathizing with these people that gave her a worldwide sphere of influence and brought her thousands of helpers to share her burden.

Mother Teresa's empathy changed lives, and it served as the foundation for all that she accomplished in this world.

Empathy in Family Business

Business leaders, including family enterprise successors, are often looking for concrete answers to the problems that they face. Unfortunately, when they get so focused on trying to solve problems, they fail to see the needs of the people right in front of them.

Similarly, in my own life I have often been too eager to find "the answer" to someone's problem when all they really needed was someone to listen. I have found this idea challenging, and I know that young successors and business people at any stage of life can find it difficult to slow down long enough to genuinely empathize—it feels like a waste of time to listen to others as they share their problems or concerns.

However, if we as leaders simply take the time to listen and offer empathy to those with whom we work, those around us will feel cared for and understood. This small shift in showing care to others has the potential to change a personal or professional situation dramatically. As Mother Teresa's life has demonstrated, if we begin with empathy, we may be amazed by the great things that follow.

NELSON MANDELA

FORGIVENESS ON A GRAND SCALE

Nelson Mandela's story is typically told as one of how the human spirit can survive and ultimately triumph over the worst circumstances. But as I reflect on his story now, it seems to better describe a man whose horrible circumstances served to shape his spirit, eventually making him into a better man.

Early on in his life, he was far from the serene and gracious diplomat that the world saw as he advanced in age. In fact, reflecting on his youth, he noted that "a steady accumulation of a thousand slights, a thousand indignities, a thousand unremembered moments, produced in me an anger, a rebelliousness, a desire to fight the system that imprisoned my people."[204]

The systematic oppression of the black majority by a white minority became South African law in 1948, and this motivated Mandela to join the African National Congress and engage in 15 years of activist opposition. The Sharpeville Massacre in 1960 (when South African police killed 69 people by opening fire on a peaceful crowd of black protestors) motivated Mandela to abandon his peaceful protests and push for the establishment of a military wing in the ANC. He was eventually arrested for participating in political sabotage and, in 1964, sentenced to life in prison.

Prison

Mandela was sent to the notorious Robben Island prison, which Mandela himself described as "the harshest, most iron-fisted outpost in the South African penal system." Prisoners slept on straw mats, crushed rocks in a quarry, and could only receive one visitor and one letter every six months. Mandela was revered as a leader amongst prisoners and, as a result, he was singled out for torture, solitary confinement, and extra punishment by the prison guards. In fact, they personally welcomed him to prison with the words "Here you will die."

Nelson Mandela, statesman and nation builder
"We must strive to be moved by a generosity of spirit that will enable us to outgrow the hatred and conflicts of the past."

Other prisoners have talked about some of the humiliating treatment that Mandela received. In one instance, "guards ordered him to dig and then climb into a grave-shaped trench in the prison yard … Then, as he lay in the dirt, they unzipped their trousers and urinated on him."[205]

> *The guards welcomed him to prison with the words "Here you will die."*

During those painfully long years, he had ample time to consider what he was going to do in response to the pain that he had experienced. In 2006, when I visited his tiny brick-walled cell on Robben Island, I was astonished that he could make the choice to forgive in spite of such hardship and profound mental anguish. Mandela, with incredible grace, made the decision to forgive even as he endured the years of humiliation and degradation.

Discovering Forgiveness

When one of the worst jailers, who was a constant abuser of Mandela, left Robben Island for another post, he called Mandela to his office to wish him the best. Mandela wrote about the surprising experience, saying that he could see there was another side to this man's nature: *"[he] was not evil; his inhumanity had been foisted upon him by an inhuman system. He behaved like a brute because he was rewarded for brutish behaviour."*[206]

He added, "It was a useful reminder that all men, even the most seemingly cold-blooded, have a core of decency, and that if their heart is touched, they are capable of changing."[207]

It seems that Mandela's heart was touched by the incident, as the brief encounter helped him to see apartheid as a corrupt system that made otherwise decent people do horrible things. In other words, apartheid was the real enemy, not the whites. It was a huge step towards a spirit of forgiveness and reconciliation, which began to soften Mandela's heart even as he suffered in prison.

Another factor that led to Mandela's change of heart was the realization that South Africa could not survive unless the majority (blacks) and the minority (whites) could work together. He concluded that "whites were Africans as well, and that in any future dispensation the majority [the blacks] would need the minority [the whites]."[208]

By choosing the road of forgiveness instead of the path of bitterness, he could create an environment that could bring healing to his country.

A Higher Purpose Through Forgiveness and Reconciliation

When he began to see South Africa as a country where blacks needed whites and vice versa, he began to think beyond himself. Forgiveness came as he realized that, as a leader, he had to consider

> By choosing to forgive, Mandela brought healing to his country.

the welfare of all of his countrymen, both black and white. He wanted what was best for them, and he wisely realized that the eyes of the world were on him. He was aware that by choosing the road of forgiveness instead of retribution, he could lead his people and create an entirely new path for them to follow.

As the world exerted greater pressure on South Africa, Mandela was mellowing in his views. In 1990, when he was finally released in an effort to negotiate an end to apartheid, "he called not for revenge, but for forgiveness and reconciliation," and as the "world took note of such a powerful heart and mind," the system of apartheid came to an end.[209]

Years later, when Mandela was about to become the president of South Africa, he was asked to provide a list of people he wished to invite to his inaugural dinner. World leaders would be there, but the only person that Mandela insisted be invited to attend was his former jailer.

Why? Because Mandela wanted to "liberate the oppressed and the oppressor both."

Mandela showed his countrymen the way of forgiveness. In doing so, he showed it to all of us.

Two decades later, Mandela is still a study in forgiveness, and scholars have urged us to follow Mandela's thinking in showing compassion to those who have hurt us. According to psychologist Dr. Janice Harper,

> Forgiveness requires compassion … remembering the humanity in each person—whether we respect or like them or not is irrelevant. Recognizing that those who harm us have made poor choices—choices that may have cost them nothing, may even have advantaged them, but for which we alone must suffer—does not mean that they are exempt from moral

> responsibility for their actions. It means only that we understand they were not acting as "monsters," but as humans. And humans can indeed behave monstrously at times.[210]

If Nelson Mandela can find it in his heart to forgive, certainly we can too.

KIM PHUC

GRATITUDE RISES FROM THE HORRORS OF WAR

It is one of the most iconic images of the 20th century. The cover photo for *Time* magazine (June 8, 1972) depicts a brutal day of horror and death during the Vietnam War. Panicked and terrorized children, the most vulnerable victims of any war, flee from their homes as the deadly chemical napalm falls like rain from the sky. Nine-year-old Kim Phuc is the naked girl at the centre of the picture. She is screaming in pain as the napalm sticks to her skin, generating unbearably intense heat as it burns.

That morning, South Vietnamese forces dropped chemical bombs of napalm, killing many of its own citizens, as it sought to eradicate the North Vietnamese troops that had seized this village. The impact of napalm is horrific; it is a sticky, firey fluid that clings to the skin and burns anything it touches. The wall of fire extinguished the fibres of Kim's clothes as she ran away from her village "naked and shrieking in pain and fear."[211]

How could anyone survive this horror? And how on earth could a story of gratitude emerge from such pain? The answers to these questions are both miraculous and inspiring.

Meeting Kim Phuc

Forty-five years after that photo was taken, I sat at a private luncheon where Kim Phuc was our guest of honour. There was complete silence as we waited for her to speak; we were eager to know more of her courage and ability to overcome, but we also knew that her words would not be easy for us to hear.

As this tiny, gracious woman took her place before the microphone, she quietly spoke her first words: "Whenever I think of that day, I thank God."

Kim Phuc, Vietnam, June 8, 1972
Nine-year-old Kim runs down the road in the village of Trang Bang, her clothes having been burned completely off by napalm.

Her voice was not much louder than a whisper, but her words struck the crowd like a clap of thunder. Perhaps anticipating our surprise and astonishment, she explained, "I was the only one in our little village who didn't die after being hit by napalm that day. *I am so grateful* that my life was spared."

> "whenever I think of that day, I thank God."

Kim's Story

Kim began her presentation by showing a decades-old video that depicted the events of that fateful day. We witnessed the towering clouds of black smoke and the blazing inferno that was unleashed by the bombs that were dropped on her village.

As she fled from the chemical rainfall, her skin was burning, and all she could shout in her panic was "HOT, HOT, TOO HOT!" A nearby soldier heard her plea for help, and, not really knowing what to do, he poured cold water over her head in an attempt to relieve her suffering. But it only made the pain worse. When napalm is exposed to oxygen, it causes a chemical reaction that heats the toxic substance even more, ultimately to an unimaginable 5,000°F (2,760°C). The pain was so overwhelming that Kim passed out.

Yet, even as she recounted this event, Kim paused again to say, almost with reverence, "*Every time I think about that soldier, I thank God.*" He made her suffering worse, but Kim graciously explained, "He reached out to me in kindness, and *I am grateful for that.*" With a wry smile, she added, "Besides, he made the napalm so hot that I passed out. So, in effect, he put me out of my pain."

> "The extreme pain he caused was overwhelming, but every time I think about that soldier, I thank God."

The next good Samaritan to come her way was photographer Nick Ut, the man who took the award-winning photograph. When Kim fainted, he scooped her up and used his Associated Press van to take her to a hospital. At first, the staff refused to treat her, believing that she could not recover from such severe burns. Nick utilized his media credentials to force them to at least bandage her wounds and then transfer her to a larger hospital in Saigon.

Abandoned in the Morgue

When she was admitted to the second hospital, the doctors took one look at her and concluded that there was nothing they could do to help. She had burns to 50 percent of her body, and they believed that it was only a matter of time before she would die. Condemned to death, Kim was sent to the morgue, where she lay, for three mind-numbing days, amongst the decaying corpses.

She was alone; she had been abandoned to death; yet, she was still alive. Little did she know that her mother had followed her trail and was walking, by foot, the three-day journey to Saigon to find her child.

Kim's mother found her in the morgue and, presuming she was dead, pulled her body close to her own and spoke to her. At the sound of her mother's voice, Kim opened her eyes. Miraculously, she had survived! Kim's mother then took her back to the hospital to demand that she be treated.

It took over 16 surgeries and years of medical attention for Kim to be nursed back to health. Over an extended period of time, she was subjected to a daily ritual of having her burnt skin pulled from her body. Each day she fell into an unconsious state during the painful procedure.

At first, Kim struggled to understand how she could have been abandoned for those three dark days! Surely it was just one more display of the cruelties she had experienced at the hands of other people. That is, until she met a doctor who specializes in treating napalm burns.

When he heard her story, he remarked, "You should be thankful for those three days."

Kim was shocked. Thankful for being abandoned? Thankful for lying with rotting corpses while maggots crawled all over her body? How could she ever be thankful for that?

Then the doctor told Kim her story from a very different perspective. If Kim had been treated when she first arrived at the hospital in Saigon, the nurses would have unwrapped her bandages and exposed her skin to oxygen, which would have fed the burning napalm once again. Given her fragile, critical condition, this would have undoubtedly killed her. But when she was sent to the cold, dark morgue, wrapped in bandages, the chemical reaction that fed the fire slowed down and eventually stopped burning her skin.

> "Whenever I think of the morgue, I thank God."

Kim concluded her thoughts with the arresting statement *"Now, whenever I think of the morgue, I thank God."*

Summarizing, Kim outlined her perspective on all that she had experienced. In the midst of the very worst circumstances, she had been given several gifts.

A well-meaning soldier who put her in so much pain that she passed out. *A gift.*

A photographer who took the time to get involved and take her to the hospital. *A gift.*

Three days in a morgue where the fire that was burning her body was snuffed out. *A gift.*

Cultivating Gratitude

Kim lives a life marked by a deep sense of gratitude. Where many see only pain, she can see a gift.

No matter what our life circumstances are, we all have much to be grateful for. As Canadians, we have freedom, and we live in a nation that is not torn apart by war.

If you are reading this book, you also have your eyesight and likely have enjoyed some degree of financial success. If you are also a successor in a business family, you have more opportunities and advantages than most and a future that you can look forward to with optimism.

So how can we cultivate gratitude in our lives? It does not require a seminar, a coach, or even a complicated change in our thinking. To begin the journey, we simply need to take a few moments each day to be thankful for what we have.

WALT DISNEY

CRITICAL THINKING AND THE MAGIC KINGDOM

The genius of Disney's creativity is to be found in the interplay between his capacity as "the dreamer, the realist and the critic."[212]

Walt Disney is remembered primarily as a creative genius and a dreamer. Yet the unique way in which he displayed that creativity and brought his dreams to life would not have been possible if he had not possessed one more key attribute: critical thinking skills. He was passionate in his efforts to gather information, take in the views of others, and produce truly novel and memorable results.

Critical Thinking Finds Ways to Improve

Author Robert B. Dilts provides the following anecdote about Disney, using it to illustrate some of the key elements of his cognitive processes and the brilliance of his critical thinking skills:

> Just prior to the opening of the … Pirates of the Caribbean … at Disneyland, Disney was making a last-minute inspection … He was dissatisfied with the [scene] depicting New Orleans. He felt something important was missing that would make [it] more authentic but could not put his finger on what it was … Disney gathered around him as many people as he could locate, including the maintenance and food service employees. He asked everyone to effectively go to "second position"—that is, imagine they were one of the characters in the scene, participating in what was taking place. Disney then systematically took everyone through each of the sensory representational systems.

© Disney

Pirates of the Caribbean, Disneyland
As a result of Walt Disney's critical thinking, this attraction
even has tiny (electric powered) lightning bugs.
This imaginative detail adds both a touch of
realism and wonder.

He asked, "Does it look right?" He had spent a lot of time and money on authentic costumes and foliage and had modelled his buildings from New Orleans's French Quarter down to the wrought iron decorations.

"Does it sound right?" he queried. He had installed the most modern audio technology with multiple soundtracks, each timed and positioned perfectly to provide the sounds of music, voices, boats and even animals.

He then asked, "Does it feel right?" He had controlled and adjusted the temperature and humidity to match that of a sultry New Orleans night.

He next asked, "Does it smell right?" He had created an elaborate setup by which he could infuse and intermingle smells of spicy Cajun food with the smells of gunpowder, moss and brine.

Everything checked out, but he still felt something was missing. "What is it?" he asked. Finally, a young man who had been sweeping one of the floors said, "Well, Mr. Disney, I grew up in the South and what strikes me is that on a summer night like this there ought to be lightning bugs."

Disney's face lit up. "That's it!" he exclaimed. The young man was given a handsome bonus and Disney actually imported live lightning bugs, at a considerable cost, until he could work out a scheme to imitate them.[213]

In this situation, Disney was not being negative or critical; he was simply looking for a better way. He wanted to ensure that the Pirates of the Caribbean attraction would meet his exacting standards. Walt's critical thinking had been purposeful and solution-oriented. He was looking for an outstanding result, and that is what he achieved by enlisting others in this quest. When he received input that made the critical difference, he was the first person to express appreciation, both verbally and tangibly.

As this story demonstrates, critical thinking, at its best, does not emphasize what is wrong or deficient. Instead, it focuses on finding a way to improve things and to make them better.

Critical thinking requires that new products and services be rigorously stress tested and not be introduced without first being carefully examined to ensure that they meet the highest standards.

© Disney

Walt Disney, animator and filmmaker
Apparently, Walt once quipped, "We don't make movies in order to make money; instead we make money so we can make more movies."

A Well Thought Out Design

Disney used his critical thinking skills to come up with new ways to resolve age-old problems while developing his revolutionary theme park. He used the following two questions as he considered how to make Disneyland both unique and significantly better:

1. What is wrong with existing theme parks? (What is the problem?)
2. What can we do to overcome these deficiencies? (What can we do about it?)

For example, when asked why he had created Disneyland, Disney said that the idea was born out of his disappointment visiting theme parks when he was a young man. His recollections included garbage everywhere, long lines and waits, as well as activities that were either too scary or too boring.

These were the problems, and so Disney looked for solutions.

He made cleanliness a top priority, and as a result Disneyland has been, from the beginning, renowned for its cleanliness. He ensured that it had a family friendly atmosphere, with activities to keep all ages entertained. By way of illustration, he introduced Disney film characters to interact with toddlers, while also developing rides with sufficient thrills and excitement to keep the teenagers coming back for more.

He even considered the time that families spent walking around the park. Disney wanted to ensure that walking was not long and tedious, so he made it an adventure just to move around the park; there were steam trains, a monorail, and PeopleMovers—all designed to make navigation easy and entertaining. Disney was one of the first to make strollers readily available for the youngest visitors, easing the trip for parents while making it exciting and easy for young children, and even babies.

These are just some of the remarkable details that make Disneyland so innovative and welcoming for everyone. Another example of Walt's critical thinking is how he responded to the problem of waiting in line for attractions.

> The rides at Disneyland are all memorable, but as a result of Disney's critical thinking skills, so is the time spent waiting in lines.

Waiting in Line

Disney wanted to change the way his visitors thought about waiting in lines, so he began to consider how he could make "waiting" a part of the Disney experience. For answers, he asked his two important questions:

1. **What is the problem?** As he thought about it, Disney concluded that the problem was not necessarily the waiting but the sense of boredom combined with the lack of progress that together created a negative experience.

2. **What can we do about it?** Disney purposed to create lines that were constantly moving, enabling visitors to remain active as they gradually snaked back and forth toward the front of the line. In addition, he artfully introduced sights and sounds that were reflective of the upcoming attraction so that a sense of excitement was gradually building as the attraction drew closer.

For example, while waiting to ride the Matterhorn Bobsleds, visitors are given a sense of what it might be like to hike in the Swiss Alps and experience the thrill of going higher as the mountain rises majestically to touch the sky.

Almost 40 years later, I can still recall the day I waited for over two hours to enter the Haunted Mansion at Disneyland. I remember being fascinated by the wrought-iron fencing, unusual architecture, and humorous inscriptions on the cemetery gravestones. It was a long wait, but it was definitely not boring!

Next time you visit Disneyland, pay attention to what it's like to wait in line for an attraction. The attractions at Disneyland are all special, but as a result of Walt Disney's critical thinking skills, so is the time spent waiting in lines.

In summary, it was Walt Disney's *critical thinking* that enabled him to assess what was wrong with America's existing theme parks and then to determine what would be truly innovative in response.

> Disney was a dreamer, a realist, and a critic.

Creativity and Critical Thinking

Disney's creativity went far beyond dreaming up the epitome of theme parks and one of the most beloved attractions for family vacations. He was instrumental in the early development of animation and the mastermind behind a film empire that has a cast of unforgettable characters, classic narratives, and moving adaptations of previously well-known tales.

He produced a vast number of short films, animated features, motion pictures, and TV shows, along with hundreds of hours of the *Mickey Mouse Club*. The simple, broad appeal of Disney's characters, productions, and theme parks demonstrates his unique ability to synthesize information, understand the context of our world, and then utilize creativity and critical thinking to produce innovations that resonated with the human spirit.

It has been suggested that Disney's unique creativity stemmed from the synergy he brought to every endeavour, by combining three key attributes that he possessed: the dreamer, the realist, and the critic.

According to Dilts,

> *The Dreamer is necessary for creativity in order to form new ideas and goals.*
>
> *The Realist is necessary for creativity as a means to transform ideas into concrete expressions.*
>
> *The Critic is necessary for creativity as a filter and as a stimulus for refinement.*[214]

© Disney

Walt Disney, 1901–1966

A Personal Note

When I was a young boy, our family developed a routine of heading to Palm Springs for winter holidays. Eventually, Mom and Dad settled on a unique destination known as Smoke Tree Ranch. It was a working cattle ranch in the 1920s and 30s, but by the time we started visiting, all that remained of the ranch was a riding stable that catered to tourists.

Over time, 84 private homes were built on the property, some by such notable family business owners as the Ford and Weyerhaeuser families. Most of the other home owners were from the Los Angeles area, seeking a private hideaway away from the lights of Hollywood. However, none of the owners was more popular than Walt Disney.

Disney had a home on Smoke Tree Ranch for many years, and as a young boy I once had the privilege of sitting beside Walt on his golf cart to have my picture taken with him. His reputation may have been intimidating for some, but his ready smile and gracious manner made him approachable, and I will always remember how gracious and kind he was to me as a child.

Walt Disney was a critical thinker. He was both brilliant and creative, yet always approachable. All of these are great attributes, which every family enterprise successor would be wise to emulate.

JOHN WOODEN

A DYNASTY FOUNDED ON PATIENCE

John Wooden was the legendary coach of the men's basketball teams at UCLA (the University of California, Los Angeles), and before we begin to discuss the significance of patience to Wooden's career, let us consider the extraordinary statistics that his leadership produced.

During the 12-year period from 1964 to 1975, John Wooden led the UCLA Bruins to

- an undefeated season, a record four times
- an unprecedented 10 Intercollegiate NCAA (National) Championships
- 7 straight championships from 1967 to 1973
- a record 88-game winning streak from 1971 to 1974
- a period with 335 wins in 357 games, an astounding winning percentage of 93.8

Never before or since has such an outstanding collegiate record been achieved. It is no wonder that Wooden was named NCAA Basketball Coach of the Year on six occasions.

Good Things Are Rooted in Patience

There are many things that set the man known simply as "Coach" apart from his peers, but his patience was extraordinary. In fact, it was his patience that undergirded his methodical approach to coaching, and it made a profound difference in his leadership.

Wooden believed that good things take time, and so we do well to be patient. He should know: When he first arrived at UCLA in 1948, he inherited the worst basketball team in the NCAA's Pacific Coast Conference. It took 16 years under his leadership before UCLA would eventually win its first national championship, in 1964.

John Wooden, 1910–2010
Pictured here with a "net necklace" just after his team
won the NCAA Men's Basketball championship

> Wooden believed that all good things take time.

Sixteen years may seem like a long time, but Wooden also had to wait 18 years for the university to fulfill its promise of a new arena for UCLA's basketball team. When he started coaching, the university had said the arena would be ready by the end of his third season (1951). Instead, it opened in 1965, just as Wooden was beginning his 18th season with the school.

There Is a Season for Patience

In an interview with *Success Magazine*, Wooden said that "progress comes slowly," and he explained how he first learned about the need for patience during his childhood on a farm in Indiana:

> There was a season to plant, a season to water and a season to harvest. The planting and the watering required hard work, but without that work and patience through the growing season, there would be no harvest.[215]

In other words, the harvest—whatever that might represent—necessitates patience. Wooden noted that young people often want things to happen too quickly and are too eager or too impatient to "wait for the necessary progress to reach the end result."

In contrast, Wooden believed that patience keeps people moving toward their goals, helps people to maintain their enthusiasm as they go forward, and creates a willingness to work hard to achieve our goals.

In the end, "When we are patient, we'll [also] have a greater appreciation of our success."[216]

Patience and Attention to Detail

For Wooden, the pursuit of a championship began with the little things. Every season, on the first day of practice, Coach Wooden would sit his players down and explain to them the proper way to put on their socks. Such instruction was probably considered ridiculous for many of his athletes, and undoubtedly it was offensive to some. But Wooden was uncompromising. With a meticulous attention to detail, he explained to even the most skeptical how to perform this elementary task.

If it required patience to go through this ritual, it required even more patience to explain why it was important. Yet, step by step, the value of this simple act was explained in this way:

> If we want to win a national championship, we will need to play better than our opposition ...
>
> If we want to play better than our opposition, we will need to practice better than they do ...
>
> If we want to practice better, we will need to practice with more intensity and consistency ...
>
> If we want to practice with intensity and consistency, we will need to give our best every day ...
>
> If we want to give our best every day, we will need to avoid getting blisters on our feet ...
>
> If we want to avoid getting blisters, we will need to put on our socks properly![217]

For many people, such an emphasis seems extreme, if not absurd. But it was typical for Wooden to patiently attend to even the smallest detail.

John Wooden, master teacher
With patience and attention to detail, he compiled possibly the greatest legacy of any coach in history.

> *Wooden patiently attended to even the smallest details, including teaching college players how to put on their socks properly.*

There Are No Shortcuts to Sustained Success

Centuries ago, in the days of lords and ladies, a young man who wanted to become a knight would begin his formal training at age 14. He would work as a squire under the tutelage of an experienced knight and mentor for seven years. It did not matter how quick a study the squire was—there was no shortening of the training time. The apprenticeship was seven years, period.

Many careers require a similar approach for the apprentice to obtain the required credentials. Professions such as medicine, engineering, accounting, and law all require years of supervised learning; similarly, apprenticeships are the norm for carpenters, electricians, and other tradesmen.

Given the extensive training required for so many professions, it is rather ironic that family enterprise successors have no such obligation to demonstrate either competence or diligence. This is also worth reconsidering because they may be stepping into circumstances where their success, or lack of it, can potentially impact the careers of many others, and so the stakes are arguably much higher. In spite of this, the mere suggestion that successors may be required to meet a prescribed standard, gain experience elsewhere, or even have performance evaluations is often rejected as unnecessary.

However, as Coach Wooden often said, "Nothing will work unless you do."[218]

> During his first season as head basketball coach at UCLA, Coach Wooden worked from 6 a.m. to noon as a truck dispatcher for a local dairy company. Upon arriving on campus with his morning job completed, his first duty was to mop the gym floor so it would be ready for practice in the afternoon. "There is no substitute for work," he was fond of saying. "If you're looking for the easy way, the shortcut, the trick, you may get something done for a while, but it will not be lasting and you will not be developing your ability."[219]

Patience and Success Are Linked

Coach Wooden thought a lot about what is required for success and documented his thinking in what he called "The Pyramid of Success." There are 25 components in his formula, each one representing an important element to success. Some of the core building blocks he lists are integrity, industriousness, co-operation, self-control, and poise, each of which holds great relevance for family enterprise successors. But, perhaps most interestingly, *patience* is listed right near the top of the pyramid and is one of the key elements required for *competitive greatness*.

I believe that being able to compete successfully is just as relevant in business as it is in sport. Therefore, learning to be patient is an important asset for any leader. In addition, if you are an aspiring family enterprise successor, learning to focus and work hard while waiting for your turn to lead will also require patience. So I would encourage you to cultivate patience.

For, as John Wooden's exemplary career demonstrates, good things come to those who wait.

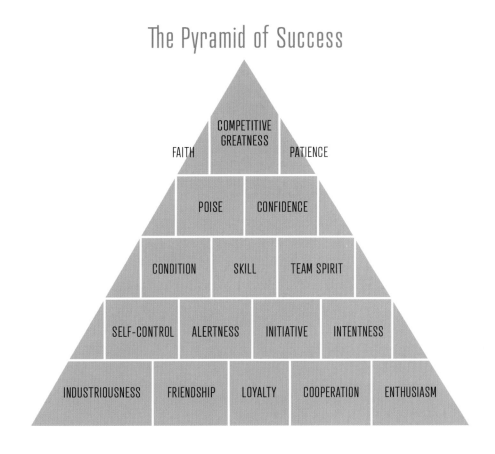

The Pyramid of Success

COMPETITIVE GREATNESS

FAITH — PATIENCE

POISE — CONFIDENCE

CONDITION — SKILL — TEAM SPIRIT

SELF-CONTROL — ALERTNESS — INITIATIVE — INTENTNESS

INDUSTRIOUSNESS — FRIENDSHIP — LOYALTY — COOPERATION — ENTHUSIASM

HELEN KELLER

CONTENTMENT IN SPITE OF CIRCUMSTANCES

When Helen Keller was born on June 27, 1880, in rural Alabama, her family likely had no idea that she would one day become a strong and influential woman whose life story would be as legendary as it is inspiring.

When she was just 18 months old, Helen contracted an unknown illness that was characterized by an extremely high fever. The doctors referred to it as "brain fever," and scientists today continue to hypothesize about the exact nature of her sickness, with most suggesting that it was probably meningitis. Regardless, when the fever finally broke, Helen's mother noticed that her daughter did not show any reaction when the dinner bell was rung or when a hand was waved in front of her face.

Helen had simultaneously lost the ability to see and to hear.

From that day on, she lived, as she recalled in her autobiography, "*at sea in a dense fog.*" Nonetheless, in spite of these deprivations, she stated most remarkably, "*Everything has its wonders, even darkness and silence, and I learn, whatever state I may be in, therein to be content.*"[220]

> Even in darkness and silence, Helen Keller learned to be content.

A Spirit of Contentment

Remarkably, Helen did not adopt the role of a victim; instead, "she filled her entire life with joy and contentment. She knew she could not heal her blindness or deafness, so she focused on what she could do; she could experience the world through words … She saw her life as beautiful!"[221]

For example, consider the delight and wonder that Helen expresses as she describes some of her life experiences:

Keller, author and educator
As she travelled the globe, she changed the lives of millions of people with visual impairments by bringing them courage and hope.

I also enjoy canoeing, and I suppose you will smile when I say that I especially like it on moonlight nights. I cannot, it is true, see the moon climb up the sky behind the pines and steal softly across the heavens, making a shining path for us to follow; but I know she is there, and as I lie back among the pillows and put my hand in the water, I fancy that I feel the shimmer of her garments as she passes. Sometimes a daring little fish slips through my fingers, and often a pond-lily presses shyly against my hand. Frequently, as we emerge from a cove or inlet, I am suddenly conscious of the spaciousness of the air about me. A luminous warmth seems to enfold me.[222]

By way of contrast, many of us who have the full use of all five senses take them for granted and often miss the remarkable beauty of a sunrise or the simple fragrance of a flower.

Dedicated to Learning

Many children complain about having to attend school and all too often resent as drudgery the requirements associated with learning how to spell. In contrast, Helen was dedicated to learning and considered it a doorway to the rest of the world. As she grew, she developed a limited method of communication with her constant companion, Martha Washington, who was the young daughter of the family cook. The two eventually created

> Though blind and deaf, Keller saw her life as beautiful.

their own kind of sign language, and by the time Helen was seven years old, they had invented more than 60 signs to communicate with each other.

Around this time, the Keller family hired a woman by the name of Anne Sullivan to be her governess. Sullivan was also partially blind but had learned to read Braille and to teach other blind and deaf children. She began to teach Helen finger spelling. She first gave Helen a doll as a gift and then spelled the word onto her hand. Connecting the object with the word spelled on her hand became a successful method of teaching Helen to identify objects around her and to spell.

For example, to teach Helen the word *water*, Sullivan took her out to the water pump and placed her hand under the spout. While Sullivan moved the lever to flush cool water over Helen's hand, she spelled out the word w-a-t-e-r on Helen's other hand. Helen understood and repeated the word in Sullivan's hand. Helen then dramatically pounded on the ground, demanding to know its "letter name." Sullivan followed her, spelling out the word into her hand. Together they moved on to other objects, and by nightfall Helen had learned 30 words.[223]

In due course, Helen began taking speech classes at a school for the deaf in Boston. She would toil for the next 25 years to learn to speak so that others could understand her. As part of her education, she also attended the Wright-Humason School for the Deaf in New York City, where she improved her communication skills and studied regular academic subjects. As her capacity developed, she became determined to attend college, and at the age of 16, she enrolled in the Cambridge School for Young Ladies, a preparatory school for women.

As her extraordinary story became known to the general public, Helen began to meet famous and influential people, such as Mark Twain. Twain was very impressed by her, and as they became friends he introduced her to his friend Henry H. Rogers, a Standard Oil executive. Rogers was similarly impressed with Helen, and he agreed to pay for her to attend the renowned Radcliffe College. By this time, Keller had mastered several methods of communication, including Braille, touch lip-reading, speaking, typing, and finger spelling. While in classes, Sullivan sat by her side to interpret lectures and texts. In 1904, Keller completed a bachelor of arts degree and graduated cum laude from Radcliffe at the age of 24.

Curiosity, Imagination, and Service

After graduation, Helen went on to become a world-famous speaker and author. According to those who heard her speak, "Helen Keller spoke of the joy that life gave her. She was thankful for the faculties and abilities that she did possess and stated that the most productive pleasures she had were curiosity and imagination."[224]

Helen spoke of the joy of service and the happiness that came from doing things for others, writing that "'helping your fellow men [was] one's only excuse for being in this world and in the doing of things to help one's fellows lay the secret of lasting happiness.' She also told of the joys of loving work and accomplishment and the happiness of achievement."[225]

Counting Our Blessings

Helen Keller was clearly remarkable in many ways, and she possessed a profound sense of contentment and gratitude that few of us will ever experience. She lived an amazing life because she focused on what she had—

> *As Helen Keller demonstrated, there are always blessings to count.*

and not on what she lacked. This is the key to living a life characterized by contentment. Her life shows how transformative it can be to count our blessings, and so we should. Especially since, as Helen has showed us, there are always blessings to count.

Concluding a book about her own life, she noted, "Thus it is that my friends have made the story of my life. In a thousand ways they have turned my limitations into beautiful privileges, and enabled me to walk serene and happy in the shadow cast by my deprivation."[226]

Helen faced many obstacles in her life, and yet she was remarkably content. Given the relative ease that most of us enjoy, it seems that we would have much to gain if we were able to follow her example.

PERSONAL REFLECTION
Ballast In the Storm

Earlier in my career, I was a member of the Young Presidents Organization (YPO). Late one afternoon, I had a chance encounter with another member as we both arrived at a private dinner. As we were walking into the venue, he said to me, "I've been looking forward to meeting you for a long time." When I asked him why, he said, "I was there when they plotted everything they did to you." His remarks both shocked me and piqued my interest.

What did this stranger know that I didn't?

He went on to explain that he had participated in many discussions where others conspired to not only destroy my career but also seize control of our family business. As he could attest, the challenges that had been thrown in my path were almost unbearable. In fact, as I entered my 30s, my professional career was in tatters.

In addition, our family legacy, which many felt rested on my shoulders, was disintegrating right before my eyes. It was a horrific time, one that I would not wish on anyone. However, my new acquaintance went on to explain that he thought that I "must be pretty special" and that my "faith must be pretty special."

What made me special? I wondered.

He then confessed that I was the only person he knew who would have been able to endure the challenges that came my way.

Having reflected on this conversation for many years, I must state that I don't think I'm special; nor do I think that my faith is particularly special. However, my colleague was right about something. My personal faith and my decision to trust God in the face of such severe testing had been essential.

In fact, God's presence was the ballast that had kept my ship from capsizing when I was caught in a raging storm. Had I not been able to articulate my problems to God, through prayer, I don't know if I would have made it through.

CAUGHT UP IN MY OWN WORLD

Unfortunately, although I genuinely desired to honour God in my life, I know that I have often failed to do this. As a young man, rather than loving Him with my whole heart or loving my neighbour as myself, I was primarily focused on my own career advancement, and this eclipsed almost everything else in my life for many years.

While it is undeniable that other factors played a major role in the disintegration of our family business, I now realize that I could have been much more constructive in the role I played. Furthermore, with the benefit of hindsight, it is apparent that my personal ambition often blinded me to my faults.

Rather than cultivating the characteristics that would have made me a good choice as the next company president, I focused on the faults of others, often being openly critical. I also worked hard to gain the knowledge and experience that I thought would help me succeed. But, unfortunately, I didn't pay much attention to my need to cultivate emotional intelligence or personal character. In short, I failed to develop in ways that are essential to becoming the kind of leader required for a family enterprise.

If you are a family enterprise successor, I invite you to look in the mirror and ask yourself whether you are becoming the type of person you would want to have as a co-owner or partner. If not, perhaps you can learn from my mistakes and begin cultivating the virtues that I have discussed throughout this book.

Your family and your business colleagues will be grateful if you do.

If I can assist you, in any way, on your journey, please let me know.

I wish you and your family much success!

Yours sincerely,

David C Bentall
September 2020

SECTION VI
Help Along the Way

TAKING ACTION:
A FEW STEPS TO GET YOU STARTED

You may dream of becoming a world champion bodybuilder, sprinter, or figure skater. However, these are not goals that are achieved without rigorous training and effort. Similarly, becoming a person of who possesses qualities like forgiveness, patience, or contentment is not something that happens without discipline and practice.

In this section, I invite you to consider a few simple steps that may help you to "take action" and to begin developing the type of character traits to enable you to work more productively and effectively as a successor in your family enterprise.

SELF-ASSESSMENT

Start by considering the following nine character traits:

HUMILITY   **CURIOSITY**   **EMPATHY**

LISTENING   **GRATITUDE**   **FORGIVENESS**

CRITICAL THINKING   **PATIENCE**   **CONTENTMENT**

Circle the two that you think you are best at. Next, identify the two where you think you have the most room for improvement (in other words, the ones that you are perhaps weakest at).

You just identified two character traits that might loosely be described as strengths and two that may be considered weaknesses.

It is important to know your strengths because you can rely on them whenever you face challenging circumstances. Like good friends, these qualities give you perspective and help you to make wise choices. They are the qualities you can rely on when faced by challenges.

In contrast, the traits you identify as potential weaknesses warrant special attention. This is because, as a leader, if you are lacking any of these characteristics, you may be vulnerable. This is especially true if you want to grow and develop in the context of your family enterprise.

As a place to start improving, I recommend that you identify one character trait that you think holds the most near-term potential for making a meaningful difference in your life. In other words, if you could significantly improve in just one of these areas over the next 6 to 12 months, which one would you select?

For me, as I write in September 2020, I think the one that I could benefit the most from would be empathy. Over the next year, this is the area that I want to cultivate much more deliberately. Which would you choose?

Write down the trait you would most like to cultivate here: _____

1) Apirations

Next, consider how you would like to be 6 to 12 months from today. Think about the one character trait you have selected to focus on, and write down what you would like to be like in relationship to this quality. The following are suggestions for all nine characteristics:

Humility: *"I recognize the value of others, and am attentive to their needs and opinions."*
Empathy: *"I seek to understand how others feel and to show them love and respect."*
Curiosity: *"I am filled with wonder, asking what other people think and why."*
Listening: *"I listen carefully, recognizing that everyone has something to teach me."*
Gratitude: *"I am thankful and gladly show appreciation."*
Forgiveness: *"I choose to live a life free of bitterness and resentment."*
Critical Thinking: *"I am objective in my analyses and decision-making."*
Patience: *"I endure problems calmly, knowing that composure breeds wisdom."*
Contentment: *"I choose to be satisfied with what is, rather than longing for something else."*

Choose one trait and write out, in your own words, what you aspire to in relation to that trait:

I _____

2) Goal Setting

Now, write out a measurable goal for the one trait you have selected. Here are some examples:

Gratitude: "*Every morning, while drinking my coffee, I will write down three things I am thankful for that day.*"

Critical Thinking: "*I will create my own six-step process for making decisions. I will make this the screen saver for my laptop and use it at least once per month to guide me in making an important decision.*"

My goal is _____

3) Read & Learn

Identify someone who exemplifies the first trait you wish to work on cultivating. To start with, you may want to read and study more about a person whom I have written about in section V of this book. To help you become more forgiving, you could focus on learning more about Nelson Mandela, or if you want to be more curious, you can read up on the life of Albert Einstein.

Consider making it your quest to read as much as you can about this person in the next 12 months and to draw inspiration from them as you seek to develop as a leader/successor.

I have seen the effectiveness of such a strategy up close as I witnessed my dad's reading habits. For decades, every night before going to sleep he would lie in bed reading, usually for about 15–20 minutes. Invariably he was reading a biography of a great leader or business executive. People like Churchill and John D. Rockefeller were some of his favourites. These leaders became my father's virtual mentors.

This was particularly important for Dad because he never went to business school or attended any executive educational seminars. However, in the privacy of his home he was studying daily, taking inspiration from some of the best leaders who ever lived. For example, the Bentall Centre, in the heart of downtown Vancouver, was inspired by reading about the Rockefeller family and by visiting the Rockefeller Center in downtown New York. Dad never met anyone from the Rockefeller family, but he was tutored and mentored by them nonetheless.

Choose one role model you want to learn more about over the next year.

Write their name here: _____.

4) Personal Hall of Fame

I want to suggest something that was inspired by the Oxford character project. The concept is to develop your own personal hall of fame. This is simply a list of those individuals whom you consciously identify as your role models and whom you aspire to be like.

As noted, my dad was both inspired and educated as a leader and as a business executive primarily by studying the lives of those he admired. Although he didn't do so formally, he created, in his mind, his own virtual hall of fame, people who animated and inspired him throughout his career. Daily, these exemplars were instrumental in Dad's thinking as he laboured to build a company that was eventually selected as one of the 100 best companies to work for in Canada.

I invite you to think deeply about the qualities and characteristics you need as a successor in your family enterprise, like my dad did so successfully. Take time to pick your role models wisely and carefully because they will have a profound and lasting impact on your leadership and on your family enterprises.

Without thinking about it, most of us have our own list of heroes or role models. They may not be written down, but if pressed we could all list a few individuals whom we notionally consider worthy of emulation. People we admire and we respect. My list of exemplars has been greatly influenced by the biographies that I have read.

In my office, I have a special collection of biographies that I keep near my desk, to remind me of the kind of person I want to become. It consists of books about those individuals who genuinely inspire me, and it includes some well-known heroes (including those that I have written about in this book). My "Personal Hall of Fame" also includes Sir Ernest Shackleton, Tony Dunghy, and Chuck Colson.

How about you? Who do you aspire to be like? Begin developing your own leadership hall of fame. You may wish to begin by reviewing all nine of the exemplars written about earlier in this book. Which ones resonate with you? Who would you potentially add?

Using the following template, begin building your own "Leadership Hall of Fame":

HUMILITY _____ EMPATHY _____ CURIOSITY _____

LISTENING _____ GRATITUDE _____ FORGIVENESS _____

CRITICAL THINKING _____ PATIENCE _____ CONTENTMENT _____

It is often said that if you want to be successful at anything, find someone who has achieved the results you want and copy what they do, and you'll achieve the same results. So, let me ask you, What results do you want as a leader, and who will you choose to imitate?

In the first year, you can focus on one of these individuals, as previously noted. Then in subsequent years you can choose additional "virtual mentors." By adopting such a strategy, over the next decade you could realistically establish an in-depth knowledge of those you have chosen for your personal hall of fame.

ASSESSMENTS & MENTORING

Finally, I invite you to consider two additional strategies that may help you to develop the type of character traits that will help you to work collaboratively and effectively as a successor in your family enterprise.

PERSONAL ASSESSMENTS

Next Step Advisors offers a complimentary assessment that can help you to determine where you are at with all nine of the character traits I have written about in this book.

If you would like to complete
our free personal assessment go to
NextStepAdvisors.ca/assessment.

GROUP COACHING & PERSONAL MENTORING

Next Step Advisors has developed virtual training programs specifically for successors. These programs include online learning, group coaching, and personal mentoring. Contact us, and we can provide details regarding the different options we offer. These have been created specifically to help you develop these nine traits and to integrate them into your personal and professional life.

If you want more information
about coaching or mentoring go to
NextStepAdvisors.ca/programs.

NEXT STEP ADVISORS

ADVISING & CONSULTING

Next Step Advisors has advisory experience and expertise in numerous areas. These include facilitating family meetings, recruiting boards, negotiating shareholder agreements, and resolving conflict.

    If you would like help with your family enterprise, we would be honoured to help.

SPEAKING & WORKSHOPS

David C. Bentall is an outstanding speaker and workshop leader. If you are interested in having him as a speaker or to lead a workshop, please let us know how we can help.

To learn more, simply go to our website:
NextStepAdvisors.ca

APPENDIX
Corrie ten Boom on Forgiveness

Forgiving someone who has hurt or disappointed us is never easy, and the greater the injury, the more challenging it will be. One of the most striking examples of forgiveness ever recorded is the true story of Corrie ten Boom, who suffered terribly during the holocaust. After the war, she came face to face with one of her former prison guards.

Below is the story in her own words, as published in "Guideposts Classics."

> It was in a church in Munich that I saw him, a balding heavy-set man in a gray overcoat, a brown felt hat clutched between his hands. People were filing out of the basement room where I had just spoken … It was 1947 and I had come from Holland to defeated Germany with the message that God forgives …
>
> And that's when I saw him, working his way forward against the others. One moment I saw the overcoat and the brown hat; the next, a blue uniform and a visored cap with its skull and crossbones. It came back with a rush: the huge room with its harsh overhead lights, the pathetic pile of dresses and shoes in the center of the floor, the shame of walking naked past this man. I could see my sister's frail form ahead of me, ribs sharp beneath the parchment skin. Betsie, how thin you were!
>
> Betsie and I had been arrested for concealing Jews in our home during the Nazi occupation of Holland; this man had been a guard at Ravensbruck concentration camp where we were sent …
>
> "You mentioned Ravensbruck in your talk," he was saying. "I was a guard in there." No, he did not remember me.

"But since that time," he went on, "I have become a Christian. I know that God has forgiven me for the cruel things I did there, but I would like to hear it from your lips as well. Fraulein"— … his hand came out—"will you forgive me?"

And I stood there—I whose sins had every day to be forgiven—and could not. Betsie had died in that place—could he erase her slow terrible death simply for the asking?

It could not have been many seconds that he stood there, hand held out, but to me it seemed hours as I wrestled with the most difficult thing I had ever had to do. For I had to do it—I knew that. The message that God forgives has a prior condition: that we forgive those who have injured us. "If you do not forgive men their trespasses," Jesus says, "neither will your Father in heaven forgive your trespasses." …

And still I stood there with the coldness clutching my heart. But forgiveness is not an emotion—I knew that too. Forgiveness is an act of the will, and the will can function regardless of the temperature of the heart.

"Jesus, help me!" I prayed silently. "I can lift my hand. I can do that much. You supply the feeling."

And so woodenly, mechanically, I thrust my hand into the one stretched out to me. And as I did, an incredible thing took place. The current started in my shoulder, raced down my arm, sprang into our joined hands. And then this healing warmth seemed to flood my whole being, bringing tears to my eyes.

"I forgive you, brother!" I cried. "With all my heart!"

For a long moment we grasped each other's hands, the former guard and the former prisoner. I had never known God's love so intensely as I did then.[227]

ENDNOTES

I The Bentall Family Story

1. W. Gibb Dyer Jr., "Integrating Professional Management into a Family Owned Business," *Family Business Review* 2, no. 3 (September 1989): 221–35.
2. Dyer Jr., "Integrating Professional Management."
3. Richard Langworth, *Winston Churchill, Myth and Reality: What He Actually Did and Said* (North Carolina: McFarland & Company, 2017), 218.
4. Winston Churchill, "Never Give In," October 29, 1941, International Churchill Society.

II Wisdom for Successors

5. "Family Enterprise Matters: Harnessing the Most Powerful Economic Driver of Economic Growth in Canada," Family Enterprise Xchange, 2019.
6. Barbara Schecter, "Family Businesses Survive Longer and Offer Less Investment Risk, Rotman Study Finds," *Financial Post*, April 30, 2018.
7. Danny Miller and Isabelle Le Breton-Miller, *Managing for the Long Run: Lessons in Competitive Advantages From Great Family Businesses* (Boston: Harvard Business School Press, 2005).
8. Miller and Le Breton-Miller, *Managing for the Long Run*, 14–15.
9. Miller and Le Breton-Miller, *Managing for the Long Run*, 15.
10. Antonio Spizzirri, "Supplement: 23 Individual Family-Controlled Company Share Price Performance Reports," Rotman School of Management, June 2013.
11. Miller and Le Breton-Miller, *Managing for the Long Run*, 32.
12. Miller and Le Breton-Miller, *Managing for the Long Run*.
13. Miller and Le Breton-Miller, *Managing for the Long Run*, 114.
14. Miller and Le Breton-Miller, *Managing for the Long Run*, 34.
15. Denise Kenyon-Rouvinez and John L. Ward, *Family Business: Key Issues* (New York: Palgrave Macmillan, 2005), 4.
16. Renato Tagiuri and John Davis, "Bivalent Attributes of the Family Firm," *Family Business Review* 9, no. 2 (June 1996): 199–208.
17. Tagiuri and Davis, "Bivalent Attributes," 200.
18. John A. Davis et al., *Generation to Generation: Life Cycles of the Family Business* (Boston: Harvard Business Press, 1997), 225–250.
19. Peter Drucker, *The End of Economic Man: The Origins of Totalitarianism* (New York: The John Day Company, 1939).
20. Daniel Goleman, *Emotional Intelligence: Why It Can Matter More Than IQ* (New York: Bantam Books, 1997), 34.
21. Goleman, *Emotional Intelligence*, xii.
22. Goleman, *Emotional Intelligence*, 138.
23. Goleman, *Emotional Intelligence*, 139.
24. Dyer Jr., "Integrating Professional Management."
25. John A. Davis and Sabine Klein, "Succession," in Kenyon-Rouvinez and Ward, *Family Business: Key Issues*, 60.
26. Davis and Klein, "Succession," 67.

27. Stephen R. Covey, *7 Habits of Highly Effective People* (New York: Simon & Schuster, 1989), 270.
28. Peter F. Drucker, "What Makes an Effective Executive," *Harvard Business Review*, June 2004.
29. Drucker, "Effective Executive."
30. David C. Bentall, *Leaving a Legacy: Navigating Family Business Succession* (Ontario: Castle Quay Books, 2012).
31. Peter F. Drucker, *The Practice of Management* (New York: Harper Business, 2006), 416.
32. "Management by Objectives: Drucker," Communication Theory, 2011.
33. "Management by Objectives: Drucker."
34. Drucker, "Effective Executive."
35. Leon Danco, *Beyond Survival: A Guide for Business Owners and Their Families* (Michigan: Reston Pub. Co., 1975), 121.
36. Jennifer Pendergast, L. John Ward, and Stephanie Brun de Ponte, *Building a Successful Family Business Board: A Guide for Leaders, Directors, and Families* (New York: Palgrave Macmillan, 2011).
37. Jack Nadel, "Best Career Advice: Find a Need and Fill it," *Huffington Post*, April 2015.
38. Richard Branson, "Richard Branson on Intrapaneurs: The business icon talks about empowering employees to break the rules," *NBC News*, January 31, 2011.
39. Antoine Mayoud, "Vision 2040 Think Tank" workshop, Family Matters Forum 2015, Business Families Foundation, Miami, FL, November 20, 2015.

III Transforming Your Leadership

40. Rick Warren, *The Purpose Driven Life: What on Earth Am I Here For?* (New York: Zondervan Publishing, 2002), 186.
41. Jim Collins, "Level 5 Leadership: The Triumph of Humility and Fierce Resolve," *Harvard Business Review*, January 2001.
42. Edgar Schein, *Humble Inquiry: The Gentle Art of Asking Instead of Telling* (San Francisco: Berrett-Koehler Publishers, 2013), 10.
43. Jennifer Cole Wright et al., "The Psychological Significance of Humility," *The Journal of Positive Psychology* 12, no. 1 (April 2016): 3–12.
44. Jennifer Cole Wright and Thomas Nadelhoffer, "The Twin Dimensions of the Virtue of Humility: Low Self Focus and Higher Other Focus," *Moral Psychology: Virtue and Character* 5 (2017): 309–371.
45. David Brooks, *The Road to Character* (New York: Random House Publishing, 2015), 9.
46. Sue Shellenbarger, "The Best Bosses are Humble Bosses," *Wall Street Journal*, October 9, 2018.
47. Cindy Lamothe, "How Intellectual Humility Can Make You a Better Person," *New York Magazine*, February 3, 2017.
48. Covey, *7 Habits*, 269–270.
49. Bradley P. Owens and David R. Hekman, "How Does Leader Humility Influence Team Performance? Exploring the Mechanism of Contagion and Collective Promotion Focus," *Academy of Management Journal* 59, no. 3 (April 2015).
50. David Bentall, "Dear Younger Me," workshop presented in Vancouver (November 15, 2017).
51. Alexandre Havard, "An Encounter with Francois Michelin," Virtuous Leadership Institute, January 20, 2010.
52. Havard, "Francois Michelin."
53. Phil Jackson, *Eleven Rings: The Soul of Success* (New York: Penguin Books, 2013).
54. Jackson, *Eleven Rings*, 96.
55. Jackson, *Eleven Rings*, 107.
56. Jackson, *Eleven Rings*, 217.
57. Jackson, *Eleven Rings*, 216.
58. Jackson, *Eleven Rings*, 217.

59. Tennelle Porter, quoted in Cindy Lamothe, "How 'Intellectual Humility' Can Make You a Better Person," The Cut, February 3, 2017.
60. Proverbs 16:18, Revised Standard Version.
61. Aaron Orendorff, "Humility, The Missing Ingredient to Your Success," Entrepreneur, August 2015.
62. Timothy Keller, "Blessed Self-Forgetfulness," *Timothy Keller Sermons*, Gospel in Life, September 13, 2019, podcast, audio, 41:57.
63. Roy Baumeister, "Analysis: Questioning the conventional wisdom of self-esteem," interview by Neal Conan, Talk of the Nation, NPR.
64. French intellectual Claude Lévi-Strauss.
65. Daniel Steingold, "Are We There Yet? Children Ask Parents 73 Questions a Day on Average, Study Finds," Studyfinds, December 11, 2017.
66. Michael Dell, quoted in Warren Berger, "Why Curious People are Destined for the C-Suite," *Harvard Business Review*, September 11, 2015.
67. Brad Lomenick, *H3 Leadership: Be Humble, Stay Hungry, and Always Hustle* (Nashville: Harper Collins, 2014), 74.
68. Lomenick, *H3 Leadership*, 77.
69. Lomenick, *H3 Leadership*, 75.
70. David Brooks, *The Road to Character* (New York: Random House, 2015).
71. Edgar Schein, *Humble Inquiry: The Gentle Art of Asking Instead of Telling* (San Francisco: Brett-Koehler Publishers, 2013), 21.
72. Amanda Lang, *The Beauty of Discomfort: How What We Avoid Is What We Need* (Toronto: Harpercollins, 2017), 304.
73. Lang, *The Beauty of Discomfort*, 2.
74. Lang, *The Beauty of Discomfort*, 4.
75. "Henry Ford Changes The World, 1908," EyeWitness to History.
76. "Henry Ford Changes the World."
77. Jack Zenger and Joseph Folkman, "What Great Listeners Actually Do," *Harvard Business Review*, July 14, 2016.
78. Zenger and Folkman, "Great Listeners."
79. Covey, *7 Habits*, 239.
80. Zenger and Folkman, "Great Listeners."
81. Covey, *7 Habits*, 255.
82. Covey, *7 Habits*, 255.
83. Rachel Naomi Remen, quoted in "Listening Skills," Skills You Need.
84. Francois Michelin, quoted in "Five Lessons from François Michelin," Family Capital, May 1, 2015.
85. William Ury, "The Power of Listening," TEDx Talk, January 7, 2015, video, 15:40, YouTube.
86. Ury, "The Power of Listening," transcript.
87. Ury, "The Power of Listening," transcript.
88. Doug Baumoel and Blair Trippe, *Deconstructing Conflict: Understanding Family Business, Shared Wealth and Power* (Massachusetts: Continuity Media, 2016), xv.
89. Baumoel and Trippe, *Deconstructing Conflict*, 177.
90. Baumoel and Trippe, *Deconstructing Conflict*, xv.
91. Allan Pease and Barbara Pease, "The Definitive Book of Body Language," *New York Times*, September 24.
92. "Listening Skills."

93. Dick Lee and Delmar Hatesohl, "Listening: Our Most Used Communication Skill," University of Missouri, October 1993.

94. Maya Angelou, quoted in Kate Murphy, "A Chat with Maya Angelou," *The New York Times*, April 21, 2013.

95. Henri Nouwen, *Out of Solitude: Three Meditations on the Christian Life* (Notre Dame: Ave Maria Press, April 16, 2004), 38.

96. Brenda Pue and Carson Pue, *But If Not: 588 Days Living with Cancer* (Ontario: Castle Quay Books).

97. Pue and Pue, *But If Not*.

98. Brené Brown, *Daring Greatly: How the Courage to Be Vulnerable Transforms the Way We Live, Love, Parent and Lead* (New York: Gotham Books, 2012).

99. Carson Pue, text message to author, October 10, 2016.

100. Brown, *Daring Greatly*.

101. Daniel Goleman, "Empathy: A Key to Effective Leadership," Linkedin, June 7, 2017.

102. Goleman, "Empathy."

103. Varun Warrier et al., "Genome-Wide Analyses of Self-Reported Empathy: Correlations with Autism, Schizophrenia and Anorexia Nervosa," *Translational Psychiatry* 8, no. 35 (March 2018).

104. Kate Thieda, "Brené Brown on Empathy vs. Sympathy," *Psychology Today*, August 12, 2014.

105. Brené Brown, *Brené Brown on Empathy*, produced and edited by Al Francis-Sears and Abi Stephenson, December 10, 2013, video, 2:53, YouTube.

106. Peg Streep, "Six Things You Need to Know about Empathy," *Psychology Today*, January 23, 2017.

107. Brown, *Daring Greatly*.

108. Stewart Butterfield, quoted in David Ebner, "Sharing Information with Slack CEO Stewart Butterfield," *Globe and Mail*, March 3, 2018.

109. Malcolm Gladwell, *David and Goliath: Underdogs, Misfits and the Art of Battling Giants* (London: Brown and Company, 2013), 305.

110. Schein, *Humble Inquiry*, 2.

111. Baumoel and Trippe, *Deconstructing Conflict*, 3.

112. Baumoel and Trippe, *Deconstructing Conflict*.

113. Baumoel and Trippe, *Deconstructing Conflict*.

114. Katie Greenman and Jonah Wittkamper, "Born to Give: A Human Approach to Catalyzing Philanthropy," Nexus, summer 2015 white paper, 11.

115. Greenman and Wittkamper, "Born to Give," 15.

116. Greenman and Wittkamper, "Born to Give," 10.

117. Dr. Dennis Jaffe, quoted in Greenman and Wittkamper, "Born to Give," 19.

118. See Paul David Tripp, *What Did You Expect? Redeeming the Realities of Marriage* (Illinois: Crossway, 2010), 288.

119. Richard Branson, "F is for Forgiveness," Richard Branson's A to Z of Business, Virgin, March 30, 2017, video, https://www.virgin.com/richard-branson/f-forgiveness.

120. Kevin Maney, "Lessons From the Great Depression: The IBM Story," Network for Solutions, October 10, 2008.

121. Peter E. Greulich, "On Thoughtful Mistakes," MBI Concepts, September 30, 2019.

122. Greulich, "On Thoughtful Mistakes."

123. C. S. Lewis, *The Four Loves* (New York: Harcourt Brace Jovanovich, 1960), 169.

124. Mahatma Gandhi, *All Men Are Brothers: Life and Thoughts of Mahatma Gandhi As Told in His Own Words* (New York: Columbia University Press, 1958, 1969).

125. Blake Morgan, "10 Powerful Examples of Corporate Apologies," *Forbes*, October 24, 2018.
126. Lawrence Tanenbaum, "Open Letter to Leafs Fans," NHL, April 9, 2012.
127. Robert Emmons, "What Gets in the Way of Gratitude," *Greater Good Magazine*, November 12, 2013.
128. If interested in this kind of experience, please go to www.ywamsandiegobaja.com.
129. Annalisa Barbieri, "Why don't I appreciate what I have? You asked Google—here's the answer," *The Guardian*, January 20, 2016.
130. Barbieri, "Why don't I appreciate what I have?"
131. Emmons, "What Gets in the Way of Gratitude."
132. Yarrow Dunham, quoted in Janice Kaplan, *The Gratitude Diaries: How a Year Looking on the Bright Side Can Transform Your Life* (New York: Dutton Publishing, 2015), 68.
133. Emmons, "What Gets in the Way of Gratitude."
134. Anonymous, quoted in Gladwell, *David and Goliath*, 47.
135. Gladwell, *David and Goliath*, 47.
136. Gladwell, *David and Goliath*, 47.
137. Gladwell, *David and Goliath*, 44.
138. Anonymous, quoted in Gladwell, *David and Goliath*, 45.
139. Lee Hausner, *Children of Paradise: Successful Parenting for Prosperous Families* (Los Angeles: J. P. Tarcher, 1990).
140. Hausner, *Children of Paradise*.
141. Malcolm Gladwell, *Outliers: The Story of Success* (London: Brown and Company, 2008), 267.
142. Gladwell, *Outliers*, 62.
143. Tim Keller, "Generosity in Scarcity" (sermon), Gospel in Life, May 31, 2009, streaming audio and MP3.
144. Bill Gates, "Bill Gates—Lakeside School," Bill & Melinda Gates Foundation Press Room, September 23, 2005.
145. Amy Gallo, "The Value of Keeping the Right Customers," *Harvard Business Review*, October 29, 2014.
146. Glassdoor Team, "Employers to Retain Half of Their Employees Longer If Bosses Showed More Appreciation; Glassdoor Survey," Glassdoor, November 13, 2013.
147. Kent Sorensen, "5 Business Benefits of Gratitude," Emazzanti, November 20, 2017.
148. Michael Kay, "Why Expressing Gratitude Is Crucial in Business," Inc., November 8, 2018.
149. Elizabeth Gilbert, *Eat, Pray, Love: One Woman's Search for Everything* (New York: Penguin Books, 2006), 348.
150. Ann Voskamp, *One Thousand Gifts: A Dare to Live Fully Right Where You Are* (Michigan: Zondervan Publishing, 2006), 45.
151. Voskamp, *One Thousand Gifts*, 45.
152. Laura Hillenbrand, *Unbroken: A World War II Story of Survival, Resilience and Redemption* (New York: Random House Publishing, 2010).
153. Armando Valladares, *Against All Hope: A Memoir of Life in Castro's Gulag*, trans. Andrew Hurley (San Francisco: Encounter Books, 2001).
154. Denzel Washington, "Denzel Washington: 'Number One: Put God First,' Dillard University—2015," Speakola.
155. Pauline Baynes, *Questionable Creatures: A Bestiary* (Michigan: William B. Eerdmans Publishing, 2006).
156. World Economic Forum, "The Future of Jobs: Employment, Skills and Workforce Strategy for the Fourth Industrial Revolution," World Economic Forum, January 2016.
157. Jack Ma, *Jack Ma: Love Is Important in Business*, at World Economic Forum, January 26, 2018, video, 55:39, YouTube.
158. Ma, *Love Is Important*.

159. Jerry Houser, quoted in Melissa Korn, "Bosses Seek 'Critical Thinking,' But What Is That?," *Wall Street Journal*, October 21, 2014.
160. "Chapter 7: Critical Thinking and Evaluating Information," *EDUC 1300: Effective Learning Strategies*, Lumen.
161. Albert Einstein, quoted in David Sturt and Todd Nordstrom, "Are You Asking the Right Question?" *Forbes*, October 18, 2013.
162. Daniel J. Levitin, *A Field Guide to Lies: Critical Thinking in the Information Age* (Canada: Penguin Random House Publishing, 2016), 2.
163. Levitin, *Critical Thinking*, 254.
164. Warren Berger, *A More Beautiful Question: The Power of Inquiry to Spark Breakthrough Ideas* (New York: Bloomsbury Publishing, 2014).
165. Warren Berger and Elise Foster, *Beautiful Questions in the Classroom: Transforming Classrooms into Cultures of Curiosity and Inquiry* (Thousand Oaks, CA: Corwin, 2000), 10.
166. Robert H. Ennis, "The Nature of Critical Thinking: An Outline of Critical Thinking Dispositions and Abilities," University of Illinois, May 2011.
167. Lisa Schirch and David Campt, *The Little Book of Dialogue for Difficult Subjects: A Practical Hands-On Guide* (UK: Good Books, 2007), 92.
168. Bertrand Russell, *Sceptical Essays* (London: George Allen & Unwin Ltd., 1928), 110.
169. Jack Ma, quoted in David Barboza, "New Partner for Yahoo is a Master at Selling," *The New York Times*, August 15, 2005.
170. Morneau Shapell and the Canadian Mental Health Commission, "Canadian Employees Report Workplace Stress as Primary Cause of Mental Health Concerns," Mental Health Commission of Canada, July 5, 2018.
171. Karen Higginbottom, "Workplace Stress Leads to Less Productive Employees," *Forbes*, September 11, 2014.
172. Murielle Tiambo, "Leaders can Cultivate True Employee Empowerment," *Forbes*, February 19, 2019.
173. Curtis R. Carlson, quoted in Sheila M. Bethel, *A New Breed of Leader: 8 Leadership Qualities that Matter Most in the Real World* (New York: Berkley, 2009).
174. Chris Myers, "Three Reasons Why You Should Be Patient in Business," *Forbes*, June 2, 2017.
175. Dov Seidman, "4 Ways to Become a Better Boss," World Economic Forum, September 12, 2017.
176. Bryan Clay, *Redemption: A Rebellious Spirit, a Praying Mom, and an Unlikely Path to Olympic Gold* (Nashville: Thomas Nelson, 2012).
177. Christine Sjolin, "NexGen Acquisition Success: Partnership, Patience, and Teamwork," *Journal of Financial Planning* 30, no. 9 (2017).
178. Sjolin, "NexGen Acquisition Success."
179. Adrianna C. Jenkins and Ming Hsu, "Dissociable Contributions of Imagination and Willpower to the Malleability of Human Patience," *Psychological Science* 28, no. 7 (May 2017): 894–906.
180. Dale Carnegie, *How to Win Friends and Influence People* (New York: Simon and Schuster, 1936), 67.
181. Liz Haq, "Canadians Believe the Average Salary They Need for 'Comfort' is $250,000," *Huffington Post*, November 4, 2018.
182. Gladwell, *David and Goliath*, 44.
183. Daniel Kurt, "Are You in the World's Top 1 Percent?" Investopedia, September 25, 2019.
184. Iain Murray, "Health, Wealth and Happiness," Competitive Enterprise Institute, October 14, 2014.
185. Jim Murphy, *Inner Excellence: Achieve Extraordinary Success through Mental Toughness* (New York: McGraw Hill, 2009), 162.

186. Tim Hansel, *You Gotta Keep Dancin': In the Midst of Life's Hurts, You Can Choose Joy!* (Illinois: Life Journey Books, 1985).

187. Merle Shain, *When Lovers Are Friends* (New York: Bantam Books, 1978), 65, quoted in Hansel, *Keep Dancin'*, 68.

188. Lomenick, *H3 Leadership*, 248.

189. Murphy, *Inner Excellence*, 162.

190. Timothy O'Keeffe, "Leading with Contentment," *American Fastener Journal* 33, no. 4 (July/August 2017): 26.

191. O'Keeffe, "Leading with Contentment."

192. O'Keeffe, "Leading with Contentment."

193. Rudyard Kipling, "If," Poetry Foundation.

194. Miroslav Volf, "The Crown of the Good Life: A Hypothesis," in *Joy and Human Flourishing*, ed. Miroslav Volf and Justin E. Crisp (Minneapolis: Fortress Press, 2015), 127–136.

195. Andrew Osterland, "What the coming $68 trillion Great Wealth Transfer means for financial advisors," CNBC, October 21, 2019.

196. Gladwell, *David and Goliath*, 51.

IV Wisdom from Successors

197. Daniel Goleman, *Social Intelligence: The New Science of Human Relationships* (New York: Bantam Dell, 2006), 54.

198. Benjamin Franklin, *Autobiography of Benjamin Franklin: 1706–1757* (Minneapolis: Applewood Books, 2008), 125.

199. Franklin, *Autobiography*, 139.

200. Franklin, *Autobiography*, 138.

201. Franklin, *Autobiography*, 139.

202. Franklin, *Autobiography*, 137–138.

203. Attributed to Albert Einstein.

204. Nelson Mandela, *Long Walk to Freedom: The Autobiography of Nelson Mandela* (Boston: Back Bay Books, 1995).

205. Stephanie Nolen, "Mandela's miraculous capacity for forgiveness a carefully calibrated strategy," *The Globe and Mail*, December 5, 2013, updated May 11, 2018.

206. Nelson Mandela, quoted in Crain Soudien, "The Provocation of Nelson Mandela," in *Nelson Mandela: Comparative Perspectives of His Significance for Education*, ed. Crain Soudien, vol. 42 of *Comparative and International Education: A Diversity of Voices* (Rotterdam: Sense Publishers, 2017), 172.

207. Nelson Mandela, quoted in Peter Rule, "Nelson Mandela and Dialogic Lifelong Learning," in *Nelson Mandela: Comparative Perspectives of His Significance for Education*, ed. Crain Soudien, vol. 42 of *Comparative and International Education: A Diversity of Voices* (Rotterdam: Sense Publishers, 2017), 38.

208. Mandela, *Long Walk to Freedom*.

209. Janice Harper, "A Lesson from Nelson Mandela on Forgiveness: If We Cannot Forgive In Our Own Lives Perhaps We Can Forget," *Psychology Today*, June 10, 2013.

210. Harper, "A Lesson from Nelson Mandela on Forgiveness."

211. Kim Phuc Phan Thi, *Fire Road: The Napalm Girl's Journey through the Horrors of War to Faith, Forgiveness, and Peace* (Carol Stream: Tyndale House, 2017).

212. Rafiq Elmansy, "Disney's Creative Strategy: The Dreamer, The Realist and The Critic," Designorate, April 6, 2016.

213. Robert Dilts, *Strategies of Genius*, vol. 2 (Capitola, California: Meta Publications, 1994).

214. Dilts, *Strategies of Genius*.

215. Craig Impelman, "How Having Patience Helps You Achieve Success," *Success Magazine*, August 9, 2017.

216. John Wooden, quoted in Impelman, "How Having Patience Helps You Achieve Success."
217. John Wooden, *They Call Me Coach* (New York: McGraw-Hill Professional, 2003), 105–106.
218. John Wooden, quoted in Craig Impelman, "Nothing Will Work Unless You Do," *Success*, April 5, 2017.
219. Impelman, "Nothing Will Work Unless You Do."
220. Hellen Keller, *The Story of My Life* (New York: Modern Library, 2003), 118.
221. Hannah Chambers, "Contentment: Hellen Keller," My Dripping Pen, February 25, 2011.
222. Keller, *Story of My Life*, 109.
223. Keller, *Story of My Life*, 22.
224. Jennifer Moss, *Unlocking Happiness at Work* (Philadelphia: Kogan Page Ltd., 2016), 41.
225. Moss, *Unlocking Happiness*, 41.
226. Keller, *Story of My Life*, 126.
227. Corrie ten Boom, "Guideposts Classics: Corrie ten Boom on Forgiveness," *Guideposts* (Carmel, New York: 1972).

Also by the Author ...

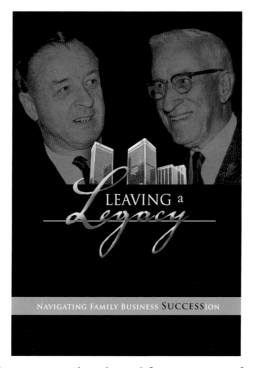

David C. Bentall shares family business insights gleaned from 20 years of working with The Bentall Group and Dominion Construction. Skillfully marrying his own experience with best practises in the field, he offers solutions to the distinct challenges faced by all families in business.

David has experienced the "best" and "worst" in family business. As a result, he really "gets it." This is a must read for anyone involved in family enterprise.
Chip Wilson—Founder and Former Chairman, Lululemon Athletica

David Bentall writes about family business with the passion and clarity that can only come from having walked many miles in those family business shoes. These are honest and powerful stories that not only teach you, they will also move you.
Allen S. Taylor—Former Chairman, Canadian Association of Family Enterprise